PREORDAINED

BOYS AS "FUTURE PRIESTS" DURING CATHOLICISM'S MINOR-SEMINARY BOOM AND BUST

Joseph F. Sheley

BL
BYRON LAREDO PUBLISHING
Sacramento, California

First published in 2020 by:
Joseph F. Sheley
via Byron Laredo Publishing
Sacramento CA

ISBN: 9798610934709

Cover designed by:
John Roina
Byron Laredo Publishing
Sacramento CA

Cover photo by: Con Tanasiuk, Alamy Stock Photo.

For my classmates, God bless 'em! ...Me too.

Tunneld. Lo Bue

Class of 1962

Acknowledgements

I owe a tremendous debt to the former minor seminarians who gave of their time and trust to discuss their seminary journeys and who encouraged me to continue a project related to who we once were and are now – "finally a chance to talk about this." I offer similar thanks to the people who have provided editorial and substantive commentary on the many drafts that led to the current iteration of this book: Bernadette Halbrook, Alexander Gonzalez, Robert Nelson, Charles Brody, J. Patrick Foley, and Patrick Ryan. I am grateful as well to John Roina for cover design and technical assistance. Finally, my wife, Bernadette, always has supported my effort to know myself better, and she encouraged me every day to stay the course in pursuit of the effects of my seminary past. That meant the world to me.

Contents

Part IV: Flight

Part V: Changing Habits

Preface

Few people beyond Catholic circles know what a minor seminary is (historically, a residential school for boys aspiring someday to become priests), and few Catholics born after 1980 have much of a clue at all. Thus, I have been asked on occasion to identify the target audience for *Preordained: Boys as "Future Priests" During Catholicism's Minor-Seminary Boom and Bust*. Social scientists? Catholics? A more general audience? Former seminarians? …Yes to all, but an emphatic yes to former seminarians as the group I desire most to reach, for this is a book about them – the institutions they entered or, more precisely, were entered into and what happened to them during and after their stay.

During the 1950s, 1960s, and 1970s, roughly 100,000 Catholic youths, the majority adolescent boys, experienced minor-seminary life. We transitioned from devout Catholic homes into a highly selective, ultra-Catholic, institutional setting within which we were socially isolated, supervised, disciplined, and kept occupied. To the extent that we entertained notions of departure, we faced significant hurdles. But depart most of us did; the only issues were when and how. The majority of former minor seminarians of the great minor-seminary "boom" (1950s through mid-1960s) and "bust" (mid-1960s through 1979) eras are still living. Most have not discussed that part of their lives with many others or in much depth. Most still grapple with the genesis of their seminary stay and the effects of their experience upon their later lives.

I have sought to train a social-science (sociological and historical) lens upon the minor-seminary experience though the approach hopefully has not rendered the book overly academic in tone. While social scientists might use my research as a springboard to further study, the research and literature citations throughout *Preordained* are offered to all – especially former seminarians – who wish to read more on the topic.

More generally, I trust that *Preordained* will inspire discussion among Catholics of all stripes regarding the wisdom of removing adolescents from their homes "someday to wear the Roman collar." Despite the common assumption that minor seminaries are obsolete in America (though not in many parts of the world), there is a substantial difference between "dead" and "dormant." The minor-seminary concept is more dormant than dead, for the church has not taken a position regarding it beyond acknowledging its financial challenges. What slumbers can awaken.

PART I

Context

CHAPTER ONE

Lambs into Shepherds

*F*reshmen sat together at meals in the refectory. Fifty of us, recently arrived, trying to sort the cues. Sophomores at their tables, upperclassmen and college students at theirs.

Sometimes we could talk during dinner; some nights a gloomy, chilly silence was imposed. Occasionally we could chat at the end of our meal, maybe have a group-sing while we passed the dishes to table's end for pick-up by the student waiters. The upperclassmen would get the song going over the clatter. We liked folk-revival tunes, easy to follow with refrains we could belt out.

Softly, from "Down in the Valley": Send me a letter. Send it by mail. Send it in care of Birmingham Jail.

And then harder: Birmingham Jailhouse! Birmingham Jail! Send it in care of Birmingham Jail!

We rookies missed it on the first go-round, and we craned our necks to hear what the upperclassmen were singing. Suddenly we got it. We sang louder, laughing, growing redder in the face.

St. Pius Jailhouse! St. Pius Jail! Send it in care of St. Pius Jail!

The padre at the elevated prefect's table slammed his hand down on his call bell. Several slams to get over the din.

"Stop! Stop it! Show some respect! This is not a jail. This is a seminary!"

Boys to the Altar of God[1]

True story the above. I was one of the new kids. The old priest was right, of course. St. Pius X, in Galt, California, was a seminary – a minor (or "junior") seminary, to be precise – not a jail, however jail-like it may have seemed to us at times. With few exceptions, minor seminaries were boarding schools for adolescents and young men aspiring someday to transition to a major (adult) seminary and ultimately to join the Catholic priesthood. They were total institutions that assumed control of most elements of everyday life, made your decisions for you, swallowed you whole. They segregated their charges from the larger world. They nurtured in many ways; no one was just a number. However, they sought also to own you: no one possessed much privacy, and the level of accountability required of students was exceptional. Further, minor seminaries sought subordination of their students' individual selves to "higher-order" community goals; the standing nail was to be bent to the floor. Consistency of message to Catholics throughout the world and the eventual priestly vow of obedience were not taken lightly even within this early vocational-development stage.

---

[1] Most Catholics will recognize the core of this phrase. It is the first said by a priest as he begins the Catholic mass. Catholics of eras prior to Vatican II heard it uttered in Latin. For most altar boys of the day, ten or so years of age, "Introibo ad altare Dei" ("I will go to the altar of God") was the first Latin phrase they memorized. It brought home the important message: priests lead; we follow. Most priests once were altar boys. Through such service, they enjoyed a particular insider's role in the mass, a peek behind the curtain.

I entered into the process of "vocation formation" for the Diocese of Sacramento in 1961. Later memories of my seminary stint are not nearly as clear as those of the first days when even the mundane was novel and details of culture and belonging seemed critical to survival. Like most of my classmates, I imagine, I recall especially vividly watching my family drive away in our tan '56 Plymouth Savoy after dropping me off at "Pius" (seminarian shorthand) on a Saturday in early September. My mother in a white dress with light polka-dots and a small hat, my dad in his blue suit and fedora. My brother and sister luxuriating in the space they now shared in the backseat and, in many ways, in their lives without their older brother around. Each turning to look back and wave at the first-born, in suit and tie, standing on the blacktop basketball courts that served as a parking lot on special days. I waved back and headed to my assigned dormitory to meet my new classmates and pursue a life I believed I had chosen but about which I had relatively no clue. I was a month shy of my fourteenth birthday.

I was not alone in answering the "call," or even one of a few – or a hundred, or a thousand. The exact count is elusive but, by conservative estimate, the number of boys and young men who passed through America's minor seminaries between the early 1950s and the late-1970s is 100,000,[2] enough people to fill the Rose Bowl or populate a city like South Bend, Indiana. At its peak in 1963,

---

[2] The estimate relies on figures provided by Anello (2018:52). Average high-school and junior-college minor-seminary enrollment combined with four-year college minor-seminary enrollment was approximately 24,000 students per annum from 1954-55 through 1963-64. Assuming a modest turnover rate (attrition, graduation, and replacement) of 20 percent as well as growth per year – a higher turnover rate would have produced even higher enrollments – 80,000 boys and young men likely passed through America's minor seminaries during the decade in question. The next decade saw enrollments plummet, but 20,000 new recruits into minor seminaries during that period similarly represents a conservative estimate.

enrollment reached nearly 39,000; the majority of enrollees were high-school students. As we shall see in Chapter Two, the seminary growth spurt (1950s through mid-1960s) that swept up so many boys like me was phenomenal. So was the enrollment crash (mid-1960s through mid-1970s and beyond) that saw minor seminaries in America effectively go the way of the dinosaur. A half-century later, the minor-seminary boom has been all but forgotten. Seminary land and buildings have been repurposed or sit empty.

I wish I could say that my seminary career was short, a small spike on a long lifeline, but that would be a decidedly untrue story. I left in 1967. Though the percentage of my life that six years represents dwindles daily, it remains significant, and the personal impact of heeding the "call" will endure, I am convinced, until I blink my last. Indeed, that is one of the main interests of this book: lasting effects of time spent in minor seminary.

In Hiding

Few of my friends and colleagues know that I was a seminarian as a kid, a product of the heady years. I worked hard to put the seminary well behind me after I had departed. It was painful in most respects to relive the experience, so it made sense to place it in a sealed box. I also did not want people to "understand" me via this element of my personal history. I worked assiduously to distance that history from my professional world so as not to color colleagues' critiques of my ideas and positions as a college teacher and researcher. Further, I was acutely aware during twenty years as a university administrator of the political hay to be made of one's past within what is a persistent tug of war over policy and expenditures in academic institutions (see Chapter Twelve).

Discussions with and accounts offered by other former seminarians indicate that I am not unique in my approach to disclosing my past (Hedin, 2003: 2-4). Our caution means that you likely know more of us than you realize.[3] You cannot spot former seminarians easily, other than those few who now wear the Roman collar. Not many volunteer their backgrounds readily, even those (perhaps especially those) who remained in the seminary for many years and thus have more than a very limited experience in earlier life to reveal. In a sense, we practice a variant of "passing," though the term generally exaggerates the importance of our secret-keeping for those of us with the secret. Really, what does it mean to pass as someone who was *not* a seminarian? The better term, it would seem, is "identity management" of the kind people with unusual pasts utilize to suggest a "normal" background.

Most of us are not so secretive as to lie outright. Instead, we camouflage our history. We offer no clues, evade questions, misdirect, say things such as, "Oh, I attended a small Catholic boys' school." Mostly, we just do not put it out there for conversation, and therefore avoid being typed as an "ex" and, as important, engaging a past that we've locked away and now often struggle to comprehend in terms of the why and the outcome. Sometimes we can spot others who also were in the "sem." They say something that triggers the recognition, although more often than not we do not follow up because it means outing ourselves.

Here's how it works according to a former classmate:

I had taken a new management job with a small company near Sacramento. I made a point right away to visit every unit to

---

[3] A partial list of notable public servants, artists, and celebrities with seminary backgrounds likely surprises as well: Supreme Court Justice Clarence Thomas, Governor Jerry Brown, Senator Joe Donnelly, Tom Cruise, LeVar Burton, Martin Scorsese, Michael Moore, Richard Simmons, Dakin Mathews, Dan Aykroyd, Gabriel Byrne, Garry Wills, and Sean Hannity.

meet everyone and to learn what was on their minds. When I looked at the roster one morning, there was the name: Charles Dresden. Could he be the guy we knew in the sem? A year behind us, nice kid, pleasant, from Sacramento, left after his freshman year. I looked up his photo on line; it was definitely Charlie from Pius. I said, this is not so good. I don't think many former seminarians forget kids ahead of them in dink-ass-size schools like Pius.

After the usual exchange about work needs and challenges, he moved first:

"I can't help but feel that I know you from somewhere?"

"Could be. You're from Sacramento too, right? Where did you go to college?"

"Pacific. You went to San Francisco State; I read that when you were hired."

"Yeah. Did we play ball somewhere together, maybe?"

"No. I like sports but was never an athlete. Are you a Catholic?"

I thought, Oh, oh ....

"Not much of one anymore, but, yes, I grew up Catholic."

"My family lived in St. Honore's Parish."

"I came from way across town – All Saints."

"Maybe you went to Bishop Armstrong High?"

"Nope."

All right, it was his move. Either "I went to the seminary for a year. Did you go to St. Pius?" or the easier, "Where did you go to high school?" To which I'd have answered: "St. Pius, same as you, Charlie." If he did not ask, he did not want to divulge without a signal from me first. Or maybe he really didn't recognize me – but he'd still ask about my high school, right? No dice. He just said:

"Well, maybe it'll come to me. I really appreciate getting the chance to meet you."

"Same here. And I look forward to working with you."

In all my years with that company, no one ever mentioned that Charlie had been in a seminary.

In short, many of us (if not most; that is among this book's major questions) repress the seminary experience and obsess about it at the same time. We consider its impact upon us as significant though not necessarily wholly negative. We are conscious of enduring personal effects of the seminary as a part of our past that seems at once a part of our present (Hedin, 2003:2; Hendrickson, 1983:25). We believe too that others type us at least somewhat in terms of that experience – or would type us, if they knew – in ways that can have consequences in social and occupational spheres.

Are we wrong? To grasp better the focus of this book, look tonight at your thirteen-year-old son or daughter (or grandchild, or some other youngster of importance to you) and imagine him or her away at a boarding school next year. Finances aside, would that even be within the realm of possibility? Now imagine that, unlike kids sent to boarding schools for status, tradition, or discipline, your child is headed off to answer God's call to embark on a lifelong religious vocation, by nearly everyone's estimate a lonely and difficult life. In this instance, your eighth-grade son says that he wants to attend a residential seminary to study for the priesthood. Would you let him go? Even were he to beg you?

Now assume that, for some reason, you said yes. Put on your son's hat and fast-forward a few decades. You are trying to fathom how and why your seminary years happened, why your parents permitted a thirteen-year-old boy to embark on such a journey – assuming that the idea was not theirs in the first place. (I never asked the how and why questions of my parents and cannot now; the same is true of most of my schoolmates.) You've become certain that much about who you are and how you handle life's challenges is linked to your time in the seminary. This was not simply a neutral or low-impact experience, though clearly neither all good nor all bad. But you cannot get a satisfactory handle on it because you've kept this part of your life locked away. You worry (or have learned) that disclosure has consequences. You now seek answers to questions that you are not even sure characterize other members of the select fraternity to which you once belonged.

Highly Personal, Not Unique

Eighteen men from the St. Pius X Seminary class of 1965 – my class – gathered in Sacramento, California in June of 2015. They were among 53 high-school mates, four of whom had passed away in the intervening years, who had entered the seminary together in 1961 or had joined the class later as high-school transfers. Some had stayed but a year, a few even less. Of the 53 classmates, 21 (40 percent) actually completed high school at St. Pius. Thirteen returned to pursue the seminary's two-year college curriculum; nine completed that curriculum; five (nine percent of the original 53) moved on to the diocesan major seminary, and one entered a religious order's novitiate.[4]

There were smiles and tentative handshakes, more than a few failures of instant recognition. However, it was clear immediately that this was not the standard high-school reunion. No guffaws, no tales of sexual prowess, car racing, and drinking as kids, no

---

[4] His stay was short. So too were those of the two other of my classmates who transferred to religious novitiates, one immediately after high school and the other after a year of college at St. Pius X.

recollection of stealing the mascot of a rival high school. The men in the room acted more like combat vets reuniting after many years. Quiet talk. Measured laughter. Less attention to post-school success or failure in life and work. Not a lot of "sharing." As the ice melted, more attention was paid to whether classmates felt the same about their days at Pius and, at least for some, the impact of their experience on their ensuing lives – something most admitted was tough to explain even to significant others. Theirs was a bond not readily understood by outsiders. To a person, they knew that only those who had entered a seminary could appreciate that the "decision" to do so at age fourteen (or fifteen or sixteen) was not easily explained. Nor were the decision to leave and the methods to accomplish departure.

Their stories appear throughout this book, but it ultimately is not about what happened to the boys of St. Pius X Class of '65, at least not entirely and directly. Few of us have lived such lives as to astound anyone, although there are many successful educators, lawyers, business people, public servants, and civic leaders in the bunch. Though many of our classmates joined the armed forces, only four, as far as we can tell, saw combat during the Vietnam War. Three of them seemed the least interested in meeting with old classmates – perhaps because the effects of their combat experience dwarfed those of their seminary experience. Only two members of the class (four percent of the original 53) ultimately were ordained priests, and only one of those two worked within the Diocese of Sacramento. A third (short-time) class member became pastor of a Protestant congregation.

The book also really is not about me directly though my own ghosts and concerns certainly framed the initial questioning and the search for answers among peers. As I sought to understand my present in terms of my past and to compare my take on both with those of other ex-seminarians, I realized that the project I had undertaken was as much about an era, post-World War II 1950s, '60s and '70s, as about the people within it. The era passed; we are its remnants. As will become apparent in the early stages of this book, the period of American Catholicism that produced the "vocations" of the Class of '65 was exceptional in the complexity of the social influences that shaped it and in the speed of the rise and fall of a social movement that called boys and young men to pursue the priesthood.

In fact, I did not begin this project as a book or even as a study. It began instead as a personal quest. In the 1980s, I was struck by what felt to me to be a veritable tsunami of life challenges: the deaths of a spouse and both my parents, a divorce, difficulties at work. I withstood them as I always did, drawing both admiration and concern from friends and colleagues. I clearly could take a punch but, as many friends said, maybe that wasn't always so good. Even I saw this as less than healthy. As I grappled with my dark clouds, the question became not, "Will I survive this?" but "Why do I feel that I have to survive every blow? Why can't I let it bring me down, at least for a while?"

The answer for me, as for most people, was partly a matter of what makes each of us who we are: the combination of biological-psychological-social factors that forms our basis at any given later point. Cradle issues no doubt account for part of who I am, as they do for everyone, but I am unaware of any of particular or unusual impact. Such issues notwithstanding, a significant part of me was fashioned at age five when my mother began championing the priesthood as her son's goal in life. Another significant part – even in my overt reaction to that part later in life – traces to the eight years that I spent in Catholic elementary school, at the time a font of religious vocations. In addition to the three Rs, students at St. Philomene School learned the rules, over and over, that would determine whether we made it to heaven – straightaway or through purgatory – or to the h-place that no one talks about anymore. Little in the way of direct relationship with God beyond asking for favors; little in the way of flexibility in behavioral choices. Who needs a conscience? Know the rules; follow the rules.

Such early influences acknowledged, biographies ultimately also are the product (more than simply the sum) of responses to myriad situations and to the larger eras that shaped those situations. Some challenges and events call up or even produce traits, good or bad. Some are so monumental that they shape us profoundly going forward (as they did, for example, for the soldiers who stormed the beaches of Normandy in 1944). Some are considerably less profound in the moment but so repetitive in their content and demand that they form patterned responses that, though important, often are not even recognized.

What shaped my response to my personal dark clouds in early mid-life? It did not take long to dismantle my biography and identify (in my mind anyway) the period that conditioned most significantly my reactions to situations for the rest of my life: I spent the second important round of my formative years, nearly all of my adolescence, in a Catholic minor seminary. Bluntly, seminarians were on their own, to succeed or fail within the institution that now honed their aspirations and values, with little daily parental influence and, during the school year, virtually no lay peer influence. In fact, so infrequent was the time we spent with parents and so lofty the reason for the absence, that greater-than-average independence was ours when we were with them. We were "on leave," even during the summer months, when we were away from our primary purpose in life. The flip-side, of course, was that we also possessed a greater-than-average sense of responsibility and obligation – holding on to our vocation – than did our contemporaries on the outside.

Within the seminary and away from it, there was seminarian peer influence, to be sure; we were encouraged to remain in close contact when gone from the mother ship. But classmates were scattered throughout the region or even the nation, so contact was difficult. More important, seminary relationships inside and outside the school's walls also were constrained and even suppressed by the nature of each fraternity member's personal relationship with his aim in life and with God's (or someone's) mission for him. We attended a school full of friends but had few friendships, always holding back our questions, secrets, and doubts, wishing not to disappoint. We were a disciplined bunch. Enduring a high level of loneliness and emotional isolation left us able to withstand considerable stress later in life. We could do time well, detach well. And there was that sense of obligation – our sacred calling – that conditioned us not to walk easily away from anything later in life, for better or worse, no matter the pain or the challenge.

To put it most simply, I believe the experience of my adolescence (in most ways, the absence of a traditional adolescence) influenced who I was and how I handled later life more significantly than did the adolescence of the average young man. As I did in the seminary, I did later. Life was about decisions made in the first-person singular, the Latin *ego*. *I* made the decision to enter the seminary. *I* made the decision to leave. *I* alone was responsible for what happened to me. Endurance was mine to muster; failure to endure was my failure. What worked was mine to own, as was what did not. The only chink in my armor was not thinking to ask why I was wearing armor.

I do not wish to mislead or exaggerate. Seminary life was not hell, nor was it oppressive in the sense of life within extreme cults. I was not banished from home by parents who wished to be rid of me; indeed, I never doubted that mine loved me. Whatever happened to me was not in the same ballpark, in the moment or longer-term, as what happened, for example, to so many foster children or to kids who were physically or sexually abused – though some of my seminary mates carry that pain too. I can hardly argue that my life's trajectory was so radically altered by my unusual adolescence that I can claim no responsibility for whatever good and bad that I have done in the ensuing half century. I am a decent, ethical person, a good husband and dad, a faithful friend, an engaged citizen, an effective leader. But how I handle those roles and what comes my way traces, I believe, in significant part to my seminary years. That realization directed me toward questions about how I got there (i.e., do thirteen-year-olds really make choices?), why I stayed (i.e., do teenagers really understand obligation?), how I got away (i.e., did those in charge simply snooze for a while?), and how it affected me afterward (i.e., why did it take me so long to ask the right questions?).

Nor do I want to suggest, this book aside, that the fact of a partial biography as a seminarian consumes my attention constantly. Quite the opposite. I have been very successful – too much so – most of my life at *not* thinking about it. I have not denied its existence, but have assumed that the effects were minor and controllable. The only times I grappled with them were when I was in the company of former classmates (who, with me, tended to downplay the significance of our lost adolescence), when I revealed my ex-seminarian identity to people close to me, and when I faced some personal demons or challenges. In point of fact, the significance of the challenges that I worked through later was as impactful as that of my adolescence. The missing piece for me was the influence of that adolescence on *how* I moved forward.

Negative feelings notwithstanding, in pure fairness, to the extent that I lay blame upon my seminary years for personal "damage," I also must acknowledge that the same cultivated personal traits that have caused me difficulties also have helped me to succeed in life and career. I learned a lot at St. Pius – discipline, focus, personal responsibility, leadership, calmness within storms – that served me very well later.

Looking for Patterns

As a social scientist – a sociologist and criminologist by training and practice – I have spent my professional life dissecting the interrelationship of institutions and individuals, seeking to decipher social patterns. It should come as no surprise, therefore, that the study that informs this book arose as I began to question whether or not my experience and more recent understanding of self were unique. Did others experience life within and after the minor seminary in the same way that I did? Did they enter and exit via similar routes? Did entry later rather than earlier in life (college vs. high school, for instance) matter, or was the experience impervious to age and level of maturity? Could I learn from others and better understand my own decisions and experiences? Did others ever even think about these things? And what about those few who ultimately heeded "God's call"? Did they regret their chosen path? Did they see it as a choice? Did they understand how they got there? Or were their lives so fulfilling that I was asking entirely the wrong questions?

Pursuit of the question of effects of the minor-seminary experience is important to me only in part because it helps me understand myself. (To the extent that those same effects characterize the later experiences of others who underwent a similar journey during adolescence, I understand myself still better.) More important, I also find myself hoping to diminish the odds that boys of a future generation are similarly "called." It is apparent already in this book, I am sure, that my feelings concerning the concept of minor seminary for adolescents lean considerably toward the negative. They began on that side of the continuum and grew clearer as I pursued the subject more systematically. I would like to believe that I have less an axe to grind than a desire to discourage rebirth of an unhealthy concept or, at least, of the institutional construct through which it was expressed.

Finally, it is important to note that I have worked to narrow the focus of my research: the effects of spending one's adolescence in a Catholic *minor* seminary. This is not a book about major seminaries and students of the age of majority. Nor is it about contemporary priests, their life situations, their joys, regrets, and sorrows – except as priests in the current study now view themselves as products of that same seminary experience. It is not a critical analysis of the Catholic Church and its place in today's world. I left Catholicism behind many years ago.[5] Beyond the disgust and outrage that I share with everyone concerning the appalling magnitude of the church's sexual abuse scandal of the past few decades, I bear Catholicism no ill will beyond that for what I consider its misguided direction of boys who experienced the "call" at mid-Twentieth Century. Even here, the goal of this book is less to criticize than to identify practices and problems that should not be repeated without exceptionally thoughtful consideration.

Seeking Answers from Others

The road to understanding the minor seminary experience and its effects more systematically began and continues with others'

---

[5] I did not last long post-seminary as a practicing Catholic. A college student in 1967, newly emancipated from regimented, no-questions-asked seminary life, I looked back at the rituals and rules that once structured my day as oppressive and boring. I also carried for a time the expected sense of guilt upon leaving the seminary and thus was a prime candidate for some form of dissonance-reduction. It occurred, not surprisingly in retrospect, as I confronted the Catholic Church's positions on birth control, sexual morality, and personal freedom. I could do what friends were doing – remain Catholic on their own terms rather than the church's terms. Or I could walk away. The exit was made much easier by my (smug) 1960s college-student conviction that organized religion was a "critical apparatus of oppression of the poorer classes within an insatiable capitalist economic and social structure." Times change and people with them.

17

thoughts on the subject. There is a considerable literature on vocational trends – the relative collapse of the supply line of priests for Catholic parishes – within the Catholic Church since the mid-Twentieth Century and an equally considerable literature on the swing of Catholicism from liberalism in the 1960s and '70s to the far more conservative movement that followed it. Much of this literature examines the difficulties faced by a 1960s-1970s generation of priests who believe that their seminary education prepared them for a role they were forbidden to pursue within the more conservative church promoted in the main by Pope John Paul II in the 1980s and forward. But little of this literature sheds light on minor seminaries.

Attention to the church's role in and response to its clerical sex abuse scandal has produced a substantial focus on the screening and training of candidates for the priesthood. Much of this comment and analysis looks at the "vocation formation" of priests who have abused children (i.e., at whether such predation emanated directly from traditional church and seminary philosophy and practices or reflects the seminary's failure to weed out "natural" predators), but little offers glimpses into the perpetrator's past minor-seminary life. The exception rests with Vincent Miles' (2012) *Boys of the Cloth* through which the reader visits a minor seminary in England in the 1960s. Miles focuses his examination of minor-seminary structure and culture on the concept of seminary created by the Council of Trent in 1563, and its possible link to the sexual abuse of minors by clergy from the 1950s through the 1980s.

Two books offer particularly penetrating accounts of the minor seminary experiences of their authors during the 1950s and 1960s. *Seminary: A Search* is Paul Hendrickson's (1983) attempt to make sense of his seven years in a religious order of missionaries. He focuses particularly upon his early childhood as the springboard for his "vocation" and offers poignant interviews of former school-mates, some of whom "made it." John Cornwell (2006) provides, in *Seminary Boy*, a similarly moving personal account of his life in a minor seminary in England in the 1950s, how he got there and how he left. He brings into the mix especially well the sense of seminary as a haven from hardship and chaos at home.

Raymond Hedin's (2003) *Married to the Church* is a personal but also more systematic look at the seminary experience of the 1950s and 1960s and its effects on others as well as on him. Hedin spent eight years in minor and major seminaries. He focuses especially on the personal and professional lives of classmates who ultimately were ordained – their trials and challenges within a changing church, how rewarding have been some of their accomplishments, how difficult has been the road for those who stayed in and those who left the priesthood. Given Hedin's foci, his description of minor seminary life is not the central element of his book. Yet, his commentary and that of his interviewees are especially useful as data against which to compare and contrast my own conclusions and the comments of my interviewees.

The late Donald Fausel (2010) offered in *From Blind Obedience to a Responsible Faith*, an account of his life as a "people-pleaser" throughout his college seminary days in the 1950s and during his days as a priest, including those spent as a minor-seminary faculty member. Perhaps as important, he recounted his journey after the priesthood as a period of recovery from unquestioning obedience followed by a period of development of critical-thinking skills. In this vein, he cast in relief the tenets of his faith as they were expressed to Catholics and, especially, priests before the Second Vatican Council (Vatican II), the Catholic Church's attempt to modernize, to pull itself out of the centuries-old defensive posture it had assumed in response to the protestant reformation (see Chapter Two).

A number of shorter, first-person accounts (including numerous internet blogs and postings) have been quite helpful as well. The late Andrew Greeley's *Confessions of a Parish Priest* (1986) offers a sense of early 1940's Catholicism and his entry into the minor seminary – in this instance, a rarer "day seminary" – and, later, of major seminary life. James Carroll (1996) looks at the stresses of the priesthood in the 1960s and traces his own vocation to his intensely Catholic parents in *An American Requiem*. Timothy Bazzett's *Reed City Boy* (2004) offers an account of how he found his way into the minor seminary in 1959 and how homesickness reduced his seminary career to a single year. Rick Carnevale recounts, in *When Pigs Fly* (2014), his adventures and misadventures at a number of seminaries during the 1960s. Supreme Court Justice Clarence Thomas writes in *My Grandfather's Son: A Memoir* (2007) of the difficulties encountered by black seminarians in the mid-1960s. More than anything, these accounts point to the universality of the seminary structure and culture across decades, at least until the late 1960s. What was different, decade to decade, was not the institution but the world around it and, increasingly, the boys entering it.

Another important study that informs this book, especially Chapter Two, is Robert L. Anello's (2018) *Minor Setback or Major Disaster?* The focus of Anello's research is the collapse of the minor seminary concept in America during the late 1960s through the late 1970s. He has succeeded in pulling together a literature that was otherwise fragmented and scattered over time and throughout various archives. The result of his hard work makes the rise and fall of the minor seminary understandable as the very complicated yet, in retrospect, almost foregone outcome of major structural and cultural changes in America following World War II. What we see today within the landscape of Catholic vocations is in most ways the product of those changes. As important, what we see through Anello's eyes provides the context for the experience of boys and young men involved in minor seminary education during its heyday.

In addition to learning from the literature, over the course of nearly three decades, I have interviewed formally 24 people who attended minor seminaries. Fourteen of these had attended St. Pius X Seminary while I was there; eleven of this number were my own classmates. The remaining ten interviewees were priests, former priests, and former seminarians whom I contacted upon learning that they had attended a minor seminary. Such knowledge almost always flowed from reference in a conversation with a third party to the individual as someone "who studied to be a priest" or was a "former priest." Over the years, I returned to many of my interviewees for further discussion, insight, and perspective. I appreciated their feedback on my tentative conclusions and received updates on their thoughts about minor seminary life and its effects as they aged and their lives changed. Everything said was held in strictest confidence. Throughout this book, then, I do not use interviewees' actual names, and when necessary, I have altered elements of their present identities and domicile. I have changed the names of most faculty members at St. Pius X Seminary as well; my focus is upon the culture of my alma mater rather than upon the identities of individuals who may have behaved less than admirably at times.

While I was conducting formal interviews, I also had dozens of less-structured discussions of the same subject matter with former seminarians and members of their families. More often than not, these occurred serendipitously and in a manner that precluded more formal interviews or the time needed to conduct them. Reunions (and, sometimes, funerals) of former seminarians, for example, often spurred conversations concerning minor-seminary years and their impact.

I discovered quickly that ex-seminarians actually wanted to talk, some quite badly.[6] It was as if they had had few occasions to share their own thoughts on that earlier period of life with someone who might understand its significance and nuances. In many instances, former seminarians noted that they had difficulty explaining to their spouses and partners what their seminary years meant to them. Interviewees who had attended St. Pius X, for obvious reasons, moved more quickly on board since they shared the same background (if not the same interpretation of it) as I. Those whom I had not known previously seemed to relax the moment that they learned that I was a former seminarian.

The potential weakness in my approach is obvious. Given that mine was not a random sample, exactly how generalizable are my conclusions – about former minor seminarians overall, those specifically from St. Pius X, and even my own classmates – will be known only when someone in fact develops and executes a fully randomized sampling frame. This will be no simple task since past minor seminary records are neither accessed easily nor easily traced to persons today. It is no coincidence that accounts of seminary life more often than not rely upon their authors' circles of acquaintances.

Sampling notwithstanding, the present findings jibe well with those of others noted earlier regarding similar topics, most of which

---

[6] Only two former seminarians whom I approached declined to be interviewed. Each had been a classmate of mine. One noted that he was not interested in "going back there. It was just a small part of my life. My memory of those days is fuzzy. And I'd rather leave it that way." (His memory may have been fuzzy, but his seminary experience was hardly only a small part of his life. He had spent his entire high-school education in two different seminaries, one of which also was attended by his older brother.) The other had spent three years at St. Pius; his older brother had spent five years there and time later in a religious novitiate. He considered the project unlikely to produce answers and worried that somehow those interviewed might be embarrassed or troubled by the findings.

focus on priests and former priests looking back on elements of their training in both minor and major seminaries. What is clear is that the decision to talk to persons who studied within minor seminaries from the mid-1950s through the mid-1970s – the earliest of the respondents' experiences began in 1953; the latest ended in 1975 – has kept at bay potential "period effects." Such effects might have occurred, for instance, were I to have mixed interviewees from the Great Depression era with those of the politically volatile 1960s. In fact, all of the people with whom I spoke had experienced Catholicism in both pre- and post- Vatican II (1962) forms (again, see Chapter Two), though one was born in the late 1950s. All had completed their minor seminary studies well before the church's sex-abuse scandal broke very publicly (see Chapter Nine). All who had been ordained had experienced the fairly dramatic shift from "liberal" to "conservative" Catholicism during their priesthood.

Finally, my greatest concern has been control of my own preconceptions and biases. I am, after all, a part of that which I have studied, and my interest in the subject is an outgrowth of my own efforts to make sense of elements of my life. This is not a new problem for most social scientists (or others who seek to describe, understand, and explain social phenomena; journalists represent a major case in point). We devote much time in training and practice to creating the appropriate distance from biases, conscious or not. Among the tools of the trade are both critical introspection and submission of ideas and conclusions to a critical audience. Also among the tools are a commitment to methods of research likely to produce "truer" and less distorted results and conclusions based upon them: considerable and critical familiarity with extant literature on the subject, decent sampling, a reasonable research timeframe, uniformity of questions asked, a willingness to let people tell their stories as they wish, always summarizing for them what you thought you heard them say and revising impressions as necessary, and revisiting ideas and conclusions with former interviewees as well as new ones.

In short, I have tried my best not to let preconceptions distort what I was reading, hearing, and interpreting and certainly not to bend others' stories to my own. Indeed, as will become apparent later in this book, those shared stories and their tellers' willingness to "correct" my sense of them and to grapple with my ideas and potential conclusions, I believe, conditioned and even subdued my take on my own story.

Moving forward, the book's chapters will examine entry into, life in, exit from, and the impact of time spent in a minor seminary. First, however, context is critical. The historical setting of my minor seminary experience and that of my interviewees – the explosive growth and decline of minor seminaries within a very short historical period – is the subject of Chapter Two.

References

Anello, Robert L. 2018. *Minor Setback or Major Disaster? The Rise and Demise of Minor Seminaries in the United States, 1958-1983.* St. Louis MO: EnRoute Books.

Bazzett, Timothy. 2010. *Reed City Boy.* Reed City MI: Rathole Books.

Carnevale, Rick. 2014. *When Pigs Fly.* Bloomington IN: Author House.

Carroll, James. 1996. *An American Requiem.* New York: Houghton Mifflin Harcourt.

Cornwell, John. 2006. *Seminary Boy: A Memoir.* New York: Doubleday.

Fausel, Donald F. 2010. *From Blind Obedience to a Responsible Faith.* Bloomington IN: iUniverse.

Greeley, Andrew M. 1986. *Confessions of a Parish Priest: An Autobiography.* New York: Simon & Schuster.

Hedin, Raymond. 2003. *Married to the Church (Updated Edition).* Bloomington: Indiana University Press.

Hendrickson, Paul. 1983. *Seminary: A Search*. New York: Summit Books.

Miles, Vincent J. 2012. *Boys of the Cloth: The Accidental Role of Church Reforms in Causing and Curbing Abuse by Priests*. Lanham, MD: Hamilton Books.

Thomas, Clarence. 2007. *My Grandfather's Son: A Memoir*. New York: HarperCollins.

CHAPTER TWO

Swift Ascent, Swifter Fall

*E*ntering a minor seminary was by design
(not the average adolescent seminarian's,
obviously) to leave the world. And we did.
*I sometimes think of myself as having entered a large
lake in 1961. By the time I climbed out of it in 1967, it
was not the same body of water, and the swimmers in
it were fewer. Yet, the majority of my classmates, even
those who climbed out early, and I had little idea that
much was occurring along the shoreline while we were
swimming. We just swam — you entered the seminary,
and you remained in or left it, period. The possibility
that there would be no seminary was neither imagined
by us nor acknowledged to us by those of our teachers and
administrators who likely understood it. How could it
be acknowledged? The whole idea was to form our vocations within the social vacuum that was the seminary.*

Sacramento's Catholic population had exploded after World War II, especially in its newer suburbs. That growth brought pressures. A man from our parish came to the house one day in late 1958 to talk to my mom and dad about a new seminary that the Diocese of Sacramento planned to build. We knew he was coming to ask for money. He needn't have bothered. Mom already was sold and knew more about the place than the pitchman did. This, after all, was where her boy was going to pursue God's call three years hence. My parents donated money to the project, perhaps a few hundred dollars – for their stretched finances, a small fortune.

Until just a few years before, the Diocese of Sacramento had no seminary of its own. It had sent boys who wished to be priests to the Archdiocese of San Francisco's minor seminary or recommended that they join a religious order. But San Francisco was producing too many candidates of its own for its seminary, and the Archdiocese was turning away boys from other places. It was time for Sacramento to step up, not just for the boys who wanted to be priests, but for a diocese that wanted to play in the big leagues.

Every Diocese needs a Seminary to perpetuate the Church by continuing the priesthood. All other dioceses on the [West] Coast and, indeed, all Dioceses of the country comparable to ours have, by the co-operative efforts of the priests and the people, already been provided with a Seminary. (Bishop Joseph T. McGucken in a 1958 appeal to members of the Diocese of Sacramento for funds to build St. Pius X Seminary)

Bishop Joseph McGucken was intent on getting the seminary built, as had been his predecessor, Bishop Robert Armstrong. For years, however, economic challenges and war had held construction projects in the dream stage. Further, McGucken faced major resistance from his own troops, the Irish clergy who for decades had filled the ranks of the Diocese of Sacramento's priesthood. In 1958, approximately 60 percent of Sacramento's parishes were headed by Irish pastors, and an even higher percentage of the priests serving under those pastors were from Ireland. It was easier and cheaper, most argued, to bring all the priests needed by the diocese straight from the Emerald Isle.

McGucken prevailed. The first iteration of St. Pius X Seminary (a "junior" seminary) had been initiated by Bishop Armstrong in 1955 via a temporary, leased, high school-level facility in California's logging country seven hours north of Sacramento. Its enrollment swelled so quickly that the diocese had to lease additional space in Sacramento to accommodate some of its seminarians. The demand made the case for Bishop McGucken, and he did not squander the opportunity. He needed $2.5 million (roughly $21 million in contemporary dollars) to build a permanent, proper seminary, and people like my parents obliged.

The new seminary was built on 320 donated acres in Galt, about 30 minutes south of Sacramento. Prime agricultural land, the parcel might well have been lifted from the prairies of Kansas. It was flat; the vista stretched for miles. When the winds blew during the winter, it was very cold. When it stormed, the wind drove the rain sideways. In May, the temperature reached the 90s and, in September, it topped 100 degrees. The social isolation thought necessary to seminaries of the day was maintained easily. Beyond the occasional farmer and a few cattle, there simply was not a soul around. Not many cars passed along the road in front of the seminary site. The nearest town was a (forbidden) three-mile walk away. The nearest public phone booth was half a mile up the road (a visit to which likewise was forbidden).

St. Pius X Seminary opened with much fanfare in April of 1961 with the relocation of the students from the temporary seminary sites. Freshmen and sophomores were housed in a dormitory building with eight large rooms, each with about fifteen beds. A second residential building housed juniors, seniors, and two-year college students in single or double rooms. "Twentieth Century Modern" in form, including state-of-the art science and language laboratories and a professional-quality kitchen and refectory (dining hall), the facility nonetheless was traditional in its primary function: promoting spirituality, academic success, physical fitness, and practical responsibility (St. Pius X Seminary, 1962:3). Its crown jewel was its chapel with the largest pipe organ in the region, gold leaf murals behind the altar, and a massive stained-glass window designed by Max Ingrand of Paris.

The seminary was staffed by members of the Society of the Divine Savior, also known as Salvatorians, an order with considerable experience in administering seminaries. In that first year, nine priests and five brothers conducted the business of the institution. Faculty size increased over the next few years as the number of students grew, and some lay teachers were added to the roster.

The first full class of freshmen, my class, arrived in the fall of 1961. Situated in the demographic acceleration of the era and the wave of enthusiasm preceding Vatican II, at the time we constituted the largest freshman class in St. Pius's history. My parish "sent" (diocesan parlance and an important element in the relationship between bishop and parish pastor) four boys to the newly constructed seminary that year; we represented about 10 percent of the boys in our eighth-grade class. We followed on the heels of four boys sent the year before; they in turn had succeeded three new seminarians from the parish in 1959. Our parish was not unusual. Most urban and suburban parishes in the Diocese of Sacramento in that era sent similar numbers to St. Pius X.

St. Pius's enrollment in the fall of 1961 was 143. Half of the students were from Sacramento; the other half came from towns and small cities throughout Northern and Central California.

Enrollment demand over the next two years forced rooms designed for single occupancy into use by three students. Total enrollment topped 180 in 1963. In response, by the time classes opened in 1965, the diocese had constructed a new residence hall as well as new meeting rooms and recreational and theatre facilities. St. Pius X now could accommodate over 200 students. More construction was planned for future growth to 300.

Spirits were high. And then they weren't. While the freshman class in 1963 had been 65 strong, the highest in the institution's history, just two years later, new freshmen numbered 43. The following year brought only 26 freshmen. Attrition rates among upperclassmen increased rapidly though their impact was blunted somewhat by the admission of "late-vocation" college students. Total enrollment for 1966 was 130, 72 percent of what it had been just three years before. For the next several years, the faculty tried desperately to attract and hold more seminarians – cars permitted on campus, students encouraged to play basketball in local recreation leagues, a tackle-football program, more free time, longer visits home.

Enrollment spiraled downward quickly; 1968 saw only a total of 76 students (less than 45 percent of enrollment just five years earlier). The exact number of seminarians over the next few years is difficult to discern because, in its effort to survive, St. Pius X Seminary became St. Pius X Preparatory School for both day and residential students, seminarians and non-seminarians. It was never clear exactly how many of the enrollees were traditional seminarians, how many were "maybe going to be a priest," and how many were simply seeking a good, Catholic "leadership" education (the stated goal of St. Pius Prep). Nothing the diocese and the seminary attempted stemmed the tide. By the mid-1970s, it was all over but the shouting.

St. Pius X closed its doors for good in 1977 after only sixteen years of operation in Galt. Just 23 of its alumni (including one from the earlier, temporary iteration of the institution) ultimately were ordained and, of these, just 16 remained in the priesthood at the time of this writing. Only 10 of the ordained alumni served the Diocese of Sacramento (as opposed to joining a religious order or serving another diocese), and, of these, only seven remained in the priesthood.

Something Happened

The focus of this book is upon life *in* minor seminaries in the 1950s, '60s, and '70s. However, it also is about the life *of* minor seminaries during the same era. Their numbers ballooned from the mid-1950s through the mid-'60s, peaking in 1963: nearly 300 high school- and college-level minor seminaries and programs (minor in the sense that they prepared young men for theology studies in major seminaries) (Anello, 2018: 18). The numbers then plummeted through the 1970s such that most stand-alone high-school and college seminaries were gone or greatly diminished by the mid-1980s and most hangers-on disappeared over the next twenty years. The context provided by these changes, then, is really better envisioned as two eras: heyday (expansion) and crash (shrinkage). And the inhabitants of minor seminaries passed through as two waves or cohorts: the *heyday cohort* (1950s through the mid-1960s) and the *crash cohort* (late-1960s through the 1970s). A quick look at the roots of the institution in which they lived and studied is helpful.

Within the Catholic Church's two millennia, the minor seminary is a relatively new concept, slightly more than 450 years old. The Council of Trent in 1563 responded to what at the time was chaos in the governance of dioceses and the production of priests. Bishops were solely and autonomously responsible for staffing their jurisdictions. Immense variability in financial and population dynamics across dioceses meant tremendous variability in the education and training of priests as well as in the number and quality of those ordained. A priest was a priest ultimately because a bishop ordained him, not necessarily because he merited ordination within some set of agreed-upon standards. The Council altered precedent by mandating that each diocese provide (or join with other dioceses to provide) facilities to educate its local priests and to offer certain elements of instruction.

Those admitted to seminaries had to be at least twelve years of age (which officially set the stage for the introduction of juveniles into priestly studies) and educationally prepared. They were to study liturgy, chant, letters, humanities, scripture, and theology. The content of the academics was to be approved by the bishop. Instructors were priests well-qualified for such instruction (eventually leading to the placement of most priestly training in the hands of religious orders that specialized in such preparation). Emphasis was to be placed upon spiritual development and discipline. Location of the seminaries was to be close to the center of the jurisdiction (primarily the cathedral) – thus, most often an urban site – so that candidates for the priesthood could be observed easily by the bishop and, at the same time, learn the basics of what made the diocese viable.

The next few centuries saw development of the seminary model along the lines of the Council of Trent's dictates not only for diocesan priests but for religious orders. The latter, especially, set the standard for separation of the seminarian from the secular world, moving his education and training from a more urban, cathedral site to a more secluded one. Younger seminarians were separated from older seminarians, a practice that ultimately cleaved minor from major seminaries. The segregation of the seminarian was further stressed by Pope Pius X – after whom, following his 1954 canonization, so many seminaries were named – in the early

1900s as he sought to counter "modernism" by reducing seminarian contact with outside influences (White, 2006). Thus was born the truly "isolationist" seminary to which many attribute (perhaps correctly but without firm research basis) the "stunted maturity" that allegedly characterized generations of priests going forward. So blatantly institutionalized was the concept of isolation that Pope Pius XII in 1950 urged seminaries to consider its potential impact upon the ability of priests to relate to the laity (Anello, 2018: 13, 27; see also Miles, 2012).

The last significant influence on the structure and style of the minor seminary in the mid-Twentieth Century came in the form of Pope Pius XII's 1950 admonition that seminaries (minor and major) should provide their charges with an education of the quality that students in Catholic high schools and colleges were receiving. The pope again sought to assure that priests were sufficiently well-educated to interact appropriately with the laity. The pope's wish effectively brought academic standards firmly into the seminary mix along with spiritual development and discipline. It also caused seminaries to seek mainstream accreditation for their curricula and faculties, an issue especially important for seminary college studies (Anello, 2018:74).

Diocesan minor seminaries during the 1950s commonly educated their students for six years, providing them with high school and two years of college before sending them on to major seminaries for completion of the bachelor's degree (two years) and movement into four years of theology studies (Anello, 2018:71-76). There were exceptions to this "six-six" model primarily within the seminaries of religious orders which typically did not initiate studies for the priesthood until candidates had completed high school (thus, a "four-four" model). The 1960s, however, found many dioceses exploring a "four-four-four" model of seminary education – four years of high school, then four years of college, followed by four years of theology studies. This model aimed to improve the academic quality of the college experience for seminarians, more easily assimilate persons with "late vocations" who had completed high school and perhaps some college, and provide remedial study in philosophy to college graduates who wished to enter the priesthood. At the same time, however, the "four-four-four" model sought to relieve the enrollment pressure seminaries were experiencing at the high-school level in the early 1960s.

The Heyday Era

Despite exploration of other models of seminary education, the typical diocesan minor seminary of the 1950s and early-1960s heyday (rapid-expansion) era subscribed to the "six-six" formula and looked like this: a boarding school with both high school and two-year "junior college" students, secluded (its students did not engage with the world outside most of the year), highly regimented and disciplined (emphasizing obedience to church authorities), promoting spirituality, and stressing academic success while also encouraging involvement in the arts and athletics. Administration of and instruction within diocesan seminaries were usually provided by religious orders via contract with the diocese, though some dioceses sent their seminarians to institutions owned and operated by religious orders.

The 1950s began with the church's (and nearly every diocese's) sense of a crisis in the number of priestly vocations. The supply was inadequate to the current number of Catholics and certainly inadequate to population projections. As if in direct response, the heyday era began taking shape in the mid-1950s as the number of minor seminarians started to increase. The growth continued into the next decade and topped out in 1963 at 38,712 students in high-school and college minor seminaries (Anello, 2018: 52). During that span, seminaries – major as well as minor – enjoyed a construction spurt to accommodate higher numbers entering minor seminaries and in anticipation of their likely impact on major-seminary enrollments.

The increase in numbers of boys and young men studying for the priesthood traces to three related sources. The first was cultural, the nation's return to "normal life" after an immense and prolonged world conflict. The Korean War and the Cold War notwithstanding, America in the late 1940s and early 1950s continued to celebrate its (allied) victory over rivals bent on destroying it. God had been on our side. Confidence was high, as was the spirit of relief and gratitude. Culture and everyday life now were focused upon family, home, religion, and job rather than upon who from the neighborhood was serving or dying where. Mom returned to the home, dad to the factory. Married couples, many now in their late twenties and early thirties, sought to grow their families quickly. Perhaps as important, Catholic elementary schools again more formally assumed the role of encouraging boys to be priests.

Seminary growth also was population-driven. New families produced children in exceptional numbers after the war. The U.S. fertility rate peaked in 1957 at 3.7 children per woman. The post-World War II baby boom generally is framed by demographers as encompassing the years 1946 through 1964. The key to understanding baby-boom effects rests in understanding changes in social structure and culture occasioned by the percentage of the population within given age brackets; to the extent that the percentage of children of elementary-school age expands or contracts, for instance, grade-school construction expands or contracts. Thus, all else equal, we would expect to have seen growth in the size of the population of fourteen-year-olds in the decades following World War II translating into a larger prospect pool for Catholic minor seminaries. Indeed, that is what happened. The first wave of baby boomers to attain high-school entrance age appeared in 1960.

The growth of seminaries and their enrollments, already driven by the post-war return to normal life and optimism, correspondingly accelerated dramatically.

The third source of seminary growth was the attention given to change within the church through the election of Pope John XXIII in 1958. His papacy followed on the heels of the longer-term reign of Pope Pius XII (1939-1958) and fostered expectations of change. John XXIII sought to position the Catholic Church better to address post-World War II global challenges. More to the point, he convened The Second Vatican Council in 1962. Vatican II aimed to celebrate Catholicism and to consider elements of the church thought to be out of sync with the times – a peasant orientation with increasingly higher levels of non-peasant membership; a laity ready for greater inclusion in the conduct of the faith; an institution that ignored or opposed rather than systematically grappled with scientific and technological advances considered vital to global peace and human progress; a hierarchical structure that potentially held sway over Catholics' political views in ways perceived as troublesome by some governments. Anticipated with considerable enthusiasm and much-discussed in Catholic schools, Vatican II brought a positive tenor to Catholicism in the early 1960s and likely inspired boys and young men to consider entering seminaries (White, 1989; Anello, 2018:14-15):

> *For most priests ordained before or during the council, the great surprise of Pope John XXIII awakened a sense of anticipation and hope unprecedented during their lifetimes. Bishops, too, felt the excitement as they reclaimed their ancient identity as members of the college of bishops. The laity, awakened and stirred by the summons to active lives of holiness, stretched their sacramental imagination and took their rightful place in the ecclesial community. Now, it was understood, everyone was called to holiness, every*

baptized person called to service and ministry in accord with his or her own gifts and talents. (Cozzens, 2000: 129)

These were heady times for American Catholicism. Yet, a description of the period as the "heyday era" by definition implies that leaner days were to follow. Times changed. The American minor-seminary bubble burst dramatically.

The Crash Era

Not everyone assumed that new seminarians would just keep coming. Observers of seminary trends during the 1960s warned that if the demographic surge subsided or Catholic support for vocations waned, there would be empty dormitories in the church's minor seminaries (Broderick, 1967). However, with exceptions (Fichter, 1961, 1968), their comments were directed less at prophecy than at prudence, and they echoed similar warnings from secular commentators concerning what might happen to all of the new public high schools then being constructed to accommodate America's rapidly-expanding adolescent population. Most of the discussion about minor seminaries within the heyday era was academic in nature, focused upon best practice rather than upon supply of boys and young men. Considerable debate centered on appropriate curricula, the potential downside of sequestration of minor seminarians, the prospect of developing true spirituality within adolescent populations, and even concern on occasion for the fate of "dropouts" (Anello, 2018: 96, 214).

As might be expected, much discussion also involved the need for quality and selectivity (i.e., assessment of an adolescent's actual prospects for becoming a "good" priest) within the classes of youths entering seminaries each year. Given the abundance of applicants, some argued that the church could be more discriminating in its seminary admission policies. The luxury of numbers also meant that seminaries could afford to experiment with psychological testing in the development of standards for admission and success, and the 1960s saw considerable attention to measures of aptitude, social and mental health, and likelihood of persistence both into and through major-seminary studies and, ultimately, within the priesthood (Anello, 2018:42).

Academic debates gave way to panicked discussions of institutional survival in the mid- to late-1960s (Davis, 1967). Seemingly overnight, the number of youths seeking admission to minor seminaries, the rate of persistence of students within seminaries, and the percentage of minor seminarians matriculating into major seminaries fell precipitously. Seminaries all over the country began closing.

Suddenly seminaries were in competition with each other for the same students. Bishops began to look critically at the number of students "poached" by religious orders from the diocesan seminaries in which they were contracted to teach. Finances became problematic for dioceses and orders; physical plant maintenance was costly whether enrollments were high or low. College seminaries faced an additional problem: unable to staff their faculties with qualified professors and rapidly running out of students, they increasingly found themselves under pressure from accreditation agencies. They began to explore mergers and amalgamations and to form relationships by which Catholic colleges (most coeducational) taught their students while the seminary itself provided spiritual oversight in "houses."

Few seminaries simply rolled over. As the pressure mounted, many sought quick fixes. They accepted boys and young men whose potential as seminarians and whose interest in the priesthood would have been considered marginal at best just a few years earlier. They tried gimmicks: more freedom for students to leave campus, lengthier visits home, more free time, "personalized" individual spiritual development, less-regimented daily routines, more lenient dress and hair-length codes, broader engagement in student governance.

Virtually none of the attempts at survival succeeded. In their final gasp, many seminaries greatly altered their sense of mission. Many became preparatory schools catering not only to seminarians but to lay students who sought simply a good Catholic education. Pursuit of the ministry came to encompass the building of a strong Catholic leadership within lay ranks as well as within those of the priesthood. Many students attended such prep schools not because they wished to be priests but to evaluate whether or not they someday *might* pursue studies for the priesthood. Many others had no thought whatsoever of, let alone plans for, the priesthood.

By 1985, for all intents and purposes, the high school-level minor seminary was an outmoded concept rarely mentioned in discussions of the production of priests (Andre, 1985; Bourgoin, 1983; Cullen, 1985). So few existed by the turn of the millennium that "seminary" referred only to college and major seminary studies, and the term "minor" was less and less often applied to college seminaries.

Hindsight

In retrospect, it is obvious that America's seminaries were highly vulnerable to a reversal of fortune. Business acumen clearly was not a strength of dioceses and religious orders that expanded their seminaries or constructed new ones. While Rome governed whether or not an institution could be designated a seminary, there was no oversight of the wisdom of building it in the first place – of financial sustainability, supply and demand, competition. If a bishop or superior general wanted a seminary and could produce the construction dollars, it was built. This level of autonomy added to the inventory of seminaries when too many already were experiencing low enrollment. In 1959, as the building boom was beginning, four in ten seminaries (minor and major) had fewer than 50 students; in 1968, as the crash was gaining momentum, the average high-school seminary held 91 students and the average college seminary held 80 (Anello, 2018: 18, 82, 172). These were not strong numbers from a financial perspective.

Somewhat more successful, day seminaries held on a bit longer. Without the costs of room and board, and located primarily in large cities such as New York, Chicago, and Pittsburgh, they enrolled significantly higher numbers of seminarians. Chicago's Quigley Preparatory Seminary, for example, enrolled 1,300 students in 1958 (Anello, 2018: 31). Some residential seminaries, faced with overcrowding during the same era, carried a portion of their enrollees as day students, though these seminarians tended to be viewed as of lower status – "day dogs," "day hops" – by the majority residential enrollees (Hedin, 2003: 15, 95; Fausel, 2010: 133).

Funding for seminaries always was uncertain; dioceses initiated drives to construct new facilities but needed to tap their own treasuries to fund ongoing operations. Religious orders counted on philanthropy and investments, always a risky financial strategy. Tuition was low (often discounted or not assessed given the economic background of many seminarians); the common $400-$500 per year rate left only about $200 per student for operating (not capital) costs after meal expenses were covered.[7] Having avoided

---

[7] Tuition (for instruction and room and board) at St. Pius X Seminary in 1962-63 was $450 per year; additional fees totaled $45. Books and supplies for classes were not included in these sums, nor were "personal expenses" such as laundry. The seminary suggested that each family deposit $40 (unused portion refundable) with the seminary treasurer to cover these expenses (St. Pius X Seminary, 1962:4-5).

the costs of their residential counterparts, urban day seminaries found their charges increasingly unable to bear the financial (and emotional) strain of long commutes. The stock of sufficiently credentialed faculty members was inadequate (especially at the college level), and accreditation pressures meant increased costs as seminaries had to employ lay teachers, primarily in the sciences. As enrollment numbers began spiraling down, seminary numbers spiraled down as well – though many institutions held on longer than good business practices would dictate.

Yet, seminary financial vulnerability by itself hardly explains why youths stopped coming. The answer did not lie in demographic trends.[8] In fact, supply of potential candidates for seminary admission was at play only in a small way during the difficult years. The second half of the baby-boom generation (1955-1964) was effectively the same size as the first half. Solid recruitment

---

[8] One demographic trend that might well have helped seminary enrollment – at least in California and the Southwest – was the growing number of Americans of Hispanic descent, primarily of Mexican heritage, in the population. Strongly Catholic and generally with larger families than was the norm among traditional white Catholics, this "newer" ethnic group was ignored in the sense of systematic pursuit of its members for the clergy, as were black Catholics in areas of the country where their numbers were greater. Though criticism and debate occurred (Anello, 2018: 308-323), in the end, the church clearly could not envision its priests as of any but Western European in heritage. Seminaries thus were white enclaves. While members of other races and ethnic groups found their way into them on occasion – as did future Supreme Court Justice Clarence Thomas in the mid-1960s – they were not well received (Thomas, 2007) until well into the 1970s (Anello, 2018: 323). One Mexican American interviewee in the present study who spent the first three quarters of his freshman year in a Claretian minor seminary near Los Angeles in 1959 put it well: "I grew up in East L.A.; everyone spoke Spanish. Suddenly I am in a school with hardly anyone like me, and Spanish is a class you take." The church missed its chance.

prospects remained. Those born in the mid-1950s, for example, reached high school age in the late 1960s and early '70s. The last of the baby boomers (1960 – 1964) were but a few years old when the crash gained momentum and, all else equal, potentially could have begun stocking seminary freshman classes well into the late-1970s. Meanwhile, members of the first wave of the baby boomers, some of whom turned twenty in 1966, were aging out of child production in the 1980s, but many of their children would reach fourteen years of age in that same decade. Gaps in seminary recruitment thus were to be expected, but not to insurmountable degrees and definitely not as early as 1964, were all else to have remained equal – Catholic culture, American class- and economic-opportunity structure, the type of boy interested in the priesthood. All else did not.

The common target of finger-pointing regarding the seminary crash is the Second Vatican Council called by Pope John XXIII in 1962. Vatican II had immediate though mixed impact. On the one hand, it alienated traditional Catholics, those comfortable with the predictable, by leaving behind centuries-old trappings such as the Latin mass. And it left some older priests and religious feeling as though they no longer belonged. On the other hand, Vatican II also energized a new generation of Catholic laity who now found themselves more involved in the liturgy and consulted to a greater degree about parish affairs. And it offered its newer priests and aspirants to the priesthood a more expressive and interactive role in the spread of the gospel and support of the laity. Its momentum in this sense should have been a boon to recruitment of boys and young men into the clergy to replace departing traditionalists.

Recruitment potential notwithstanding, Vatican II negatively affected clerical recruitment and retention because the church did not deliver more meaningfully on the promise of change and ulti- mately produced mistrust of its hierarchical authority (Greeley, 2004). Not only were markers of serious change not apparent in the ensuing years, but a prominent traditional marker was reinforced aggressively: the church's conservative position on marriage and divorce, birth control, sexual orientation, and sexual mores. In particular, Pope Paul VI's *Humanae Vitae* in 1968 dictated an approach to reproductive freedom and responsibility that seemingly spoke to Catholics of past centuries and signaled for the average Catholic a religion that was anything but contemporary (Greeley, 1986: 241-243; 332-344). Additionally, the church's attempts to clarify the difference between democratic involvement of the laity in church affairs and permission to participate to a greater degree in the liturgy and parish matters fostered cynicism. That this occurred during a period of more general cultural upheaval and questioning of authority in America, the 1960s (Gitlin, 1987), served further to distance Catholics from their church leaders.

Vatican II concluded in 1965 and ultimately dampened rather than stoked the hopes and ambitions of newer priests to go forth, spread the word, and affect change. By the mid-1970s, it was clear that priests and religious were being asked to run harder but not differently. The fallout from Vatican II in terms of the production of priests was not so much flight of the laity (and its offspring) from Catholicism as it was the distancing of Catholics from church authorities and, by implication, from priests. Catholics remained in the church but were not likely to encourage their sons to pursue a formal role in the church's clerical structure. Many priests and religious left their vocations behind in the 1960s and 1970s, unsure of their calling and uninspired by their leaders. Many more simply grew quiet and no longer served as major recruiters for the priesthood.

But Vatican II, by itself or in concert with financial challenges, did not bring down minor seminaries. However critical its role in the shape of the Catholic priesthood in decades to follow, something else was at play in the actual, rapid demise of the minor seminary. Ancllo (2018) argues persuasively that the trend away from pursuit of the priesthood by Catholic teenagers preceded Vatican II. While the baby boom brought a higher volume of recruits into the seminary, production could not meet demand as the Catholic population grew significantly. Further, minor seminary attrition rates were increasing; fewer students were persisting through high school and fewer among those who stayed were moving on to the college level and then into major seminaries. The seminary "success" rate — minor seminarians ultimately ordained — dropped from about one in seven in the late-1940s to about one in ten in the mid-1960s and fell further thereafter (Anello 2018: 54; Dougherty, 1968). When Chicago's Quigley Preparatory Seminary closed in 2006, it had produced only one alumnus since 1990 who ultimately was ordained (Donovan and Falsani, 2006).

The steep decline in the production of priests despite a larger candidate pool raised questions about whether the "right" kind of boy was being recruited into seminaries. The better question was whether the same "right" kind of boy existed anymore. The 1930s and 1940s were tough years economically. The priesthood was, for many young men, the only alternative to an otherwise very constrained range of opportunities in a world in which even high-school completion was not a given. The 1950s, as Halberstam (1993) tells us, were quite different. They were marked by economic growth, massive highway and school construction, a burgeoning middle class, suburban development, the GI Bill, Sputnik and federal investment in the sciences, new tensions and perspectives regarding race in America, increased national communication and advertising through television, a car in every garage, McDonald's, and *The Man in the Gray Flannel Suit*.

Catholic populations dispersed quickly in the 1950s from urban and rural ethnic enclaves built around the neighborhood church and school to more ethnically heterogeneous suburbs and new Catholic parishes. Brand new schools – public and parochial – appeared almost overnight. Catholic parents, the children of immigrants, began to imagine their own children going to college and having careers. In short, alternatives now existed and their achievement was decidedly within the realm of possibility. The new middle class also asked more questions. Where once a parent may have doubted the wisdom of isolating boys in seminaries but assented because the church knew best, a parent now more likely said, "I don't think so; let him get through high school first" (Stravaniskas, 2018). The upshot of this cultural change was that boys and young men who entered seminaries indeed were less "committed" to vocational pursuit than were their predecessors. Though perhaps not fully consciously, they understood that they were not without options. And their parents were quicker to accept their decisions to leave the seminary; it was not an automatic ticket to a limited future.

Against this backdrop, then, it is not surprising that seminaries saw higher attrition rates in the late 1950s and early 1960s, even as enrollment numbers mounted. It is equally unsurprising that, as the 1960s became the decade of Vatican II, questions and protest, and skyrocketing college enrollment, seminary recruitment efforts produced fewer dividends. Catholic boys, their families now more distanced from the Catholic clergy, entered minor seminaries in smaller numbers. Entering freshman classes of seminarians became smaller than those of upperclassmen, themselves marked by increasing attrition. The great era of the Catholic minor seminary in America ended as quickly as it had begun. As the years have passed, it now seems only a blip within the Twentieth-Century timeline, a fad, a cruel (self-) deception, certainly a distraction. Were we to remove the "vocation spike" – the late 1950s through the mid-1960s – from the Twentieth Century, we'd see the same problem year after year: the church's failure to align priests with parishioners in number and, many would argue, in substance.

Yesterday's Impact upon
Today's Catholic Priesthood

On those rare occasions on which I attend a Catholic service (a wedding, a funeral), I nearly always find it led by an immigrant priest, but not one from Ireland as was customary when I was a boy. Now he is from the Philippines, Mexico, Nigeria, India, Viet Nam, Colombia, or China – places once considered destinations for Catholic missionaries. Historically, the United States more often than not has had too few priests for too many Catholics. Nations like France, Portugal, Germany, and Italy once sent priests to America to tend to recent emigrants from the old country. However, with more priests than its bishops could afford to support, Ireland was for years far and away the major exporter of priests to America to serve parishes of all kinds, not just those of Irish emigrants. Poorer countries are today's new Irelands. They have an excess of freshly ordained clergy and have become a critical part of the global supply chain. America's bishops need the labor and are quick to sign them up (Gautier et al., 2014).

Bishops must contend with a Catholic population in America that has swelled since 1965 from over 46 million to almost 70 million. The church has not kept pace. Statistics provided by CARA (the Center for Applied Research in the Apostolate, 2017, 2018) indicate that, since the mid-1960s, the number of priests in America has declined from nearly 60,000 to under 40,000 (69 percent of whom are diocesan priests). Large numbers of priests in dioceses and religious orders have died or retired and not been replaced. Over 90 percent of priests in 1965 were active in the ministry; in 2017, 63 percent were active. Many priests left the clergy – seemingly in droves during the late-1960s and throughout the 1970s – and also were not replaced. In 1965, 994 new priests were ordained nationally. 2017 saw only 504 ordinations. The steep drop has not been confined to the diocesan world. In the same period, 1965 to the present, the number of priests in religious orders has been halved. Some orders have been hit particularly hard; Jesuit membership in the United States, for example, has declined from 8,000 to 2,300 (McDonough and Bianchi, 2002; Reilly, 2016).

The downward spiral in number of clergy translates into the church's decreased capacity to serve its membership. CARA (2017, 2018) data indicate that in 1965 there was one priest for every 789 Catholics. In 2017, there was one for every 1,842. The average number of active diocesan priests per parish in 2017 was one; in 1965 the corresponding number was two. Masses are fewer, and younger priests find themselves becoming pastors sooner than was the case in past decades. Parish mergers and closures are increasing rapidly. As late as 1990, there were nearly 20,000 Catholic parishes in America; today there are 2,500 fewer. Some 3,500 extant parishes nationwide – one in five – lack a resident pastor.

There seems little chance of a reversal in the shortage of domestically-produced priests anytime soon. The cradle of religious vocations, the Catholic school system, also has seen its numbers tumble (CARA, 2017, 2018). There were fewer than half as many Catholic elementary schools in 2017 (serving 1.3 million pupils) as there were in 1965 (serving 4.4 million). The number of Catholic high schools has decreased by 20 percent, and the number of students within them by 16 percent. The schools still here have few religious teaching within them. In 1965, the Catholic Church had about 180,000 nuns in America; in 2017, just 46,000 (a high percentage of whom were elderly and a high percentage foreign-born). Religious brothers numbered about 12,000 in 1965 but only 4,000 in 2017.

The freefall in the size of the pool of potential replacements for aging priests in America has abated but definitely not been reversed; the pool remains inadequate to affect seriously the ratio of priests to Catholics. Current pool size also reflects the precipitous drop in seminary numbers since the mid-1960s. In the fall of 2017, there were 3,369 men enrolled in "graduate-level" seminary programs (i.e., post-college, "major-seminary," theological studies prior to ordination) (Gautier and Do, 2018). The corresponding number in 1965 was 8,325. Minor seminary programs – high school-level and college-level programs – designed to prepare candidates for the college degree and theological studies, enrolled, by generous estimate, 1,639 students in the fall of 2017 (Gautier and Do, 2018); in the mid-1960s, in the heat of the minor-seminary boom, the corresponding number was nearly 39,000 (Anello, 2018. 466).[9]

Who Knew?

My heyday peers and I saw only progress. Our difficulties were personal rather than institutional. Our spanking-new campus and its expansion shortly after we arrived conveyed confidence in St. Pius X Seminary. When we told people outside how many students attended our school, they seemed genuinely amazed that we went to a "real" school. The facility expanded; Salvatorians sent elsewhere always were replaced. I recall not a single priest at St. Pius – or in my home parish – leaving the priesthood while I was a seminarian. The only inkling of trouble surfaced as a rumor among upperclass-men in 1966 that the Salvatorian order had encountered financial

---

[9] Estimates of seminary programming and population at all levels prior to the late 1960s are challenging because wholly reliable census figures for the 1950s and 1960s are not available and because the nature of seminaries against which to make comparisons has changed drastically. Many seminary programs now exist within broader institutional settings. It thus becomes difficult to sort which students within them are, in fact, seminarians and which may be engaged in other vocational-education tracks leading, for example, to deaconate or lay-ministry roles.

difficulties (Avella, 1994). St. Pius alumni then studying within the order had gossiped to us about real-estate investments gone sour, and one poor old priest who had tried to call attention to the debacle had been transferred to our campus. But what had that to do with us, with our school?

Within Catholicism more generally, change was happening though it was not clear yet that truly difficult times were to follow. Recollections of Vatican II for most former minor seminarians of the era are primarily memories of liturgical change. Latin to English overnight. New prayer books and hymnals. Protestant hymns in Catholic churches. Guitars and folksongs at mass. Priests facing us rather than the altar and wearing colorful, contemporary vestments. Suited boys at the sanctuary lectern offering readings from the Book of Someone. Fasting before communion gone along with meatless Fridays.

We could see unhappiness on the faces of some of our teachers, the more traditionalist of them, old timers. But others seemed not the least fazed by the changes, even happy with them. Bad singing in Latin became even worse singing in English, of course, but the change made virtual Mario Lanzas of the hammier of our priests. We saw the same at home during holidays and summer: grumpy priests and parishioners, happy priests and parishioners. Altar railings gone, altars moved. Women doing the readings at some masses!

When I left St. Pius in 1967, incoming classes were smaller, but the average of us did not add two and two. Members of the crash cohort, however, encountered a very different seminary and surely sensed the obvious. How could one miss the implications of steadily shrinking class and faculty sizes and the move to "prep school" status? The physical plant became shabby. By the mid-1970s, everyone knew what was coming for the institution, though few sensed what awaited Catholicism in the decades to come.

Such was the saga of boom and bust of the minor seminary in post-World War II America. What began with a roar ended with a bleat. My classmates and I were swept in during the ascent, the heyday. We aged out of the minor seminary, those of us who had not already departed, just as the crash was gathering steam. The difference in the seminary's effect on its students pre-crash versus the effect on those post-crash was meaningful, as we shall see in coming chapters. Heyday-cohort seminarians failed, in the jargon of the time, to "persevere" in their vocation and left feeling accountable. For crash-cohort seminarians, it was the institution – perhaps even the church itself – that failed to persevere. For both cohorts, at issue always was the notion of "vocation." It is to this concept that we turn our attention in Chapter Three.

References

Andre, Daniel. 1985. "High School Seminaries –The Changing Picture." *Ligourian* 73 (February):43.

Anello, Robert L. 2018. *Minor Setback or Major Disaster? The Rise and Demise of Minor Seminaries in the United States, 1958-1983.* St. Louis MO: EnRoute Books.

Avella, Steven M. 1994. *The Moment of Grace: One Hundred Years of Salvatorian Life and Ministry in the United States, Part II, 1947-1992.* Milwaukee: Society of the Divine Savior.

Bourgoin, Mary Fay. 1983. "Seminarians as Endangered Species." *National Catholic Reporter* 7 (February 25): 19-24.

Broderick, John F. 1967. "Empty Seminaries in Prospect?" *American Ecclesiastical Review* 156 (4): 217-27.

CARA (Center for Applied Research in the Apostolate). 2017. "*Frequently Requested Church Statistics.*" *www.cara. georgetown.edu.*

_____. 2018. "*Frequently Requested Church Statistics.*" *www.cara. georgetown.edu.*

Cozzens, Donald B. 2000. *The Changing Face of the Priesthood: A Reflection on the Priest's Crisis of Soul.* Collegeville MN: Liturgical Press.

Cullen, Paul. 1985. "High School Seminaries: Keeping the Doors Open." *Our Sunday Visitor* (www.osv.com, October 13).

Davis, Thurston N. 1967. "Vocations to the Priesthood Are Falling and Falling Fast." *America* 116 (19): 707.

Donovan, Lisa and Cathleen Falsani. 2006. "Quigley Seminary Will Close: Only 1 Student Became Priest in Last 16 Years." *Chicago Sun-Times* (September 20, p. 8).

Dougherty, Denis. 1968. "The Rate of Persistence to Ordination of Minor Seminary Graduates." *Sociological Analysis* 29: 30-38.

Fausel, Donald F. 2010. *From Blind Obedience to a Responsible Faith.* Bloomington IN: iUniverse.

Fichter, Joseph. 1961. *Religion as an Occupation.* South Bend IN: University of Notre Dame Press.

_____. 1968. *America's Forgotten Priests: What They Are Saying.* New York: Harper and Row.

Gautier, Mary, Melissa A. Cidade, Paul M. Perl, and Mark M. Gray. 2014. *Bridging the Gap: International Priests Ministering in the United States.* Washington DC: Center for Applied Research in the Apostolate (CARA).

Gautier, Mary and Thu Do. 2018. *Catholic Ministry Formation Enrollment: Statistical Overview for 2017-18.* Washington DC: Center for Applied Research in the Apostolate (CARA).

Gitlin, Todd. 1987. *The Sixties: Years of Hope, Days of Rage.* New York: Bantam Books.

Greeley, Andrew M. 1986. *Confessions of a Parish Priest: An Autobiography.* New York: Simon & Schuster.

_____. 2004. *The Catholic Revolution: New Wine, Old Wineskins, and the Second Vatican Council.* Berkeley: University of California Press.

Halberstam, David. 1993. *The Fifties.* New York: Random House.

Hedin, Raymond. 2003. *Married to the Church (Updated Edition)*. Bloomington: Indiana University Press.

McDonough, Peter and Eugene Bianchi. 2002. *Passionate Uncertainty: Inside the American Jesuits*. Berkeley CA: University of California Press.

McGucken, Joseph. 1958. *Pioneering for Christ*. New York: Lawson Associates.

Miles, Vincent J. 2012. *Boys of the Cloth: The Accidental Role of Church Reforms in Causing and Curbing Abuse by Priests*. Lanham, MD: Hamilton Books.

Reilly, Patrick. 2016. "American Jesuits Are in a Free Fall, and the Crisis is Getting Worse." *The Cardinal Newman Society* (https://newmansociety.org/ american-jesuits-free-fall-crisis getting-worse/) (July 29).

St. Pius X Seminary. 1962. *General Bulletin*. Galt CA: St. Pius X Seminary.

Sravaniskas, Peter M.J. 2018. "Pre-Publication Endorsement." In Robert L. Anello, *Minor Setback or Major Disaster? The Rise and Demise of Minor Seminaries in the United States, 1958-1983*. St. Louis MO: EnRoute Books. P. ii.

Thomas, Clarence. 2007. *My Grandfather's Son: A Memoir*. New York: HarperCollins.

White, Joseph M. 1989. *The Diocesan Seminary in the United States: A History from the 1780s to the Present*. Notre Dame IN: University of Notre Dame Press.

_____. 2006. "Perspectives on the Nineteenth-Century Diocesan Seminary in the United States." *U.S. Catholic Historian* 19: 21-35.

PART II

Pushed or Pulled?

CHAPTER THREE

Who Called?

*S*t. Francis asked God, *"Lord what will you have me do?" God told him to "Go and repair my church." Francis was a grown man. I was a kid, with, as Boyne (2014) puts it, "no more sense than a thimble," when my mom pointed me toward the priesthood. I never heard a thing, just did as I was told. The older I got, the less I heard or maybe wanted to hear. Must have lost the call a few days after my mother gave it to me. It didn't matter; I was hypnotized, and hypnotists can make you do things.*

Vocati Sumus
(Latin: "We Have Been Called")

Men and women in pursuit of "doing God's work" (i.e., more than striving to live in harmony with his dictates) invariably refer to themselves as "called" to minister to others in his name. Indeed, the term "vocation" by which we more formally refer to this sense of invitation or command derives from the Latin verb, *vocare*, "to call." Priests, preachers, ministers, brothers, nuns, monks, monastics, deacons, missionaries – from John the Baptist to the Apostle Paul to Jeanne d'Arc to Martin Luther to Martin Luther King, Jr. to Thomas Merton to Mother Teresa to Jimmy Swaggart – believe themselves called to spend their lives responding as directed. For most who accept it, the religious calling involves an exceptionally difficult and often lonely walk for a lifetime, however ultimately spiritually and emotionally rewarding the journey may be. Many live with a high degree of uncertainty about why they were chosen and whether they are conducting their ministry as God truly wishes.

Having walked the path, there are priests and other religious on their deathbeds today who believe fully that God invited them into special service, that they did their best, hard as it might have been to please him, and now will enter the afterlife in peace. And there are others who cannot say with certainty that they ever had a religious calling. They hope so given that they committed themselves to a particular form of service to God and want neither to have wasted their lives nor to have disappointed him.

There are those too who have concluded that they devoted their lives to something that was not real. They have decided that God does not call persons to such service or, in any case, did not call them specifically. Many are fine with this; they tried their best and did good things for people; no regrets. Others are bitter, feeling that they got stuck in a maze from which they could not extricate themselves.

Finally, there are those who embarked upon but never completed the journey along the path. Joined the race; left the track before the finish line. Their numbers encompass the vast majority of those who entered minor seminaries in the mid-Twentieth Century.

In Pursuit of Vocation

Many priests who attended minor seminaries describe themselves as "knowing I wanted to be a priest" at a very early age. One retired priest in the Diocese of Sacramento and alumnus of St. Pius X Seminary, for example, "knew at age four." Another had the "seed planted" in the sixth grade. Yet another from St. Pius knew at age ten that he wanted to become a priest and return to his grade school to give everyone his first blessing. In short, while their resolve may have been tested along the journey to ordination, the fact of vocation was indisputable for these men. Their twelve years of minor and major seminary education and training were never about vocational "discernment" (the term applied to today's seminary experience as a process of determining whether one is called) but about the "preservation" and "nurturing" of the vocation they *knew* they possessed. Called from the cradle, they have given virtually their entire lives to the priesthood.

On the face of it, the sense of God's call is what a study of boys and young men on the road to the Catholic priesthood in any era should entail. Thus, we could approach the topic of boys made into priests as a matter of whether or not individuals are called: God calls, and the boy says yes; God calls, and the boy says no; God does not call, but the boy thinks he did; or the boy can't determine whether or not God is calling. Or we could assume that "many are called but few are chosen," and focus on the capacity of the church and its seminaries to sort out real from misheard or mistaken callings and to shepherd those truly chosen. The latter path leads easily to discussion of the size and condition of the net cast by the church and the manner of the cast. In either case, it is God doing the calling and the church acting as the conduit.

Conversely, we could approach from the other direction, leave God out of the call, and define a vocation as whatever the church says it is. Within Catholicism, one does not simply hear the call and proclaim himself a priest. The church picks and chooses its priests. While it must behave operationally as if a priest is a person chosen by God to minister, the tap on the shoulder from God is not the issue. Instead, the priesthood is license granted and continually overseen by the church to engage in certain acts and behaviors. The church alone determines the terms by which persons are so licensed. As indicated in Chapter Two, just how liberal or conservative is the church in screening "candidates" for the priesthood is era-specific. To the extent, for example, that the Catholic Church *needs* more priests – as when fewer people perceive themselves to have a vocation or the population of Catholics expands beyond current supply, or both – the door to the seminary is easier to open and the church's willingness to grant ordination expands, theoretically even to the point of becoming indiscriminant.

What happens in most cases, of course, resides somewhere between these poles. For vocation is in part a perception held by an individual, subject to change over time, its concreteness or ambiguity known only to the person pursuing it, struggling with it, happy or miserable in it. It is in part as well a matter of how the church at any time defines, measures, or recognizes vocation; that too always is subject to change. Thus, it may be easy enough to define "vocation," but it is difficult to apply the term to a specific case – including one's own – and equally difficult to measure vocations in quality and quantity at any point in history.

Put simply, the notion of vocation in any practical sense is complex and involves decidedly adult, high-stakes decisions by those who perceive themselves to be called (in the matter of minor seminarians, likely because someone convinced them of it) and by the church that determines whether to recognize and foster that person's perception. The term *seminary* refers literally to a place where seeds are cultivated. Yet, the process of priestly "formation" (the precise term the church employs) includes the weeding out of candidates who appear unsuitable for ordination. Thus, with both individual and church as actors in the production of a priest, one can heed the call, miss the call, resist or run from the call, mistake the call, or have the call acknowledged or denied by the church. Indeed, all of these outcomes potentially exist for a single individual during the course of a life's vocational pursuit.

Given the above, the concept of vocation is not mere contextual material for a look at how boys in the 1950s, 1960s, and 1970s did or did not pursue the priesthood. Rather, it is the ambiguous mechanism by which fairly naïve and uninformed teenagers were invited into and retained in Catholic minor seminaries during those decades. Adolescents were pursuing adult objectives. The natural question, then, is: what was the sense of "call" experienced by the average minor seminarian before and after entry?

Seminarians' Sense of Calling

My interviews and readings of first-person accounts put to rest quickly the notion that former minor seminarians easily could describe, let alone explain, their perception of having been "called" or of realizing that they were not. Their grasp of what they were doing was slippery at best. Twelve-year-olds do not undergo experiences like Saul's on the road to Damascus, and teenagers generally are unclear about both what constitutes a call and the consequences of choosing not to respond. What brought them to the seminary?

As noted previously, seminarians tended early on to assume responsibility for their vocations – the ball was theirs to carry or to drop. Personal care of one's vocation, after all, was a major element of minor seminary culture. Sorting the history of their special calling was difficult for boys and young men while in the seminary and made their decisions to stay or leave challenging. Distance (and age) tended to permit former seminarians to parse the source of this element of their lives years later, yet even men who long had been away from the seminary frequently were at a loss to pin down what had happened. One interviewee, for example, detailed his family's connection to the church and its willingness to let their children explore what they wished, including a religious vocation. But he had no idea why the priesthood had attracted him in the first place. It was not until late in the interview that he suddenly said of his days in the seminary, "I knew I did not want to go back home because the old man drank too much."

Another interviewee who had attended a minor seminary for two years similarly had no sense of what got him there. He recalled no family influence upon the decision; it was his alone, he said. His aunt was a nun but, in his view, she had not pushed him toward the priesthood, perhaps had even discouraged entry. During his interview, he noted that he also did not recall exactly why he chose to enter the diocesan seminary at thirteen when he really had his sights set upon entering the Jesuits after high school. This led to the following exchange:

JFS: I don't get it, Owen. You knew no Jesuits, but you wanted to be one. You grew up in a small rural town with one parish, and it was Franciscan. Where did the Jesuit idea come from?

Owen: I don't know, other than that my mother used to refer to me as her little Jesuit scientist.

Owen froze and turned very pensive. He then spent much of the remaining interview sorting out the extent to which his mother had influenced his decision to become a priest. He recalled waiting until the last minute to tell her he was not returning to the seminary because he knew it would disappoint her terribly. He told me sometime later that he was still wrestling with his inability over the years to recognize his mother as the major source of his "vocation."

Similarly, a former priest from Chicago noted that he had no idea why, since childhood, he wanted to become a priest. Perhaps it was his devout grandmother's influence, he said, but he had no memory of her ever saying a word about it. His mother (who later made it very difficult for him to leave the priesthood) seemed not to push, and his father never broached it. Our exchange proceeded:

Don: Beginning in the second grade, I used to get up at five in the morning, every day, and ride my bike to six o'clock mass [at a Chicago suburban church]. Sometimes I'd get there even before they opened the doors, and I'd sit on the cold step.

JFS: Your parents let a seven-year-old kid leave the house unattended every morning at five AM to go to church?

Don: Yeah, I guess that was a little odd, huh? I never thought about it.

Seminarians' sense of being called to serve God may have differed across individuals and may or may not have been strong and clear. Nearly invariably, however, their sense of what they would do as priests someday was straightforward. They knew what priests did because they saw priests doing it.

Early Role Models

Ask any seven-year-old who wants to be a police officer upon growing up what it is that cops do and, unless the kid has a relative who is a police officer, he or she will tell you: catch bad guys. Children who want to be nurses believe they'll take care of sick people.

Future astronauts will circle the earth. Soldiers will fight battles. Teachers will, well, teach. And what will a priest do? Youngsters who see themselves as a priest someday invariably will tell you, "Priests say mass and hear confessions."

> *[As a boy] I would offer in my play a piece of bread… the gift of the Eucharist. I put an old satin dress of my mother's around my shoulders. Shaking with excitement, I carried the piece of bread around the room slowly; bobbing up and down, I muttered in pretend Latin over a vase.* (Cornwell, 2006: 35).

> *[In sixth grade] I was very fascinated with the mass. At school when they role-played the mass and the sacraments, I once got to be the priest which was an honor. And I had an altar* [at home]. *I was saying mass in my room long before I entered the seminary.* (Retired priest from San Diego.)

> *Yeah. I used to play at saying mass in my room as a kid. I'd put a blanket over a lamp and call it my sanctuary light.* (Redemptorist priest from St. Louis)

As the mid-Twentieth Century boy who wanted to be a priest moved into early adolescence, he gained a sense that the job was perhaps a bit more complicated than celebrating mass and hearing confessions. Especially if he had been an altar server, he likely knew that there was more to the funeral or wedding than the mass alone. Maybe he had seen a baptism, so that too was added to the job description. And every kid knew that priests visited the parish school, told a few jokes, answered some questions, and gave the class his blessing. The point is that, sans a priest-relative (and maybe with one), a thirteen-year-old priest-prospect acted upon what he had seen. During the heyday era of huge seminary growth, when he shared his dream with adult members of the Catholic community of which he was a part, his intention was celebrated (certainly more so than today in the wake of the sexual-abuse scandal): "So you want to be a priest? Wonderful. We need priests. I'll pray for you."

That is the easy part of understanding what children thought they were getting into when they set their sights on the priesthood. The harder question in this look back at the 1950s, '60s, and '70s is: if boys had a fairly rudimentary notion of priests' work before they entered the minor seminary, when and how ultimately did they gain a more sophisticated sense of that work? The answer, at its root, is: they did not; minor seminarians (rookies and veterans alike) possessed a sense of a priest's life little different from that which characterized their pre-seminary counterparts. A priest's role was, for the minor seminarian, what the boy or young man saw priests doing. There was no introductory course on priests' work. There was no spend-the-day-with-your-favorite-priest. And no priest took the seminarian under his wing and showed him the ropes.

Another true story:

In May, 1961, a meteor fell from the sky onto the head of Father Charles Fagan on the playground of St. Philomene School in Sacramento. Well, not a meteor actually, but a baseball which surely felt to him like a meteor when it struck. Fr. Fagan was a good-natured and likeable priest who would stop and talk to kids on the playground after school as they awaited their rides home or practiced with their school sports teams. On the day in question, he hit a few grounders to the infielders on the base-ball team – placing his hands on the bat in reverse (incorrect) order "because it felt better." Then he walked out to the (asphalt) outfield and began a conversation with a group of outfielders shagging flies. It was there that he was beaned by a fly ball off the bat of Bennie Carbon, an eighth-grader soon to enter St. Pius X Seminary. Fr. Fagan did not return to baseball practice.

Why, you ask, would a grown man walk among a pack of kids shagging flies, back to the hitter no less, totally oblivious to the fact of baseballs raining from the sky? Try this: he was a recent Irish immigrant who knew zilch about baseball!

During the era in question, unless he was from a Franciscan or Jesuit parish, the average seminarian at St. Pius X shared with his fellows a common notion of a parish priest: an Irishman who came to the U.S. directly from the seminary which itself was all he had known of the world. In the Diocese of Sacramento, Father Fagan was "every priest," the prototype. He had a brogue. He dropped by our grade-school classroom every week, and we strained to understand what he said after Sister Ann adoringly introduced him. He celebrated Mass on weekdays and Sundays, and parishioners strained to understand him. He heard confessions and rarely chewed us out, though we were not sure because we did not always understand what he said. He was spoken of and spoken to in respectful terms by our parents and would come to dinner at our house on occasion. He officiated at our sister's wedding and our grandmother's funeral. If he patted our heads, we beamed. If he was annoyed at us, we were crushed. If we bonked him with a baseball at practice, we were very scared. If he brought a complaint to our home, the roof fell in.

Of course, we also learned about priests from reruns of "priest movies" on television during the 1950s: *Boy's Town* (1938), *Angels with Dirty Faces* (1938), *Going My Way* (1944), *The Bells of St. Mary's* (1944). The priests depicted in those movies were incredible in their impact upon the sheep in their flocks. We also had Bishop Sheen – from Illinois, not Ireland – a television star in his long black cape. We learned too about the hardships faced by missionaries – priests and nuns – in Africa (*The Nun's Story* debuted on the silver screen in 1959), India, Latin America, and Communist China. And we read books about Father Damien and the lepers of Molokai. Our parents generally were not keen on us becoming missionaries.

To know our parish priests was not necessarily to view them as saints. One associate pastor was especially officious and condescending, for example, and I remember my mother saying unkind things about him. Our pastor, on the other hand, was humble, shy, and soft-spoken. But he also had a serious drinking problem easily discerned by the altar boys each morning when he arrived at the last minute for eight-o'clock Mass tucking his white t-shirt into his pants. He mumbled his Latin so that we had difficulty knowing what to respond and thence earned "the glare." Invariably he demanded two pours, rather than one, of altar wine into the chalice. Still, he was a priest, as pastor a very important one. He and the other priests in our parish received every bit of the respect and deference that Catholics throughout the world gave the clergy in that day.

In sum, what we knew about priests upon entering the seminary in the 1950s, 1960s, and 1970s — though Vatican II was changing perceptions a bit by the '70s – was what we knew about the priests in our parish.[10] They were the "cultic" clergy (Basik, 1999), occupying the "sacral" role (Rausch, 1999), i.e., men apart, immersed in the sacred, holy and obedient to the church hierarchy, holy and paternalistic toward the laity. Rarely one's friend but most times

---

[10] Looking back in the wake of the sexual-abuse scandal that has demoralized Catholics and good priests over the past several decades (see Chapter Nine), it is likely that at least a few of my seminary schoolmates had another sense of what some priests did. For those boys were the abusive priest's victims, sitting ducks, looking forward to entering the seminary, hanging out at the church, spending time with the "good father." The "good father," unfortunately, had other plans. He also spent considerable time visiting in the boys' homes, and no parent could have been prouder than to have had such a special visitor in the neighborhood. Maybe someday their boy would be a priest too, God willing.

friendly, priests walked above us even if sometimes failing to inspire while doing so:

> *The priest dealt with sacred matters in a sacred language. He was versed in the mysteries of the faith. He was holy by the mere fact of being a priest. He was highly educated and wise and had unquestioned authority in every facet of the parish. It did not matter if he could not preach very well. The really important thing was that he could celebrate Mass. ... The specifics of his personal life were shrouded in mystery. He seemed happy....* To be a priest was the highest life a boy could aspire to. ... [I]t meant being respected and revered almost as Christ himself.* (Pilarczyk, 1986: 140).

Later Role Models

Inside the minor seminary, a second set of role models emerged – the priests who taught us and evaluated us as potential clergy. As indicated in Chapter Two, at St. Pius X Seminary, these priests were Salvatorians (members of the Society of the Divine Savior). Theirs was an order with origins in Germany and, in this country, in historically German, rural Wisconsin. Of the seventeen Salvatorian priests who taught at St. Pius over the years I was there, thirteen had attended the same Salvatorian minor seminary. Ten were from Wisconsin, and most of those had left the farm or the small farm town during the Great Depression because the priesthood offered one of the few ways out of an opportunity structure that could not accommodate all of the youths in the area. Six of the faculty members had acquired advanced degrees in their areas of curricular interest, but the average instructor had completed the college philosophy major within the major seminary and had not pursued topics beyond his mandatory theological studies.

Here is what we saw: men who were (for us) teachers first, disciplinarians second, priests third. We knew them best in the role in which we interacted with them on a daily basis. They framed the subject matter we studied, and they graded us "on merit." They directed the plays in which we acted. They coached the basketball teams on which we played. They balled us out, and they sometimes gave us compliments. We respected them as teachers much as our secular contemporaries respected their teachers – some better than others, some very good, some simply awful. We challenged and picked on some of them, and others we dared not rile. One faculty member, for instance, was a gruff man of legendary temper and prodigious strength. He once lifted and then lowered back to the floor the desk of a student – the boy still in it – who was slow responding to a question.

Many interviewees and writers have noted one important outcome of attending minor seminary: we saw the human side of priests. Those of us at St. Pius could see childishness and bullying as well as kindness, maturity, and wisdom among the priests who taught us. We knew which priests had a drinking problem, sometimes manifested through the confessional screen in the early morning. Some of our faculty were approachable while others were completely the opposite. Some clearly were happier in their vocation than were others. Many likely were bored to tears since, like us, they were isolated from the world on a remote patch of flat valley floor in rural California. Every priest was a disciplinarian in the sense that he had to deal with teenagers being teenagers. Some handled it well; others did not. Some were secure, some insecure:

I used to cringe when [Father] *Charles would hit kids, really slug them, and then tell everyone that "What happens within these walls stays within these walls."* (Alumnus, St. Pius X Seminary)

69

Once when a bunch of us were goofing around with [Father] *Sigmund, he didn't like something I said, so he whipped me across the face with his cincture* [a knotted, heavy cord worn around the Salvatorian's waist]. *He just missed my eye. He was laughing, but it was that kind of nervous laugh – like he knew he had just screwed up. It hurt so bad I had to fight off tears and sneak away.* (Alumnus, St. Pius X Seminary)

Remember the time Jones asked [Father] *Marvin a question in* [college] *history class, and Marvin did not get it or didn't know the answer but didn't want to show it? So he says, "Ask questions that matter, Jones. And write me a 1,500-word paper on this one, due Thursday." (Alumnus, St. Pius X Seminary)*

We also saw priests – a few of our teachers, anyway – as social activists. This was, after all, not only the era of Vatican II but of significant civil rights and anti-war movements. Catholics saw Father James Groppi lead marches for fair housing in Milwaukee and priest-siblings Daniel and Philip Berrigan engage in activities against U.S. involvement in Viet Nam. In California, priests and nuns joined social-justice activists in support of better working conditions and wages for farm workers; priests and seminarians from St. Pius X took part in activities in support of Mexican grape-pickers. And some of our number traveled with a seminary priest to minister to Catholics in rural Appalachia during summer break.

Our role models in the minor seminary, then, made clear that priests could be teachers and, if they wished, social activists. They lived in a communal setting (sometimes an isolated one) and reported to a rector; indeed, every year, the Salvatorians lured to their novitiate a few of the St. Pius high-school graduates or two-year college students in pursuit of the life they admired in our faculty members. But when did we see our teachers and disciplinarians as priests who engaged in behaviors that might characterize life in a diocesan parish? At mass and confession and at mandatory prayer – the same look we were afforded at our parish priests. (On Sundays, many of our teachers drove off to neighboring churches to help out with mass and confessions.) What did we see that would prepare us for a future as a diocesan priest, a priest doing everyday priest-work, a professional priest? Less actually than what we had seen in the parish as children and surely less than what we would have seen had we simply remained at home as halfway-observant high-school students. In short, few minor seminarians of the day (i.e., few adolescents) could describe in any depth that which they hoped someday to become. We sense that depth as we explore the work of priests in Chapter Four.

References

Bacik, James. 1999. "The Practice of Priesthood: Working through Today's Tensions." In Karen Sue Smith, ed., *Priesthood in the Modern World*. Franklin WI: Sheed and Ward. Pp. 51-65.

Boyne, John. 2014. *A History of Loneliness*. New York: Doubleday.

Cornwell, John. 2006. *Seminary Boy: A Memoir*. New York: Doubleday.

Pilarcyk, Daniel. 1986. "The Changing Image of the Priest." *Origins* July 3: 140-141.

Rausch, Thomas. P. 1999. "Priestly Identity: Priority of Representation and the Iconic Argument." *Worship* 73:169-79.

CHAPTER FOUR

Bless Me, Father

W hat exactly was the prize that we seminarians hoped someday to capture? On the one hand, the value of the priesthood seemed known; why otherwise would everyone tell us what a wonderful thing we were about to do? On the other, no one ever really told us what a priest did beyond what we observed with our own eyes. The notion of vocation was nebulous if not downright confusing to us. Was its outcome, the practice of the priesthood, any clearer? Could priests themselves have explained it to us? Andrew Greeley (1986: 116) suggested in his autobiography that "once the rigid social control of diocesan and rectory life were lifted [by Vatican II], many of us revealed that we had no idea of what a priest was...." Making the point yet more emphatically, a former priest among my interviewees described how he had kept his eye on the prize for his entire seminary career. The problem was that the prize, for him, was ordination. The priesthood that ordination permitted had largely not

been considered by him, and, "When I got there, it was
not really something that I wanted to do."

Priesthood as Profession

Older priests often refer to their years in the priesthood as their "career." In contemporary parlance, career generally is associated with the notion of profession. Profession suggests more than the fulfilling of tasks and reporting to a boss or manager. Members of professions claim higher and more complex levels of specialized knowledge than do standard job holders, and the claim generally is honored within society. Most professionals base the claim in part on the lengthy and rigorous education, training, and evaluation they received in order to practice.

Professionals are granted considerable autonomy in decision-making within the work sphere. Yet, many, if not most, professionals are supervised either by a manager (a "higher-up") in a product- or a service-delivery organization or, oftentimes, by professional associations that ultimately determine the suitability of the individual to practice. Many professionals do not have to "clock in," instead determining the pace and amount of their time devoted to work – including working far longer hours than do others within their jobs. Many specialize in certain areas within their profession, again often licensed to do so by professional associations. Finally, professionals adhere to codes of ethics that govern their decisions, behavior, and how they treat clients. By virtue of these features of career, professionals generally earn more money than do nonprofessionals and are accorded more than ordinary social respect and status.

Is the priesthood a profession? Some priests say no: it is neither job nor profession; it is a special calling directly from God. However, it decidedly is a profession in almost every sense of the above discussion. Priests spend years in rigorous (seminary) education and training on the road to ordination. They are granted license to work by their professional organization, the church. While always accountable to a supervisor (a human one as well as the divine one), they have considerable autonomy in on-the-ground decision making (e.g., the disposition of a penitent within the confessional; advice to persons whose marriage is in trouble). Many specialize in particular areas of professional expertise (e.g., canon law, administration, social services). They definitely are bound by a code of ethics and, by virtue of the church's rules and bureaucracy, are well-versed in complicated church practice. And, the recent sexual abuse scandal notwithstanding, they are well-respected socially.

In short, no one calls the priesthood simply a "job." Yet, we can argue that the priesthood differs from (or perhaps exceeds the scope of) other professions in the sense of vocation as a way of life. Vocation is a complicated phenomenon that requires choices, maturity, and persistence. The priesthood demands commitment of roughly the whole life of the practitioner. Service, ministry, contemplation, and prayer are neither compartmentalized nor turned off at the close of the workday. Time "on call" virtually is twenty-four hours per day, at least for the average diocesan priest. Priests do not have spouses and children and, thus, forego both the pleasures and the distractions associated with family.[11] They lack decision-making autonomy regarding anything that is policy-related. Finally, the priestly vocation does not translate into higher-than-average financial compensation. The profession lacks the buying power of

---

[11] It is common within Catholicism to speak of those with religious vocations as "married" – nuns as "brides of Christ" and priests as "married to the church." The point brings home the absolute commitment of the religious to the organization perceived to have been founded by Christ as well as highlighting the commitment of the individual to the concept of celibacy.

the "regular" professions. Indeed, priests are not expected to possess that capacity; quite the opposite.

By way of its ownership and oversight of the priesthood, the church also recognizes an error term in the screening, preparation, selection, and retention of those it deems worthy of the cloth. Though ordination creates a "priest for life," one cannot actively remain a priest (in the sense of officially conducting priestly duties within Catholic parishes and communities) if the church withdraws its designation of one's status as "active." The church can expel bad actors (child molesters and embezzlers, for example) from the ranks of the active priesthood via what is termed "involuntary laicization." Short of exercising such expulsion rights, it also reserves the right to deny "incardination"; every priest must operate under the jurisdiction of a bishop (in the case of diocesan priests) or superior (in the case of religious orders, i.e., groups of priests, brothers, or nuns who live set apart and communally under guiding principles established by the group's founder). He has no right to a particular assignment or placement or to change dioceses or orders without permission. Permission to practice is the bishop's or religious order's to own.[12] Indeed, one cannot even leave the priesthood in good standing, in the church's view, without its blessing. The Vatican reserves the right to "laicize" a man who wishes voluntarily

---

[12] This generally is not a matter of whimsy but of bishops and superiors acting in good faith to integrate the priest's strengths and weaknesses with the needs of the diocese or religious order. Further, the process is regulated by canon law. That said, I encountered two priests in one Midwestern diocese who described their bishop as ignoring canon law regarding placement. He simply refused to provide assignments for the two, leaving them to drift as priests without practice (and income). Further inquiries indicated that this has become increasingly common as religious leaders seek to avoid the hint of scandal of any kind in the wake of the larger sexual abuse scandal that has cost dioceses hundreds of millions of dollars in recent years.

to leave, a right dispensed differentially in varying eras.[13] Nor can the priest who voluntarily became inactive and wishes to remain in good standing within the church marry without a papal dispensation. Bluntly, a vocation to the priesthood is the church's to determine, before, during, and after ordination.

Priests' Work

*Maybe there are some young men present here who have this call in their hearts, the aspiration to become a priest, the desire to serve others in the things that come from God, the desire to spend one's entire life in service in order to catechize, baptize, forgive, celebrate the Eucharist, heal the sick… the whole of one's life in this way…. If some of you have heard this call in your heart, it is Jesus who has placed it there. (*Pope Francis, 2014)

To characterize the priesthood as a profession falls short of describing what it is that priests actually do, of the expectations and actions that make a priest a priest. We know that, universally and at the very least, priests pray, contemplate, and minister. This sounds simple enough, but it is hardly so. Priests must pray daily (generally and mandatorily through recitation of specific prayers). They must contemplate seriously and proactively (but within bounds set for them) the life of Jesus Christ, what Christ wishes for and from

---

[13] Contrast this situation with that of the itinerant preacher or the protestant minister in a formal congregation (perhaps even with a seminary education). He (or, within many religions, she; Catholicism is among the few denominations to maintain the purely fraternal approach) may or may not continue to "practice" the ministry. He can depart or even be fired by the congregation he serves. He can change denominations at will. He can walk away from the whole thing. It is between God and him. Thus, we meet people in various walks of life who describe themselves as once having been a minister in the same way that others note that they once were doctors or lawyers or teachers but no longer practice.

the faithful, and how best through example and action to serve in Christ's stead for the faithful on earth. The priestly ministry always involves "preaching" or "spreading the word of God" – again within prescribed bounds. Beyond that, the ministry involves assignment by the priest's superior to any number of pastoral activities, not the least of which, for the diocesan priest, is the administration of the parish in which he has been placed. Finally, the priesthood is first and foremost about exclusivity in the administration of the "holy sacraments" that form the basis of communion between the faithful and Jesus Christ – more on this below.[14]

The second avenue toward an understanding of priests' work is to note what they do (or should) *not* do: they do not act independently and unilaterally; they do not have sexual relations with others, and some (priests in many religious orders) are called upon to pursue not just celibacy but a life of chastity; and they do not make money in the sense that the majority of society envisions financial security. These prohibitions are captured in what, somewhat inaccurately, are assumed to be pledges by all priests upon ordination – vows of obedience, chastity, and poverty.

In fact, the priestly vows or denials in question are perhaps better comprehended via the distinction between diocesan priests and those in religious orders. Every priest has a boss, a superior whom he has promised to obey. In most cases, the subordinate role takes

---

[14] Perhaps the best vehicle by which to gain a sense of both the substance of and the rules governing life as a priest in contemporary society and, for the most part, the latter half of the Twentieth Century, is the *Directory on the Ministry and Life of Priests*, a fairly lengthy and detailed document aimed at specifying "those doctrinal elements which are the basis of the identity, spirituality and continuous formation of priests." Produced by the United States Conference of Catholic Bishops and signed by Pope John Paul II on January 31, 1994, it also clarifies the church's notion of boundaries of involvement in church business by the laity.

one of three general forms: service to a diocese (e.g., work in a Catholic parish), membership in a religious order (e.g., the Dominicans, the Franciscans), or (also as a member of a religious order) monastic life. Within those three organizational forms, priests engage in some combination of prayer, contemplation and ministry.

Some (most diocesan priests) work in parishes, preaching, counseling, organizing, and comforting. The supervisory manager (the priest's boss) is the bishop of the diocese. For those who join religious orders, the supervisory manager is the provincial or general superior. Priests within orders work in missions at home or abroad (as do members of the Maryknoll order, for example) or in schools, colleges, and centers of learning and teaching, including most seminaries. Some members of religious orders administer parishes under contract with a diocese; still others focus their activities upon provision of social services to communities. Finally, we encounter priests who are members of congregations living in monastic, contemplative communities, some working in virtually complete silence, some in agricultural settings, with an abbot as supervisor.

Beyond their promise of obedience to a bishop or superior, all priests are expected to be celibate, to steer clear of sexual engagements whether of a heterosexual or a homosexual nature. By definition, marriage is out of the question (though, in rare instances involving the conversion of an Anglican (i.e., protestant) minister to Catholicism and the priesthood, the church may ordain men who already are married). Members of most religious orders are expected not only to practice celibacy but also take a vow of chastity by which they pledge proactively for the rest of their lives to resist thoughts, let alone acts, of a carnal nature. Diocesan priests, on the other hand, are expected to be governed by God's commandments in this regard but are pressed less to pursue the level of cerebral hygiene that accompanies a vow of chastity; their focus is upon their promise of celibacy.

Finally, priests within religious orders take a vow of poverty, a pledge to rely upon their order to provide for their needs. This translates essentially to dependence upon the order of which they are members to care for their immediate and future physical and financial wellbeing. The flipside of this arrangement is that any monies that the priest may bring into the religious order (prior wealth, earnings, or inheritance) now reside with the order. Diocesan priests, in contrast, do not take a vow of poverty; to whatever extent prior wealth, side-earnings, or inheritance occur, they are the priest's. Practically speaking, however, though not impoverished, most diocesan priests are far from financially secure. Room and board usually accompany the parish assignment; the diocese generally covers health insurance and provides a salary considered meager by most standards. Looking toward retirement, most diocesan priests are given the opportunity to move some of their salary into a pension fund; the choice is to meet today's needs or those of tomorrow. Cars are expensive to buy and maintain, for example, but are indispensable to most parish priests' work. Leisure activities and vacations can be costly too; savings are difficult to accumulate.

The Essence of the Priesthood

The vows of poverty, chastity, and obedience characterize membership in most religious orders, whether of priests, nuns, monks, or brothers. Indeed, the work assignments of diocesan priests and those in religious orders – parish work, missionary work, scholarship, teaching, providing social services, agriculture, spreading the word of God, prayer, and contemplation – are the activities in some combination of virtually everyone, man or woman, who pursues a religious life. What, then, differentiates the priesthood from other forms of serving God within Catholicism?

That which makes a man a priest, according to the church, is the delegation to him, under the strictest of rules and guidelines, of the responsibility and authority to administer what Catholicism terms the "holy sacraments." The sacraments are believed to have been instituted by Jesus Christ and entrusted to the church as a means of communion of the faithful with Jesus and as vehicles by which individuals increasingly attain and maintain a state of grace. They may be received only by Catholics who are in such a state (i.e., not in a state of very serious, "mortal sin"). Belief in their efficacy is thought to bind Catholics to each other within a shared community globally and temporally.

The sacraments are seven in number,[15] but two win the administering priest an especially exalted and respected status. The first is the eucharist. The church posits that Jesus Christ, through the priest's consecration of bread and wine during the celebration of the mass, gives his body and blood to the faithful. Only an ordained priest may perform the sacred consecration; the circumstances of the performance are determined by his bishop or superior (Wills,

---

[15] The sacraments include baptism (ordinarily administered by priests and by which persons enter the church and Christianity more generally and without which the other sacraments may not be received), the eucharist ("holy communion"), confirmation (by which the relationship of the individual to Jesus and to the church is reaffirmed and strengthened), penance or reconciliation (by which those who have sinned regain their positive relationship with God, are absolved of their sin by the priest-confessor acting *in persona Christi*, and are given by the priest-confessor specific acts of penance to atone for the sin in question), matrimony (the entrance of a couple into marriage via a ceremony officially "witnessed" by a priest), holy orders (by which men are ordained priests by a bishop), and the anointing of the sick by which those suffering from illness are anointed by a priest with special oils. (Once called "extreme unction," this sacrament at one time was reserved only for those in danger of death and served both to comfort and to prepare the individual for passage into the afterlife.)

2013). Importantly, the church's position is not that the host represents or symbolizes Christ's sacrifice (his death to atone for the sins of mankind), but that the consecrated bread and wine literally *embody* Christ's body and blood. The substance of the church's position regarding what it terms "transubstantiation," is one of the two most important "mysteries" of Catholicism.[16] According to the church, priests (and the laity to a lesser degree) *must* believe. Since mysteries are by definition inexplicable and must be accepted truly on faith, perhaps the better characterization of the priest's position is one of actively not disbelieving. To the extent that a priest has doubts on the matter (believes, for example, that the host *symbolizes*, rather than *is*, the body and blood of Christ), he may not so indicate publicly.

Assignment of administration of the eucharist to the priest by the church places him in the setting for which he is best known: leading the faithful in the celebration of the mass. Catholics attend mass (mandatorily every Sunday) and, each time, reaffirm the sacred role of the priest in gathering the flock in prayer, preaching, and performing the act of "transubstantiation." Priests are strongly urged though not mandated to celebrate mass daily. And the requirement that the faithful be in a state of grace (the absence of "mortal sin") in order to receive the eucharist places the priest in the second of his best known, exclusive roles: confessor. Priests are known to the world as persons designated by the church to act in Christ's place to forgive a Catholic's sins and to establish the terms of atonement for those sins. They are known too for their vow of silence; priests may not, under any circumstances, divulge what is said by the penitent within the confessional.

---

[16] The other great "mystery" involves the church's sense of the "Holy Trinity," i.e., the notion of God as being one but consisting of three "persons" (not three gods): God the Father, God the Son (Jesus Christ), and God the Holy Spirit. Again, as a mystery, the Holy Trinity must be accepted on faith.

Returning to the initial focus of this section, that is it: whether in your view it is huge in importance or less so, what priests do that no one else does is administer the sacraments.[17] In the chain of command and permission granted, priests within a diocese represent their bishop who represents the pope who represents the church to which Jesus Christ is believed, at least until fairly recently, to have entrusted stewardship of the one true path to eternal salvation. For the truly faithful, this is the clear source of the tremendous respect accorded the priesthood for centuries. For those less inclined to accept the church's position on the matter, priests may be well-respected personally but nonetheless are viewed simply as cogs in a vast global bureaucratic, controlling, and financial machine (Wills, 2013). *In either case, no one else administers the sacraments.*

Hard Life

Most priests work very hard; they always have, though the decline in number of priests over the past several decades has made "workload" seem a more contemporary problem. The vocational pursuits of others may duplicate many of the priest's assignments beyond administration of the sacraments, but those pursuits by men in clerical collars occur in a considerably magnified sphere and within a set of expectations (from the laity if not from the church

---

[17] There are exceptions to this exclusivity. In extremis, for example, someone other than a priest can administer baptism so that an unbaptized person can attain salvation. Further, there exists an area in Catholicism, beyond administration of the sacraments, wherein no one but a priest can conduct church business: the pastorate. Only a priest, on behalf of his bishop, can be the pastor or associate pastor of a parish. This insures that neither local governance nor lay takeover of a parish can occur. It insures also a universal sense of community and of bureaucracy, the necessary consistency across all dioceses globally in the manner of conduct of Catholic life and decision making.

hierarchy) that allow for little human frailty (Greeley, 1990). For diocesan priests in particular, the everyday activities of the ministry bear witness to the difference between vocation as a complete and lifetime surrender of self to a cause, and profession as pursuit of a line of occupational activity shared with other societal commitments and responsibilities.[18] By way of a final pass at the substance of the diocesan priest's role, a look at the challenges and at time and energy expended in pursuit of that role is useful.

Much is asked of a priest. The church promises that "The community will be able to count on his dedication, availability, untiring work of evangelization and, above all, his devoted and unconditional love" and thus envisions a cleric "consecrating to [the church] all his energies and giving himself with pastoral charity in a continuous act of generosity" (United States Conference of Catholic Bishops, 1994). He is asked to administer the sacraments, to preach with the zeal of a missionary, to say mass in a way that inspires, and to remain current on all church positions, including those occasioned by advances in the sciences. And, while he is at it, he should pray continuously, promote vocations, and proactively honor Mary, the Mother of God. For support and growth, he should fraternize with other priests in a manner that reinforces commitment to his

---

[18] Since the focus of this book is upon minor seminaries that represented the first phase of production of a diocesan priest, the current discussion falls short of describing well the challenges and difficulties faced by members of religious orders, including cloistered communities, most of which have never utilized the high school-level minor seminary structure in preparing priests. Emphases may vary but challenges exist nonetheless: loneliness, uncertainty of one's closeness to God, unhappiness with assignments, and so forth. Overall, the clearest difference between diocesan priests and those in religious orders is the latter's satisfaction with an order's shared and supportive community (Bishop, 2006; Hoge and Wenger, 2003; McDonough and Bianchi, 2002).

vocation, replenishes his spirituality, and provides assistance to fellow priests in crisis.

The priest is "on call" at all times, driving in the middle of the night, for example, to anoint a dying parishioner, comforting the family of that parishioner upon her death, making certain that the funeral is done sensitively and inspirationally. The priest also must be ready to counsel parishioners on all matters under the sun – the parents of the 25-year-old who still lives at home and shows no sign of looking for a steady job, the family of the gang member, the young wife who thinks her husband is drinking too much or cheating on her: "What do we do, Father?" And there are baptisms. And marriages, and the long hours of required counseling leading to them, speaking about marital issues the priest has never experienced (though, one priest-interviewee observed, years of counseling experience make up for a lot). Keeping straight the religious calendar, the proper vestments to wear at mass, the appropriate homily delivered well and economically.

Priests encounter routinely in their work what most of us do far less often: personal traumas and anguish, people dying. They possess the daunting responsibility of the confessional wherein the faithful bare their souls (Hoge and Wenger, 2003: 27, 28). Confessional duty is important, but it also is time-consuming when so much else must be done. Early morning mass, after calls during the middle of the night, must still be said in a manner that continues to reinforce in parishioners the church's reverence for the "mystery of transubstantiation." And there are the practical problems: keeping the trains running – maintenance of the church and its grounds and often of the accompanying parish school. The routine visits to the school classrooms. Asking for money. Pastors' assignments to associate pastors, the grunt work (Fichter, 1961, 1968). The work with parental and lay groups in support of the parish and school, often trying to hold the line against aggressive lay control. Closing down that school when attendance has consistently dropped below the level needed to pay for it.

Many priests worry about health and about money:

…[S]omething has to be done to be sure that priests stay in communion with people… and not go it alone at night. [Otherwise] … they won't eat or they'll eat out. …It will kick back to bad health later – high blood pressure, cholesterol, bad stomach, the whole works. It builds up as time goes on. (Diocesan priest interviewee, Hoge and Wenger, 2003:38)

In my early years as a priest, it was typical for rectories to have a cook and/or housekeeper who did the food shopping and prepared the meals. Those arrangements are all but entirely gone and have been for many years. [Now] parishes that used to have two or three or more priests often have one (who has all the duties previously shared with the other two or three). For example, a few weeks ago I visited a parish in Iowa where one priest (native of another country) is serving as pastor of four parishes, in four different small towns, with lots of driving in between. That's the norm, not the exception. One consequence is that such priests often have little time for preparing healthy meals (assuming they have the necessary skills), and are more susceptible to the health issues that result from a poor diet. I've seen this happening in rectories all over. (Priest interviewee from Sacramento)

I remember driving through town shortly after ordination, wanting to stop at McDonalds for a hamburger; I avoided doing so because of lack of money. …My salary as a newly ordained priest was $400.00 per month plus mileage and I was making monthly payments on a student loan, a car, and other *personal items. ...It was the beginning of my disillusionment with the priesthood.* (Former priest, Henry, nd., from *leavingthepriesthood.com*)

And then there are the dangerous people, folks who try to get into the rectory or church, folks who are not mentally stable, folks who might attack you. A homeless, former convict killed one priest and wounded another in a church in Phoenix, Arizona on June 11, 2014, for instance (Kiefer, 2017). On New Year's Day 2014, Father Eric Freed, a popular priest in Eureka, California was tortured and murdered by a mentally troubled man who had broken into the rectory of St. Bernard's Catholic Church which he then sought to burn down (Houston, 2016).

A former-priest interviewee from Chicago recounted his brush with danger:

I was at a parish downtown and this guy held a knife to my throat. He left and the police found him and arrested him. He was schizophrenic, and I did not know it. No one had explained it as part of the experience of counseling downtown. I was shaking. I went back to my room and called all sorts of people to talk. Next morning, this asshole – another priest – says, "Oh, it'll happen again. You'll get used to it."

The Challenges

Beyond the above drawdown on time, energy, and spirit, most priests have faced three especially difficult challenges no matter the era in which they were ordained and most active as a cleric (DeJong and Donovan, 1988; Hoge and Wenger, 2003; Gautier et al., 2012): social isolation, treatment as a non-professional, and disagreement with some church doctrinal positions.

Social isolation in some senses traces from the pedestal that characterizes the traditional role of priest – a set of expectations and privileges that prevent "common" behavior. Beyond that, however, social isolation often is built into the living and working situations of priests. It surely occurs when a priest is assigned to a rural site, living by himself, perhaps covering masses and confessions in multiple parishes. What does one do when he comes home from dinner at a nice Catholic family's home, no longer on stage? The evening is still young, and there are too few Catholics in the area to assume that his services will be needed during the night. How many times can he look at the budget – likely always in the red – for what is a very small church and congregation? How many hours of the evening can he give to prayer and contemplation?

But social isolation can occur even in the big city. It happens when the pastor who supervises the young priest has little to do with him outside of the time necessary to clarify parish assignments or to critique progress, sometimes in a less-than-charitable manner. Alone in the cold. It may happen too when the parish itself is less than hospitable:

> *In my first parishes, no one knew me ... and didn't particularly care. They weren't very impressed. ...Many nights being up till four or five in the morning, I really did want to die. ...Basically because of loneliness. What I wanted was relationships.* (Priest interviewee, Hedin, 2003: 113)

Foregoing sex is an obvious sacrifice, but most priests seem to come to terms with it (some simply by not honoring the vow; see Sipe, 2003) or leave to seek what they have missed. Lack of intimacy is the bigger challenge, the absence of a close relationship with someone – a very close friend, a partner, a family to whom to return each night. Emotionally fulfilling relationships are hard to come by within what many assume should be but in truth is not always a very supportive fraternal order. (One priest-interviewee in the present study attributed many of priests' health issues to a lack of fraternal support.) Fewer than one in three priests looks to peers as his main source of support (Hoge and Wenger, 2003: 202). Some see fellow priests not only as unsupportive but often as competitive and malicious (Greeley, 1986:133).

I entered the seminary thinking that I would find the kind of supportive religious community that I could see in my parish rectory as a kid. I didn't know then that some of the priests in that rectory had not spoken to each other for ten years. (Priest interviewee from Sacramento)

I remember feeling so bad when [a priest colleague] left active ministry and I lost contact with him. I knew that I had lost a large part of myself; I had lost my history. There wasn't another human being around that I ever related to that had known me for more than two or three years. They never knew me the way I used to be. They didn't know my struggles or my experience. (Priest interviewee, Hedin, 2003: 90).

Further, the priest's higher-order relationship with God, generally achieved through prayer and spirituality – and likely to sustain him in the absence of close human companionship and intimacy (Turton and Francis, 2007) – is fragile and often elusive. Most priests drift back and forth in their level of satisfaction with this relationship, at times experiencing crises of faith:

I believe men leave religious life for the same reasons that people separate and divorce from married life. They fall out of love..., sense that they are alone. Religious life is a love affair, a love affair with the Lord. Your friends can help you… but ultimately the love affair is not with other men and women but with God himself. (Priest interviewee, McDonough and Bianchi, 2002:32)

I think we need to encourage guys to find spiritual directors and do spiritual direction. Too many guys are out there that don't seek spiritual guidance. …You have to have a strong spiritual life, because if you don't, you're up there blowing wind. Who should believe you? (Priest interviewee, Hoge and Wenger 2003: 144)

The second major challenge for priests is what many view as a lack of respect on the part of church authorities for what they know and do, for their intellect, and for their professional opinion. They are educated and sensitive men who wish to be treated as something more than "workers." Yet, many feel they are being directed to shut their eyes and plod on. An elderly Sacramento priest told me:

What bugs me is what the church intellectuals do: think and talk and no action. They tell us how to think and pray and what is important and what is not. They have no clue what we actually do out here. We are the ones who make everything happen, or keep the wrong stuff from happening. From the brain side of the church, we are seen as assembly-line workers. You know: just shut up and do your job.

There is merit to the complaint to the extent that the priest believes himself a professional who has or should have influence, or, at least, a chance to speak, concerning what the church tells Catholics to do. Instead, many view themselves as taken for granted and destined in perpetuity to administer the sacraments, explain the church's position on important issues to parishioners, and make sure the parish's buildings are locked at night. While none of these is viewed negatively (indeed, quite the opposite in the case of the sacraments), priests often feel that they have become "functionaries," a state in which they are seen as unidimensional and, thus, further isolated socially. The difficulty is in some ways exacerbated by the church's encouragement of priests to seek even deeper communion with Christ in order to understand why this must be so (United States Conference of Catholic Bishops, 1994).

The third challenge is common to most professionals: disagreement with company policy and the question of whether to voice it. This is nothing new within Catholicism, of course, as Martin Luther demonstrated in 1517 with his *Ninety-Five Theses* and the church demonstrated in 1521 with his excommunication. Yet, it is never easy when, for example, a priest must articulate the church's position on matters such as birth control with which, in fact, he does not agree. It is difficult when a priest who is homosexual in orientation (though not necessarily sexually active) must articulate a position that defines homosexual relations as immoral even among partners committed to each other for life.[19] Nor is it easy to champion a "charity and love" approach to issues of poverty in the United States when one believes in the necessity of structural change through social activism as the more appropriate remedy.

A hard life often exacts a serious toll. It is no coincidence that many priests suffer from persistent stress and depression (Virginia, 1998; Zicker et al., 2008). Nor is it particularly surprising that rates

---

[19] It was precisely this issue that occasioned the placement of a 1960s schoolmate of mine on inactive leave from the ministry by the Diocese of Los Angeles in 2012. See *Catholic News Agency* (internet news site), September 12, 2012.

of closeted alcoholism among priests are high or even, some believe, that the problem derives from a culturally condoned approach to drinking within the priesthood (Donahue, 2013; Rastrelli, 2016; Schorsch, 2012). Some priests find other ways to cope. Some leave. Some live unhappily within the priesthood feeling trapped by the absence of any skills remotely marketable. An elderly Atlanta woman who grew up during the Great Depression described the situation of her brother:

> *We were ten of us kids in our family. We were Catholics in a small town, and it was always assumed that some of us would become nuns or priests. A good Catholic family was expected to give some of its children to religious life. That came from my mother. My sisters Ellen and Jane entered the convent. My brother David became a priest. He was never happy with it. It was more what my mother wanted. I always thought he wanted to leave. He drank too much, and I know he had at least one affair. But he could not leave while my mother was alive and, after she died, he was in so deep that all he could do was stick with it. He had no other training. I think he actually made his peace with it then and went on to work with other priests who had alcohol problems.*

Satisfaction and Fulfillment

The above catalogue of priestly trials and tribulations notwith-standing, study after study finds that most priests – those who have not left the active priesthood – are generally happy and sat-isfied with their lives, a bit more so than are other male profes-sionals of similar age (Hoge and Wenger, 2003; Knox et al., 2005; Rossetti, 2011). Many believe, as one priest put it, that they have "one of the hardest and coolest jobs there is" (Gordon, 2011). This is true even among American priests who have had historically the most difficult ride: the cohort that entered the priesthood in the late 1960s and early 1970s with the Vatican II-inspired expectation of substantial change in the church and the priest's role and saw the expectation largely unfulfilled (Greeley, 1972; Cozzens, 2000; Hoge and Wenger, 2003; Gautier et al., 2012). Eight in ten active priests, younger and older alike, in Hoge's and Wenger's 2003 study of Catholic priests described their desire to remain in the priesthood as "definite," and another 16 percent considered persistence "probable." That this was not merely dissonance-reduction or accommodation to the fact of no other options available was demonstrated by the sample's response to the question of whether they'd choose the priesthood again were they granted essentially a "do-over"; close to nine in ten respondents replied that they would.

While there are decided age (cohort) differences regarding how priests frame the level and source of their happiness (DeJong and Donovan 1988; Hoge and Wenger, 2003), it is clear that administration of the sacraments and leadership in the practice of the liturgy are the most fulfilling elements of the priestly role across generations. Indeed, 50 percent of diocesan priests and 35 percent of priests from religious orders would be at least somewhat satisfied were their priestly duties limited only to sacramental and liturgical activities. Further, 77 percent of diocesan and 63 percent of religious-order priests consider consecrating and administering the eucharist and hearing confessions the essential elements of their priesthood (Hoge and Wenger, 2003: 201, 213 – 215).

The best part of my experiences has been … [s]aying Mass, hearing confessions. Confessions are wonderful. Being sacramentally present to the people, being priest for the people. Trying to be Christ present to them.… And to be able to point the way to

God.... And preaching too. That's all wonderful. (Diocesan priest interviewee, Hoge and Wenger, 2003: 27).

Who Knew?

We've come full circle, it seems. Boys were recruited into the priesthood during America's minor-seminary boom in pursuit of saying mass and hearing confessions – that's what priests did. Many years later, as members of that cohort who were ordained slow down their active priesthood, it is the notion of mass and the sacraments that gives meaning to their retirement, keeping them priests forever, making their vocations lifelong. As one of my interviewees, in his late sixties and looking toward retirement, noted: "I can't imagine not being able to say mass. I have done it all my life. It is special. It is what priests do."

We see in priests the combination of pleasure and pain in their role that we see in most adults who have dedicated their lives to a cause. There are periods of doubt and periods of immense satisfaction. Loneliness often gnaws at the soul; community and relationship with God fill the void for many. The critical question in the context of boys and young men who entered the minor seminary during the heyday and crash eras is: did these young people have anything resembling clarity about challenges and satisfactions associated with the role and life of a priest? The answer from those I interviewed, not unexpectedly, was no. And, were they to have had more clarity about the priesthood, would things have gone differently? Perhaps, though immaturity and facts ordinarily or necessarily do not produce rational decisions. But they did not, in fact, possess clarity. They were kids when they first thought of pursuing the priesthood. Most were teenagers throughout their time in minor seminary. What they saw as children was but a veiled glimpse at life wearing the Roman collar. What they saw as seminarians – their teachers' lives – provided a sense of the priest as human but little else. Beyond administration of the sacraments and, for cohorts in the mid- to late-1960s, the possibility of joining other religious and lay persons in pursuit of social justice (see Chapter Three), their role models engaged in little that hinted at the complicated and sometimes quite difficult priesthood they someday might live. Minor seminarians would offer – could offer – essentially the same response to "What do priests do?" that they offered as children: "Priests say mass and hear confessions."[20]

References

Bishop, A.J. 2006. "Age and Gender Differences in Adaptation and Subjective Well-Being of Older Adults Residing in Monastic Religious Communities." *Pastoral Psychology* 55: 131-143.

Catholic News Agency. 2012. "LA Priest on Leave for Advocating Gay Marriage." (www.catholicnewsagency.com/news/la-priest-suspended-for-advocating-gay-marriage) (September 12).

DeJong, J.A. and D.C. Donovan. 1988. "Age-related Differences in Beliefs, Attitudes, and Practices of Priests." *Journal for the Scientific Study of Religion* 27:128-36.

Donahue, Wendy. 2013. "When Father Has a Drinking Problem." *U.S. Catholic* 78 (6): 23-27.

Fichter, Joseph. 1961. *Religion as an Occupation*. South Bend IN: University of Notre Dame Press.

_____. 1968. *America's Forgotten Priests: What They Are Saying*. New York: Harper and Row.

---

[20] Times have changed. Minor seminaries are rare today. Men of adult age enter major seminaries with their eyes open wider or possess the faculties by which more quickly to size up the pros and cons of life within the priesthood. See Chapter Fourteen for further discussion.

Gautier, Mary, Paul M. Perl, and Stephen J. Fichter. 2012. *Same Call, Different Men: The Evolution of the Priesthood Since Vatican II*. Collegeville MN: Liturgical Press.

Gordon, Charles. 2011. "Why I Am a Priest." *University of Portland Magazine* (Autumn): 28-31.

Greeley, Andrew M. 1972. *The Catholic Priest in the United States: Sociological Investigations*. Washington, D.C.: United States Catholic Conference.

_____. 1986. *Confessions of a Parish Priest: An Autobiography*. New York: Simon & Schuster.

Hedin, Raymond. 2003. *Married to the Church (Updated Edition)*. Bloomington: Indiana University Press.

Henry. Nd. "Various Reasons for Leaving the Priesthood." (blog) *www.leavingthepriesthood.com*.

Hoge, Dean R. and Jacqueline Wenger. 2003. *Evolving Visions of the Priesthood*. Collegeville MN: Liturgical Press.

Houston, William. 2016. "Bullock Guilty of Eureka Priest's Murder-Torture." *Eureka Times-Standard* (https://www.times-standard.com/2016/04/11/bullock-guilty-on-all-charges-in-murder-torture-of-eureka-priest/).

Kiefer, Michael. 2017. "Ex-Convict Pleads Guilty to Avoid the Death Penalty." *The Republic* (https://www.azcentral.com /story/news/local/phoenix/ 2017/02/24/gary-moran-father-joseph-terra-kenneth-walker-murder-phoenix/98373080/).

Knox, Sarah, Stephen G. Virginia, Jessica Thull, and John P. Lombardo. 2005. "Depression and Contributors to Vocational Satisfaction in Roman Catholic Secular Clergy." *Pastoral Psychology* 54: 139-155.

McDonough, Peter and Eugene Bianchi. 2002. *Passionate Uncertainty: Inside the American Jesuits*. Berkeley CA: University of California Press.

Pope Francis. 2014. *General Audience in St. Peter's Square*. (March 26): Vatican City: Libreria Editrice Vaticana.

Rastrelli, Tom. 2016. "Confessions of an Ex-Priest: Learning to Drink Like a Catholic Cleric." *Huffington Post* (https://www.huffpost.com/entry/confessions-of-an-ex-priest_b_1838037) (February 2).

Rossetti, Stephen. 2011. *Why Priests Are Happy: A Study of the Psychological and Spiritual Health of Priests.* Notre Dame IN: Ave Maria Press.

Schorsch III, Albert. 2012, "A Day of Atonement for Blasphemy in the Seminary, 40 Years Later." *Sanity and Social Justice.net* (December).

A.W. Richard Sipe. 2003. *Celibacy in Crisis: A Secret World Revisited.* New York NY: Brunner-Routledge.

Turton, Douglas W. and Leslie J. Francis. 2007. "The Relationship between Attitude toward Prayer and Professional Burnout among Anglican Parochial Clergy in England: Are Praying Clergy Healthier Clergy?" *Mental Health, Religion & Culture* 10: 61-74.

United States Conference of Catholic Bishops. 1994. *Directory on the Life and Ministry of Catholic Priests.* Washington DC: U.S. Conference of Catholic Bishops.

Virginia, Stephen V. 1998. "Burnout and Depression among Roman Catholic Secular, Religious, and Monastic Clergy." *Pastoral Psychology* 47. 49 67.

Wills, Garry. 2013. *Why Priests? A Failed Catholic Tradition.* New York: Viking Press.

Zicker, Michael, William Balzer, Aziz Shahnaz, and John Wryobeck. 2008. "The Moderating Role of Social Support between Role Stressors and Job Attitudes among Roman Catholic Priests." *Journal of Applied Social Psychology* 38:2903-23.

CHAPTER FIVE

Family Matters

A single word could constitute this chapter, and the majority of former minor seminarians would understand perfectly: Mom. *As we shall see below, rarely can we talk about a boy or young man being called by God to the priesthood without talking about his mother, "part of that utterly unique class of devoted Catholic mothers who labored tirelessly to get a Roman collar around one of her sons" (Rohde, 2011). In the heyday era, mothers were more often than not the driving force behind their sons' vocational journey either as long-term initiators of their priestly studies or as the enablers of a goal set for them by someone else (Fichter, 1961: 21-22; Miles, 2012). In either case, rarely could a boy walk through seminary doors without his mother's blessing. Nor could the young man later walk away from the seminary without grappling with his mother's disappointment. For those ultimately ordained, nearly always, departure from the priesthood brought agony to the mother and corresponding guilt to the son. Such were the stakes, and such was the pressure. A former priest once told me of the inscription on a gravestone he saw in a Catholic cemetery: "Agnes Flaherty, Mother of a Priest." That was a vocation if ever one existed.*

It was not at all rare in the mid-Twentieth Century to encounter Catholic families with multiple children pursuing religious vocations – priests, nuns, brothers, seminarians, postulants, novices – as if God had called the family rather than just an individual within it. Paul Hendrickson (1983:40), for example, discusses seminarian siblings and notes that he and his brother joke that if they combined the years each put into his seminary studies, their mother would have nearly the priest she always desired. And Timothy Bazzett (2010) recalls being buoyed as he prepared to enter the seminary by the knowledge that his brother and another set of siblings from his parish also attended.

Of the 377 seminarians I encountered during my six years at St. Pius X, 66 (18 percent) were siblings; this included two sets of twins. In my first year, three of the six second-year college men had brothers in classes below them. Seven of the boys in my freshman class had older brothers at St. Pius. Having a brother in the same institution seemed to have no impact upon persistence. No two siblings defected simultaneously though many left only a year apart. Only three pairs of brothers continued further studies for the priesthood after finishing at St. Pius; none of those six men was ordained.

Sibling seminarians may or may not have been close as brothers. I recall schoolmates whose brothers left or were dismissed, and it seemed to have had no effect on the one who stayed. Others clearly were upset. Hendrickson (1983:291) remembers his older brother's departure as the beginning of his own slow movement away from his priestly studies. One of the interviewees for this study similarly was shaken when his younger brother did not return after only a year in the seminary. I too remember riding my bike with my friend Ed during the summer before we both entered St. Pius. Uncharacteristically quiet, he suddenly blurted that his brother, two years our senior, was leaving the Maryknoll minor seminary. I was quiet too because I knew that Ed, like me, would now be the only one to shoulder his parents' dream of having a priest in the family – even then, we sensed the pressure.

Boys from the same family may well have heard the same call or may have entered the seminary for different reasons. Some brothers were competitive from an early age and continued the contest into the seminary (and after). Some younger brothers had no desire to compete but were hoping to capture at least some of the affection and attention showered upon their older seminarian siblings. My younger brother, for instance, flirted with a religious order in upstate New York clearly in hopes of gaining some of the strokes accorded his older brother. Our mother said no and that, if he wanted to go to seminary – notice the lack of encouragement – he could go to the same one as I (and live in my shadow there too). Needless to say, his "vocation" evaporated quickly. My mom, not my brother and I, determined the terms of vocations in our family.

In short, family mattered in a young person's decision to pursue God's call – if not by virtue of outright encouragement, then at least by virtue of qualified assent. Encouragement or assent may have taken any of a number of forms. That possibility leads to a search for similarities and dissimilarities rooted in family that might explain why and how a boy or young man found his way into a minor seminary during America's minor seminary boom. In this vein and based upon my interviews and readings, I have identified three *basic* types of minor seminarian, each with a vocational anchor in the family: *anointed boys* (or young men if they entered after age eighteen) who self-identified early as future priests and were nurtured seemingly by a cast of thousands into studies for the priesthood, *parental offerings* who from an early age were steered proactively toward the priesthood by a parent, more likely the boy's mother, and *runaways* who found their way into the seminary to avoid problems, usually at home.

None of the three cells in the above typology accommodates a particular case unambiguously, for many, if not most, minor seminarians were to some degree a mix of types. The issue is the overall disposition; was an individual *primarily* an anointed boy, a parental offering, or a runaway? Patterns of entry, stasis, and exit flowed from this variable.

Anointed Boys

Anointed boys were marked, generally early on, as future priests. The sisters at school and the parish priests knew of and supported them in their vocations. The reinforcement that was offered a boy who identified himself as destined for the priesthood was positive, plentiful, and persistent. It is easy to imagine the strength of the label, "future priest," for a second grader – the pats on the head, the attention, the pride observed in one's parents, the assignment time and again of major school responsibilities (altar boy, choir boy, traffic-crossing guard) reserved only for the best of "good boys." Seminarians (future priests) were *special*; they knew it and thrived on it (Hedin, 2003; Hendrickson, 1983). Vincent Miles (2012:6), a former seminarian, recalled his motivation to pursue the priesthood at eleven:

> *My main reason for wanting to become a priest was simple: the attention and approval it would bring me. Attention from the world in general, and approval from my mother in particular. ...I wanted to be the star of the show.... My "vocation" was ...*

a product not of conviction but of ambition, inherited in abun-
dance from both of my parents.

A former seminarian-interviewee from the Midwest similarly recalled:

I can't remember not wanting to be a priest. I came from a big
Irish family and had cousins who went to the seminary. It was
prestigious to go though no one ever forced it on me. My family
and their friends always slapped me on the back and said what
a wonder I was because I wanted to be a priest.

Anointed boys were products of what were considered model Catholic families. Those families tended to be large. They took up most of a pew in church, and their children seemed to be in every grade in the parish school. They were, as one former seminarian referred to his family, "aggressively Catholic." They had their houses blessed by priests and said the rosary at home and on long family car trips. The family patriarch wore a suit and tie to church functions and walked into a room ahead of his brood. He took a leadership role in lay matters for the parish and even at times for the diocese. He was president of the parents' club. He was an usher at Sunday mass. He carried the collection basket from aisle to aisle. Everyone knew his name. If he or his family owned a shop or business, parishioners patronized it. His wife also was respected in the parish as a woman who was keeping her family well on the road to devout Catholicism. She too was prominent as a volunteer for parish organizations and functions.

Model Catholic families were immersed in Catholic life, and their children grew up with a decidedly Catholic identity. Their exposure to priests was greater than average since their fathers often were friends with the parish pastor, and priests routinely were dinner guests in their home. It was not a surprise when boys from these families said as children that they wished someday to be priests. The anointing then began in earnest as the family was viewed as yet more devout, and its status in the parish increased. Anointed boys' parents were supportive of their sons' entry into the minor seminary even if many had reservations (very common within anointed boys' families) about a thirteen-year-old's ability to make such decisions. The practice was established in Catholic circles; a vocation was affirming; a priest in the family was a good thing. In fact, in later life, former anointed boys commonly noted that, while their parents did not pressure them toward the priesthood, their pride and pleasure should they choose that path were obvious. As one Sacramento priest put it: "From second grade forward, I was proudly introduced by my parents as, 'This is our son. He's going to be a priest.'"

Frank, a former-seminarian interviewee from Sacramento, described his decision to enter the seminary:

> I knew my parents would love to have a priest in the family. It was their dream. It was part of being Catholic. I was the oldest and the spotlight was on me, but my folks never really pressured me. In fact, I applied late in eighth grade without even seeing the recruiter. I was not a good student so I don't know who was more surprised when I was accepted, them [his parents] or me. But they were really pleased. My mother was the emotional driver of the household, and my dad was the disciplinarian. I managed to win her love and my father's approval.

Cal, a former priest from Milwaukee, recalled a different form of anointing:

> By the seventh grade, I was practically ordained. It had little to do with my parents. My mother was a convert and befuddled.

My dad had mixed emotions and was wary. It was the clergy. Teachers and priests encouraged bright kids to become priests. It was the most significant thing you could do in our culture. Pure adulation followed.

Catholic mothers were particularly respected and supported in their sons' quest for membership in the clergy. Former priest Donald Fausel (2010: 181) remembered a conversation with a "pew duster" (his term) church woman:

Oh, Father, I understand your brother will be ordained in a couple of years. Your mother must be so proud. Just think, there'll be two priests in the family! How blessed she is. She'll never lose her two boys.

John Cornwell (2006: 42) has similar memories:

Mum looked at me with a mournful smile. Then she said with tears in her eyes: "If only my mother were alive to see this day. Fancy, me having a son a priest. It's surely an answer to her prayers."

While the family set the tone for its child's aspiration, the common mechanism for designation publicly as an anointed boy was the question asked by a nun in an early grade: "How many boys in here are going to be priests someday?" A former priest among my interviewees (see also Hedin, 2003:7) considered this moment pivotal in his ultimate decision to enter the minor seminary:

I was in the first grade. Our teacher asked what we wanted to be when we grew up. One kid said a movie star, and everyone burst out laughing. When it was my turn, I didn't know what to say, so I said that I wanted to be a priest – I have no idea where it came from. But everybody said ooooh. I got major attention for it. That was it. I was a priest from first grade on. Everyone at school thought of me that way. I don't recall my mother planting the idea, but, boy, did she ever get on the band wagon. She was very strong, very influential in my life. She would say to other people – everyone – "He wants to be a priest."

Having declared his intentions, the anointed boy's status within the school accelerated. Teachers praised future priests, and the boys assumed a certain celebrity. Even one's siblings gained stature by virtue of the association (though perhaps younger brothers also resented the pressure to achieve similar prominence). For the most part, other children were supportive. The only bump in the journey forward came in the seventh and eighth grades as young adolescents began to have parties and to pair off in early romances. It was then that the seminary-bound boy felt distanced a bit from the social scene because he was "going to be a priest." One interviewee noted that in the seventh grade he was invited to parties but also invariably asked what he was doing there; "in the eighth grade, I was not invited to parties anymore." Another reported good-natured teasing from eighth-grade peers who started calling him "Father Frankie."

If a potential seminarian somehow had flown beneath the nuns' radar in the early grades, the boy likely was tagged in a later grade, sometimes as late as high school (see Cornwell, 2006: 6; Fausel, 2010: 118), by a parish priest who sensed his potential:

I guess I had impressed Father Wood somewhat because over the next few years he began to tell me I might have what it takes to become a priest. So being an impressionable 13 year old I joined the "seminarian club" with about ten other guys where we learned what having a "vocation" was all about. (Carnevale, 2014)

The label, "future priest" thus attached, the process continued with referral by the nun or the parish priest to a seminary recruiter who visited the elementary school annually. One former priest recalled:

My teacher set me up in eighth grade. She gave me the keys to the library and told me to go and let Father Smith [the recruiter] into the room. As we walked there, he asked if I had considered becoming a priest. I said yes, but planned to go to high school first. He said, "Why wait? Let's talk." The rest is history.

I too remember the recruitment process very clearly: my seventh-grade teacher sent several of us boys during class to talk to the seminary recruiter about our aspirations, already well-professed, and my eighth-grade teacher sent us again the next year to close the deal. We were glad to get out of class, to be sure, but the sense of being special was more important. The transaction was cemented for those of us who went to St. Pius X Seminary by Father Cletus LaMere, a Salvatorian who for years recruited throughout Northern California for the Diocese of Sacramento. I remember him well: a black suit rather than a cassock, the whitest collar I had ever seen, Clark Kent glasses, a straw fedora. His skin was alabaster and his nails manicured. Father Cletus was nice, mild-mannered, and very smooth. He motivated you by asking the right questions about your motivation and your family and by explaining seminary life and the process by which to enter it. (Obviously, he also could decide on the spot that you were not the right candidate material.) If the deal needed sealing still further (mine did not; my mom needed no convincing), he would meet with your parents; in any case, it was he who had the appropriate literature and brochures sent by mail to your home.

Were the anointed boy in question unable for some reason to enter minor seminary immediately after elementary school or to have declared his intent to join an order whose membership was initiated after high school, shepherding duties most often transferred to a priest, sometimes a parish curate, sometimes a teacher at the boy's Catholic high school, but always a man whom the boy very much respected. A former Jesuit seminarian from New Orleans remembered:

> *At Jesuit High, fourteen of us graduated in my senior year and entered the novitiate. We had been identified as freshmen as future Jesuits. The Jesuits were smart. They assigned men on their way to ordination, scholastics (advanced seminarians), to their high schools. These were young guys who seemed to us to be real cool dudes. They held us together as a group, kind of a high-status fraternity. We attended lectures as a group, went to plays together, were treated as intellectual elites.... There was never a moment when we were not reminded that we were special; we were going to be Jesuits – and cool, just like the scholastics.*

Commitment to a vocational path as a boy or young man hardly would (or should) seem binding, but it felt exceptionally so for many seminarians. As many priests and former priests have noted, anointed boys were "people-pleasers." Concurrent with the praise and status came the concern about letting down those who championed the boy's dream. An interviewee in Hendrickson's seminary memoir (1983:268) recalled considering departure from the seminary:

> *I had never really questioned before whether I belonged in a seminary, had pretty much never thought about another kind of*

life. I knew that I wanted to be a priest from second grade, and told people so. And I don't break my word.

Decisions to leave the seminary, though in no sense as grave as those to leave the priesthood (i.e., in that era, to become a *fallen* or *spoiled* priest), were by no means insignificant within model Catholic families. Parents and even siblings had invested seriously in the vocational quest by virtue of identification as a family that God had called upon to produce a priest. One interviewee observed that not only was his identity attached to the seminary but so also was his mother's; her son's status was her status. People asked after her health only after leading with "How's Chuck doing at St. Pius?"

Yet, pressures to persist acknowledged, interviews and related literature indicate that most anointed boys sensed that their families ultimately would support their decision to leave the seminary should it come to that. They would be sad certainly, perhaps quite upset for a short while. Vincent Miles's (2012) mother, for example, was angry because he had made the decision to end his seminary career after seven years without consulting her. Raymond Hedin (2003: 44) remembers his mother crying and his dad nodding softly as, in tears himself, he told them he was leaving after eight years in the seminary. Like Miles and Hedin (see also Murray, 2018), most of my anointed-boy interviewees who left the seminary recalled their parents' disappointment over their decision to leave, but noted emphatically that they backed the decision.

Anthony, a diocesan priest, captured the dynamic well since his was the more unusual case; he was an only child:

My becoming a priest was not my parents' idea though the decision kind of traces back to them – they were really involved in the parish, and I admired that even as a little kid. It was other people who put the priest idea in my mind. They saw me serving mass and would ask me if I was going to be a priest someday. And I liked what I saw in religious communities, the nuns and the priests. When I told my folks, they were supportive, but also ambivalent. Members of our family, who also were supportive, kept asking them what about carrying on the family name if I became a priest. And with no one else around after I left, it was hard on my folks. But they were always there for me because it was what I wanted, and that's what counted. If I had changed my mind, they would have been fine with it. Same if I chose to become a lawyer or a doctor.

Model Catholic parents often understood much about the priesthood. Andrew Greeley (1986: 96, 51-53), whose autobiography signals anointed-boy status, suggests that his parents' support of their son's entry into the minor seminary was genuine but qualified (i.e., "not exactly against their better judgment, but against some gently spoken reservations"). It traced to their sense of how challenging the priestly vocation truly was:

Both my parents felt that fourteen was "too young" to know one's own mind about a vocation. My father, I suspect, knew too many unhappy priests to want me to risk the same fate. ... I think I understand my parents' fears. In those days I thought that stories about men becoming priests because of parental pressures were fairy tales. You only became a priest because you wanted to, right? My father knew better.... [H]e was involved, through the Knights of Columbus, in helping alcoholic priests. He had no illusions about the sanctity of the priesthood.

Looking back, I now sense that anointed boys, most of whom were captured into their vocations as youngsters, were more fortunate than many of us seminarians. Their folks ultimately had their backs. That was less true of the other two minor-seminarian types.

Parental Offerings

My seminary days ended as they had begun:

> *I left the seminary in June of 1967, having given to that point a third of my life to my potential vocation. My parents were with me that last day as we drove away from St. Pius X. My classmates (only a few remaining in what was a two-year college program after high school) and I had just kissed the bishop's ring as he bestowed upon us the certificate of completion that deemed us worthy of transition into the major seminary for another six year, much more serious round of preparation. I had indicated to family and classmates some time before that I was done.*

> *I sat in the front seat as we drove away, and I recall clearly my mother's voice from the back seat: "Well, Joe, this has been your home for a lot of years. Will you miss it?" Without emotion, I answered simply, "No Mom, I won't miss it." But I knew that she would. My vocation was far more hers than mine.*

Parental offerings were boys or young men who were deliberately steered toward the priesthood by one of their parents, usually the mother (Hendrickson, 1983:30).[21] To the casual observer, children who were "offered up" differed little from anointed boys. Both

---

[21] I have chosen not to characterize boys (myself included) who were parental offerings as "mama's boys" though more than a few interviewees employed the term to describe themselves and other seminarians. The term suggests a profile that, absent knowledge of a boy's biography, one would never have thought to apply to him. And it obscures the fact that the parent behind some offerings was the boy's father. That said, the choice of the term by some men to characterize the force behind their own entry into the minor seminary speaks volumes regarding the strength of maternal influence in this regard.

types almost always declared quite young (usually as small children) that they were going to be priests, and both were celebrated and rewarded throughout elementary school and within Catholic circles on the basis of their aspiration. However, the difference between types was marked, at least as each type later reflected upon his seminary career. Former anointed boys tended in interviews to refer to both parents in discussions of family influence upon vocation while former parental offerings nearly invariably spoke of a sole influential parent. Anointed boys someday would ask, "Why did my parents let a thirteen-year-old decide to pursue the priesthood?" Parental offerings, on the other hand, would ask, "Why would my mother [or, for some, my father] set me up from childhood to become a priest, and then hold me to it at the risk of breaking her [his] heart?"

Several interviewees conveyed easily the sense of a parental offering:

There are pictures of me at three years old wearing a priest's biretta [three-peaked clerical hat]. (Redemptorist priest from St. Louis)

When I was three, my mother would tell everyone that I was going to be a priest. And they'd all say wonderful, and everyone would look at my mother. (Former minor seminarian from Chicago)

I never made the decision. Family lore has it that my mother said as a child that she was going to be a priest. She was told that girls could not be priests, but they could have a son who could be one. My mother did it. By high school, there was no question, and I never had any doubts. Don't let down the church, God, or my mother. (Diocesan priest from New Orleans)

It was my mother and my grandmother, my mother mainly. She planted the seed early enough that I said it and got a lot of praise. So I said it some more. She made sure I was an altar boy. She took me to mass all the time. She would invite priests to dinner and put her arm around my shoulders – "This one will become a priest one day." (Former Jesuit seminarian from New Orleans)

In most cases, the parent behind the offering was the mother though on occasion the father drove his son's early ambition to become a priest. The scenario effectively was the same: early planting of the seed; the aspiration made public by the parent or by the boy in grade school, considerable positive reinforcement of the goal in school and in Catholic circles, later concern on the part of the seminarian or priest that to leave his vocation would be to cause his parent great pain.

At four years of age, I knew I was going to be a priest. My mother was not expressive, but my father was very encouraging – he would like to have been a priest. My family was big into it, particularly my aunt. They nurtured it. We lived in a Franciscan parish. My uncle was a Franciscan. It was not just that I'd be a priest. It was always that I'd be a Franciscan. I never considered anything else and neither did my father. (Franciscan priest from San Diego)

My father was the one I had problems with when I decided to leave. My mother was sympathetic, but he was really hurt. It was like I had disgraced him. (Former priest from New Orleans)

To be clear, I am not, in describing the dynamics of the parental offering, recounting the plot of *The Manchurian Candidate*. The offering in question was genuinely religious, made for a higher-order cause championed within the Catholic faith, what James Carroll (1996:7) refers to, in his mother's case, as the "lifelong Irish dream" of a "staunch, chin-high Catholic woman." The parent sought to further that faith in the best way possible. The sacrifice trumped the parental urge to hold a son close. However, unlike the parents of the anointed boy whose pride in their son's vocation was essentially reactive, the sacrificing parent proactively "conditioned" the son in early childhood, actively generated positive reinforcement to build his interest and commitment, and employed guilt to preserve the sacrifice.

Carroll (1996) attributes his mother's fervor for his vocation at least in part to the fact that her husband left the seminary just short of ordination to marry her. I too suspect that, in offering me to the priesthood, my mother sought redemption for some mistakes she had made as a young woman, seeking to be a good girl again. Yet such knowledge or intuition is unusual, since most "offered" boys have difficulty accounting for what happened even after years have passed. Interviewees whose mothers were behind the parental offering generally expressed the mother's motivation as hyper-internalization of what it meant to be a good Catholic girl-woman. Many believed that their mothers actually felt closer to God by virtue of their sacrifice. Fathers who promoted their sons' entry into priestly studies more often were viewed (later) by those sons as having sought atonement for a mistake or personal shortfall. Most sacrificed boys ultimately ceased seeking answers as men – too hard to comprehend, too painful to inquire about. "She was just trying to be a good Catholic," they would say, "and once you were in, she feared that if you quit, she'd be seen as a failure by other Catholics."

Parents who offered their sons to the priesthood nearly always did so alone. This raised the obvious question during interviews: "Where was your other parent when all of this was happening?"

If the offering parent was the father, interviewees rarely suggested that there was any mystery to the mother's decision to permit the sacrifice: "My mother took a backseat to my dad. He was the dominant one in the family." If the mother was the offering parent, on the other hand, interviewees had more difficulty explaining why their typically assertive fathers had deferred to their wives in this critical matter (Hendrickson (1983: 41). Often, they believed that the subject never had been discussed between their parents (Cornwell, 2006: 42), and, as boys, they had not discussed it with their fathers.

In most cases, looking back, men whose mothers steered them toward the seminary sensed that their fathers did not want them to go:

> I think he assumed it would never really happen. (Former priest from Sacramento)

> [My father] never said a word until long after I had left — he supported me going into the priesthood but did not want me to go into the Jesuits. And then there's my grandfather. When I was about to graduate from high school and about to join the Jesuits, he waited for me outside school one day and offered me a car if I'd postpone going in until after college. (Former Jesuit seminarian from New Orleans)

> During the reception after my ordination, I heard my father tell a guest that the church had stolen his son away. (Former priest from New Orleans)

If not opposed to their son's vocation, at the very least, then, most fathers of mother-driven parental offerings were ambivalent.

Perhaps they were too consumed with work to muster the necessary questions or objections. Perhaps they drank too much. If they were themselves Catholic, they also had been raised to view positively the notion of God's call to the priesthood. Yet, the single best explanation for the father's "passive" (the word used most often by interviewees) approach to his son's entry into the seminary is the fact that he was outnumbered. His wife had been pursuing her dream for years. Hers was now also his son's dream. To object was to earn the wrath of both spouse and son.

When I left the sem after high school, it was my mother who walked around the house crying. It was my dad's turn to walk around smiling. I had never sensed his reservations. He was a Minnesota stoic. "The seminary, huh? Well, Pard, okay, best of luck." (Alumnus, St. Pius X Seminary)

... [After the seminary recruiter had met with my parents,] I knew I had won. ...My father was on the downside of any argument to get me to stay home and go to the new Catholic high school up the road. (Hendrickson, 1983:59)

It is clear too from the literature and interviews that the offered son rarely understood the dynamic in question, let alone the parent's motives. Indeed, sacrificed-son seminarians, nearly to a man, viewed pursuit of the priesthood originally as their idea and its abandonment as theirs alone to own. The standard version of their guilt framed withdrawal from the seminary as the forfeiture of the prize in which *they* had encouraged parental investment. (This was especially true if the parent was the mother of the seminarian.) It is not even wholly clear that the offering parent fully recognized the extent to which she or he was predetermining the desired outcome, as opposed simply to working to establish the medium in which hopefully it might bloom. In either case, once the son's declaration happened, the parent stayed intently vigilant.

The high-school minor seminary was a critical component of the offering parent's effort to produce a priest within the family. Her or his attention was fixed on the ultimate goal; the seminary was but a mechanism to achieve it. The odds of having a son enter a seminary and ultimately achieve that goal decreased if he attended a standard high school even with the specific goal of seminary entrance afterward; distractions were inevitable. Stated differently, the pressure associated with parental stewardship of a vocation increased by four years if the boy did not enroll in a high-school seminary.

My own status as a parental offering includes an episode that demonstrates exactly this point. In the summer before entering eighth grade, I came into the house after playing baseball at a nearby park with buddies. My mother was folding clothes in the living room while my younger brother and sister were watching television. Somehow, as my mother good naturedly asked after my game, I stated that, yes, "someday I am going to be a major leaguer." The room went cold immediately as my mother snapped, "Oh, stop that! You're not good enough for that!" It was not that she was wrong (quite the opposite) or that my boast was anything more than a harmless kid-statement at the end of a fun afternoon of baseball. I could not comprehend why she had jumped so uncharacteristically down my throat, and I headed to my room with my tail between my legs. In hindsight, of course, the reason for the outburst was obvious. Mom was literally only a year from moving me to the next, very critical stage of her goal for me, and *nothing* was going to get in the way, including consideration of going to the local high school to play ball, just in case that was on my mind.

That she had created and invested in my vocation was indisputable. My first memory of her mission was the positive response of a visiting aunt when, at age five, I did as my mom told me: proclaimed that I was going to be a priest when I grew up. I recall the constant references to her cousins, Charles and Mike, who were priests. I remember the uptick in my stock with teachers as she managed to weave the theme into parent-teacher conferences. The work she put into helping me in the fourth grade master the Latin responses to the priest during mass. The visits to the rectory in the parish in which we once lived to "say hello to the nice priests." The small statues of saints that filled my room, not to mention that little, white, plastic altar with the tiny tabernacle and the tinier gold chalice within it. The holy cards. The bus trip downtown to attend an ordination at the cathedral. The family drive to see the new seminary under construction – "Where Joe will go to school next year." My mother put tremendous effort into getting me there and, like so many of my fellows who were similarly offered up, I exerted tremendous effort to make her happy.

I remember my dad, not a Catholic, saying nothing – "passive," as my interviewees would describe their fathers. I'd ask his ghost today:

Where were you, Dad? I mean, you said nothing, not even, "Don't worry, son, you can come home anytime you wish." I get that you had pledged to permit your kids to be raised Catholic which meant that most of the educational decisions were in Mom's hands (though in your paycheck). Maybe you had no idea where this was all going when Mom started it so early on, and by the time you sensed how big it was, there was little you could do without offending both her and me. I remember how hard you hugged me the first time you saw me after letting me go away at thirteen. But what about later when, after my junior year, I tried to get out (for the third time), telling Mom

that I wanted to go to public high school for my senior year?[22]
You came to me and said, "Mom is going crazy –'What is Joe
going to do?' She's told Tom [my brother] that he has to go to
Jesuit High, and she can't turn around and let you go to public
school." I caved and said I'd go back to Pius. Why didn't you
stand up for me, say: "Let the kid go to public school; he's just
spent three years in a seminary, for God's sake!"? [My nor-
mally assertive dad normally talked this way.] But you said
nothing. …Or did you?

Runaways

Many of the boys and young men with whom I attended the seminary were running away from something bigger than they could
handle. Often it was conflict within the family, perhaps even physical threat. Sometimes, it was a sense of drift, perhaps of hitting a
wall, the feeling of having no appealing options in life; this was a
common profile among young men with "belated vocations." The
thread that bound these boys and young men was a desire to feel

---

[22] The irony is that my brother, with more guts than I, simply got himself
kicked out of Jesuit High School midway through his freshman year and,
thus, into the public high school that I had wanted to attend. In truth, I did
not want to attend the only Catholic high school for boys my age in Sacramento at the time. It was administered by Christian Brothers, and we all
heard in elementary school how brutal they were – even putting on boxing
gloves to go at it with "tough guys." A former classmate expressed the same
fear in exactly the same words. For him, the seminary was the preferable
option. On the other side of the coin was an interviewee who chose the
seminary in part because in his small town, there was only a public high
school: "I had gone to Catholic school all my life, and I was worried about
public high school. Were they like me? Would I be able to fit in with them?"

better about themselves. For them, the minor seminary offered structure instead of chaos, asked little about the trouble they had left behind, and told them that they were special. Seemingly overnight, many told me later, their status in the world changed and, with it, their respect for themselves.

More often than not, the problem that loomed so large was dad, and his problem was alcohol. Dads could hurt you, as a former classmate recalled:

Remember Williamson? When I was in the eighth grade, his dad, a Navy captain or pilot or something, drove him and me to a school baseball game. Williamson made an error at first that cost a run. After the game, the two of us got in the car while his dad was talking to some of the men. I was in the backseat, and I think his dad forgot about me. When he finally got in the car, he slapped Williamson so hard you could hear it outside. "Don't you ever mess up like that again!" The next fall, guess what? Williamson shows up at Pius in our class.

Nor was it just young boys who ran from their fathers to the seminary. Peter, twenty years old with two years of college behind him when he entered St. Pius X Seminary in the mid-1960s, also was escaping his father:

My entry into the seminary happened in five days – the week before I was to start back to college. [He lived at home and commuted to college classes.] My dad dominated everything. My mother let him. He always wanted my brother and me to get further than he got as a kid. So he dictated every move we made, including the courses we'd take in college. My brother went into the Navy and left me to deal with dad at twice the level as before. My mother was Catholic, my dad not, but I was not raised super-Catholic. I don't even know exactly where the priest notion came from. Looking back, it's funny. There was a spiritual quality to my decision – I thought I was going into a monastic environment! I was too immature and dominated to consider other options, I guess. I just was desperate and went to the rectory and knocked. I told the priest who answered that I wanted to find out how to become a priest. He was a "late vocation" guy himself and, before it was over, he got me into Pius and showed up at my house to help sell it. My parents were stunned. My mother was confused but also happy. My dad was blown away for me, it was kind of like "take that!" – but did not fight it because he'd have to take on "your mother's religion." Five days, and my whole life changed.

Things with dad sometimes were more difficult than most of us could have imagined, as a former priest from Seattle attested:

I grew up in an Irish Catholic household with a lot of kids, absolute bedlam which, for some reason, I thought was my fault. Everyone thought we were a good family. We hid behind our religion to camouflage our dysfunctions. I grew up thinking God hated me. That was my fault too. So what does a Catholic kid do to feel good about himself? He becomes a priest! That's me. Thirty years in the priesthood never confronting why I was there. I was not a good priest – I did not have a relationship with God, did not pray, and I did not believe a bit of what I preached. But the biggest thing I was running from was that, from the time I was ten until I was twelve, my dad sexually molested me. It felt good, and I liked the intimacy even though I knew it was wrong and blamed myself for it. During those two years, he treated me really well. We were close. And then it stopped, just like that. He paid no more attention to me ever again. And I thought it was my fault then too.

Occasionally, a mother precipitated her child's flight. A former schoolmate, who to all the world seemed, and was primarily, an anointed boy, told me, "Shoot no, we weren't a holy family. Our mother was nuts. We [his seminarian brother and he] had to get out of there." Another anointed boy labeled his home "tempestuous" and his mother a "shrew." More likely, however, the role of the mother in the life of a runaway was providing encouragement, since her son's (sometimes, multiple sons') entry into a seminary meant safety for them. And she would continue her attempts to protect the rest of her children as she always had: choosing carefully the hills on which to die, keeping a lid on trouble, seeking things for her children without upsetting her husband, working to earn the money he failed to earn or frittered away, distracting him when he was tanked, getting the kids out of the house when she could not distract him, sometimes taking a physical beating herself, but always putting on a good face for the neighborhood and parish.

Runaways, especially those from abusive situations, commonly described their entry into the seminary as a vehicle by which to feel good about themselves, not by design but in effect. Andrew, a former seminarian from a small Northern California town, noted:

Thirteen-year-old boys do not really make decisions. They flow where they sense reward. I was in a nasty alcoholic family with a lot of conflict. One of my friends in the eighth grade was going away the next year to an expensive Catholic boarding school. We could never afford that, but maybe that's what first put it in my mind. Somewhere in the eighth grade, probably around the time the seminary recruiter came to school, I started thinking of becoming a priest. Priests were good, sinless, authority figures. If I became one, it was somehow a way that would guarantee that I'd be a good person. My parents approved – this made the family look good. The nuns really liked it at school. I felt vali-dated. There had not been much validation for the human being that I was within my family. It was all about looking for a way to like myself. All of a sudden, I began to feel good about who I was. I had a new identity. Not just "Ted's kid" – and everyone in town knew what that meant. And my mom and dad had me – the son who was going to be a priest – and that was a bit of sunshine for them too.

In all candor, the church did not want boys like this (Anello, 2018: 88). Future priests, it reasoned, should not carry family baggage: mental illness, suicide, alcoholism, sexual abuse, criminality, or divorce. These attributes surely would reappear later in some form that created problems for everyone. But the church could not always distinguish the "runaway" from the "good boy." For the family often put up the perfect Catholic front – involvement in the parish and at school – and their children did not blow the whistle. One of Hedin's (2003: 21) interviewees recalled:

I couldn't admit [my family's alcoholism and parental conflict] to anyone because you don't tell people – you're supposed to come from a good family. So in a way I had a little lie, and I lived it to its fullest by saying how I come from such a good family. I'm going to be a priest. And how can I come from a bad family if I am a priest?

Not all flight stemmed from difficulties in the past or present; some chose the seminary because they feared the future. Young men who entered the minor seminary after high school often described themselves as having hit a wall. Arnold, who grew up near San Francisco, for example, faced a quandary when he graduated from high school. He entered a minor seminary because

123

I had no place to go. No job other than menial ones that I knew were a trap. No career plans. Not much interested in the community college. I always respected priests, so I thought I'd give it a shot.

Jerry, who entered a minor seminary at twenty-three along with several other young men who had completed stints in the military, also recalled the sense of being at a dead end:

You were supposed to have an idea about where you were going. I had no idea. I did not want to stay in the Air Force. I did not want some boring job. I could not imagine sitting still in college classes. I felt like a loser. Becoming a priest was a worthy thing to do.

Not everyone I interviewed remembered runaways during their seminary days. Those who attended day seminaries, for instance, had little recollection of boys in flight, perhaps because attendance at a day seminary offered no escape at night for boys who needed one. Former seminarians from the 1950s, especially, were likely not to recognize runaways as at all common. They tended instead to distinguish two types of schoolmates: "real men" (the majority of their classmates, themselves included, smart and athletic) and "effeminates" (adolescents who seemed softer, mama's boys, sissies, "probably homosexual"); in Hedin's (2003) minor seminary, for example, students were "jocks" or "knitters." The sharpness of the distinction appeared tied to the size of the seminary; the easier it was to avoid contact, the easier it was to attribute type to individual. One former priest stated: "There were hundreds of guys in our school. We did not interact with [the 'effeminates'], and they stuck with their own."

Interviewees from 1960s cohorts were more likely to recognize runaways among their classmates, if not during their time together, then certainly after the fact. They commonly were considered few in number. As well, some interviewees felt, in retrospect, that the seminary attracted a small number of boys who were having trouble with sexual identity, uneasy about but not yet cognizant of their sexual orientation. The seminary offered an escape, a place to fit in, few questions asked. Again, interviewees sought to ground their own typology in the sexual identity of these youths later in the seminary or after the seminary.

For the record, with one exception,[23] I have not encountered, via interviews or literature, a single individual who sought refuge within a minor seminary to escape the feeling of being out of sync with common sexual-preference identities. Nor have I met anyone who personally knew someone who entered the seminary for this reason. Even older minor seminarians who entered the institution after being active in the gay culture of the day did not enter because of a sexual-identity crisis or to seek homosexual encounters (which, most believed, they could or should forego as celibates) This is not to say that many boys and young men did not wrestle with their sexual orientation in the seminary (see Chapter Eight), especially given its gender isolation, or that most ultimately have not resolved their dilemma. Rather, these were boys and young men who entered as anointed boys, parental offerings, or runaways (for another reason) and moved over time toward a more pronounced homosexual orientation. Many of these individuals in fact were, to borrow the jargon of the 1950s' seminarian, "real men."

Some runaways ultimately became priests. Most left the seminary, however, when they had gained the emotional independence

---

[23] Father Robert Van Handel, ultimately sexually abusive of young boys and now a registered sex offender, entered St. Anthony's Seminary in the early 1960s petrified of "sex, women, men, and my father." According to Van Handel (nd: 4), the seminary seemed a place to escape these feelings.

(and, often, physical strength) to return to their homes or to move out and go to work or college. Nearly all who came from abusive homes looked back upon the seminary as safe harbor that offered a structured routine rather than chaos: "Hey, it was so much better than walking in the front door every afternoon wondering if this was one of the days I was going to get hit." While they would grapple with their family issues for most of their lives, nearly to a person they credited the minor seminary with providing a platform for self-esteem.

My interviews have convinced me that there likely were far more runaways in the seminary than anyone suspected. They hid it well. Even among anointed boys and parental offerings, there lurked a bit of the runaway. Frank, an anointed boy, for example, reveled in the freedom he had from his strict-disciplinarian father. Another anointed boy noted that "there were some problems in my family that you couldn't see from the outside." Still another referred to his father as a "night-time alcoholic." I have come to understand too that, while I clearly was a parental offering, I also possessed elements of the runaway. This became apparent when, looking back, I realized that I had none of the homesickness that many seminarians suffered (see Bazzett, 2010; Cornwell, 2006; Hinsvark, nd). One schoolmate interviewee, for example, noted that he cried not only when he first arrived at the seminary but every time he left home for St. Pius, that he moped for days, that he missed his family terribly.

I experienced none of that sadness and loneliness even though I did not wish to be in the seminary the better part of my time there. I was not homesick; I did not want to go home. For there was a cloud at home that I dreaded even if I could not put my finger on it. My parents' marriage was not made in heaven. I think they loved each other in the sense that they had paired up and wanted the best for one another and their offspring. They did not seem *in* love, however, or were too busy and stressed to attend to love. My siblings and I would see more clearly later in life that which we sensed during our childhood – our parents' resignation and sadness. They had "settled" when they had tied the knot in their mid-thirties like so many people who had postponed marriage during the Great Depression and World War II. My dad went from the Army into marriage and lower-scale jobs before getting a better position but still never earning much money. Trapped. Always worried. My mom went from career secretary in Chicago with lots of friends and parties to few friends and three little children in a small-box house in a small, new, American-style suburb. Life now required a car; my mom did not drive. Trapped. Speaking to babies all day. Starved for an adult conversation. Driving my dad nuts.

I recall the shadow of tension at home. Perhaps it was Catholicism itself that brought it. My dad was not Catholic. He came from a small Illinois Methodist town that had little tolerance for papists. He seemed not particularly intolerant but fairly disinterested in religion. In order to enter into a "mixed" marriage, he had promised to raise the children as Catholic. He went to church with us at Christmas and Easter, and that always gave us hope that he would convert and thus avoid going to hell as we were assured would happen to non-Catholics. He seemed convinced that Catholic schools provided a better education than public schools though he chafed, I am sure, at the price tag for twelve years of superior schooling for each of his three kids.

My mother was very Irish Catholic, from a seriously Catholic Iowa farm town. My father probably had little sense of what he was getting into when he married such a devout person. Mom worked to make us a *really* good Catholic family. Lent seemed especially to motivate her. Always the first to the altar rail to receive communion, her three ducklings race-walking to keep up. Helping out at church functions. Going to Catholic social events. Getting us to mass (Dad dropped us off) every Sunday and holy day and always researching the nearest church and its mass times when we were away from Sacramento.

Perhaps the tension traced to the whole idea of the priesthood for the first-born son. My dad may have viewed it as a dirty trick on a little boy. In my mom's mind, it was not as if she were shipping her son off to drug-trafficking school. Priests were great. Short of the respect accorded bishops, cardinals, and the pope (and, hey, one never knew, right?), that given to a priest was the highest known in Catholic circles of the day. Men of God. What was not to like about the idea?

Who Knew?

"Vocation," in the sense that we have examined it in this and the last few chapters, embraced the notion of individuals being called by God. But God clearly worked in mysterious ways. His summons came through family in one fashion or another: the model Catholics whose connection to faith made the notion of priesthood appealing to their young son, the parent whose own vocation was to produce her or his son's vocation, and the dysfunctional family whose son fled to save his sanity or physical wellbeing. The church too had a hand in producing those vocations: nuns and priests wooing boys onto the path, parishioners celebrating the quest, and recruiters sealing the deal (or killing it on the spot). In those days, the church was getting its numbers.

Time and again my interviewees told me that the word "vocation" meant little to them prior to entering the seminary and not a lot more once in it. Even within the seminary, the term was not used a lot by seminarians. Retreat masters would talk about it, guidance counselors would warn about its loss over the summer, and angry disciplinarians would throw it out there in an attempt to link one's current foul to a much larger playing field. At St. Pius X Seminary, the word also appeared with regularity in the school's news magazine, aptly named *The Call*. The magazine was published quarterly during the seminary's heyday, edited and written by seminarians, overseen by a faculty advisor, and aimed at both external and internal audiences. In most editions, an article would remind seminarians that they must seek ever-stronger spirituality if they hoped to respond appropriately to God's plan for them, must be there to help others who were having vocational doubts, and proactively stand ready to ward off temptation during summer recess.

Hear and read about it they might, but most seminarians rarely discussed their calling privately with other seminarians. Ironically, it was not the priesthood that anchored the seminarian's vocation; it was the minor seminary itself. Boys and young men wrestled with whether or not to remain in the seminary (with their friends); attending minor seminary *was* their vocation. The espoused end-product of their venture made its appearance only when an outsider asked the common question; "Where do you go to school?" and, if evasive responses ("a small Catholic high school out of town") did not serve, followed your answer with "So, you are going to be a priest?" ("Um, uh… yes.") The focus on seminary rather than priesthood carried for many well into the major seminary. Peter, the former minor seminarian who fled his domineering father at twenty, explained:

> *The seminary helped me get away from home even though I did not think of it in only that way at the time. It hit me just as I was to become a deacon. That meant that I was going to be a priest, and it was as if the thought had never crossed my mind before. I had been going to the seminary, not learning to be a priest. That's when I left.*

"What was it like in that place," people ask, "the place that became your vocation?" That is the question pursued in Section Three of this book.

References

Anello, Robert L. 2018. *Minor Setback or Major Disaster? The Rise and Demise of Minor Seminaries in the United States, 1958-1983.* St. Louis MO: EnRoute Books.

Bazzett, Timothy. 2010. *Reed City Boy.* Reed City MI: Rathole Books.

Carnevale, Rick. 2014. *When Pigs Fly.* Bloomington IN: Author House.

Carroll, James. 1996. *An American Requiem.* New York: Houghton Mifflin Harcourt.

Cornwell, John. 2006. *Seminary Boy: A Memoir.* New York: Doubleday.

Fausel, Donald F. 2010. *From Blind Obedience to a Responsible Faith.* Bloomington IN: iUniverse.

Fichter, Joseph. 1961. *Religion as an Occupation.* South Bend IN: University of Notre Dame Press.

Greeley, Andrew M. 1986. *Confessions of a Parish Priest: An Autobiography.* New York: Simon & Schuster.

Hedin, Raymond. 2003. *Married to the Church (Updated Edition).* Bloomington: Indiana University Press.

Hendrickson, Paul. 1983. *Seminary: A Search.* New York: Summit Books.

Hinsvark, John. Nd. "Remembering St. Joseph Seminary." www.*stjosephscollege.org/memoirs.*

Miles, Vincent J. 2012. *Boys of the Cloth: The Accidental Role of Church Reforms in Causing and Curbing Abuse by Priests.* Lanham, MD: Hamilton Books.

Murray, Joseph C. 2018. *Ex-Seminarian Guy: A Memoir.* Exsegu Publishing.

Rohde, Marie. 2011. "The Prophet." *Inside Milwaukee* (http://www.insidemilwaukee.com/Article/9192011-TheProphet).

Van Handel, Robert. Nd. *Sexual Autobiography* (www.documentcloud.org/ documents/555084).

PART III

Containment and Control

CHAPTER SIX

Protective Custody

*S*trangers in town, lots of us, roaming nervously *in small packs, peering into windows of empty shops (all six of them) on Main Street, as if we were characters in a* Twilight Zone *episode. We were fourteen-year-olds descended upon the small, very quiet, rural community of Galt, California on a Sunday afternoon in September of 1961. Everyone just stared at us... except the Dairy Queen owner who made a killing that day. Our seminary was brand new, built on farm land in the middle of nowhere, and people in the neighboring town had no idea what was going on in "that new place over on Twin Cities Road." Perhaps that's why the rector had given everyone permission to go into town that afternoon.*

We were excited to get away though we wondered why only freshmen seemed interested in the offer. Could have been the terms of engagement: you had to go in groups, and you had to wear your suit and tie. And, by the way, you had only three hours to accomplish the three-mile

hike each direction. (Yes, we had to walk into town.)
The straightest route was via the train tracks. You could
make it one way in about 45 minutes once you mastered
the rhythm necessary to traversing railroad ties. After a
few minutes, we grew accustomed to the old beer cans,
whiskey bottles, and sliced cadavers of rabbits and skunks
that had failed to yield to oncoming trains the night
before. Forty-five minutes each way left us about an hour
and a half to invade and explore. Far too much time. We
returned early and cleaned the black-specked dust off our
shoes and pant cuffs before chapel and dinner. Back into
our box, lid again sealed firmly, peep holes covered.

True story. I walked the tracks, wandered Galt's streets, peered in the windows, and went back into the box. What was it like inside that box? When I asked former seminarians to recall life in minor seminary, a few actually flinched, some quite dramatically. Others pondered long and hard. But everyone paused. Anointed boys, parental offerings, and runaways came at it from different angles, especially given the exit options available to each type (see Chapter Five); why you were there and how trapped you felt affected how easily and warmly you remembered your seminary days. And number of years in the institution colored the experience whatever the seminarian type. Yet, the hesitation before responding, however measured, was a fairly natural one. Men were scanning their adolescent-experience inventory and, likely not for the first time, remembering their days in the seminary as a mixture of pleasure and pain. Pleasure linked to camaraderie and humor was a constant. Situational pleasure, even among general detesters of the experience, also was nearly universal – the memory of the sporting event, the theater production, the scholarly achievement, the good joke pulled (always on someone else, of course). The ache of loneliness and the pressure of "vocational responsibility" similarly were nearly constant, and everyone could envision vividly moments of situational pain – a beating, a humiliation, a betrayal (sometimes delivered rather than absorbed, as reflected in one interviewee's self-assessment: "I could be a real asshole.").

The minor seminary experience was intensely personal, the more so when examined after so many years. For most participants, it is a set of memories in a box in a closet – behind other boxes, accessed via a stepstool, very hard to reach. To reopen it entails recognizing direct effects of the experience on who you are and how you think and behave all these years later. That means looking at everyday life in the seminary as something more than a set of activities within routine schedules. Making sense of those activities and schedules is hard enough; explaining them to people who have little intuitive insight into them, i.e., most people within the former seminarian's social sphere, is yet more difficult. The more systematic effort begins with what the seminary had in mind for its wards.

Give Us Your Sons

America's minor seminaries – high schools and colleges – held nearly 39,000 boys and young men in 1963, the peak of the seminary heyday era. Seminaries differed little from each other in purpose and method. St. Pius X Seminary, for example, sought to

> ... *assist its students, in proportion to age and academic level, to develop into well-informed, intelligent, self-reliant, and vigorous men, capable of shouldering the responsibilities of the priestly state and able to meet the expectations of Christ and his Church ... [through training in] solid spirituality, academic competence, physical fitness, and practical responsibility (St. Pius X Seminary, 1962:3).*

135

This was a tall order, but the church believed it understood how best to accomplish it:

Since the first institution of Seminaries, the Church has always advocated that candidates for the Priesthood should be taken apart [sic; the reference is to physical isolation] *at an early age and trained in an atmosphere favorable to the development of their spiritual life. While fully aware of the importance of the education received in a good Catholic home, the Church has nevertheless insisted on the need of Minor Seminaries in which the vocation received by many boys at an early age may be fostered and protected until their minds and characters have been formed along the right lines.* (Giuseppe Cardinal Pizzardo, Prefect, *Sacred Congregation of Seminaries and Universities,* in a published message of congratulations to the Bishop of the Diocese of Sacramento upon the dedication of St. Pius X Seminary on April 23, 1961.)

Given the above and with notable exceptions, most seminaries were boarding schools,[24] and that status serves to frame a discussion of everyday seminary life in terms of what sociologists call a *total institution.* Total institutions generally are organized around a specific theme or purpose, and their residents – often even their administrators – are separated from the larger world, not simply physically but also in the sense of information and communication flowing into and

---

[24] As noted previously, day seminaries differed considerably from residential seminaries. The goal was the same – eventual movement of boys and young men into a major seminary. However, the relationship of student to institution and that of student to parents were quite different. Day seminaries lacked the substantial control of the seminarian for which residential institutions strove. The students also interfaced quite differently with their parents – home at night with people who watched over them and were part of the vocation-formation experience.

out of their bounded social environments. Decision making in most such institutions rarely is democratic, at least as far as the residents are concerned (and especially so if the resident population is adolescent). Life in total institutions is highly regimented. Behavior is dictated prescriptively; anything not dictated should be assumed to be proscribed (as in, "Who told you that you could be in this room?"). In the extreme, nearly every element of life is determined for the resident: when, where, and what to eat (institutional food; "take it or leave it"); when to use the latrine and shower; when and where to move about. Total institutions may differ from each other in many ways, but each ultimately features a social control-oriented structure.

Boot camps, military academies, orphanages, prisons, and mental hospitals are offered routinely as examples of total institutions. So are boarding schools and, therefore, minor seminaries (Anello, 2018: 27-28; Appleby, 1990: 22; Hoge and Wenger, 2003: 10; Ingleby, 2006: 122; Sipe, 2007: 79). While prisons, mental hospitals and orphanages pursue some form of containment and care (and sometimes punishment or reform) of their wards, institutions such as boot camps, military academies, and seminaries strive to fashion raw social material into products that will carry forward the organization's mission: fighting men and women who will run through walls if so ordered, priests who will shepherd their flocks as directed.

Military boot camps seek to convert individuals into interchangeable pieces of the organization, each member subordinating self-interest to that of the larger unit. This is accomplished in part by the immediate removal of basic individual identity symbols: hair is shorn, uniforms are worn, and jewelry is forbidden. To a lesser but still significant degree, minor seminaries in the 1950s and '60s sought to downplay individual expression, in part to emphasize commitment to the common good and in part to fend off economic class distinctions, intended or otherwise. Permissible hair length was prescribed conservatively. Facial hair was forbidden. A suit was mandatory day-wear in a few seminaries. One interviewee for this project recalled wearing an ROTC-style khaki uniform with a black tie, and another former seminarian noted that the rule at his school was black pants always. For the most part, however, students in minor seminaries were expected to dress "as becomes a candidate for the priesthood": "a suit of conservative color, white dress shirt, and tie" on Sundays and holy days and, on school days, "a dress shirt (white or colored) and tie; clean, pressed slacks or wash pants; shined dress shoes or clean bucks (no white bucks); long-sleeved sweater, sport coat or blazer" (St. Pius X Seminary, 1962:5). Watches were permitted; rings were not.

Total institution that it was, the minor seminary sought not only to subordinate individuality to group needs and goals, but also to emphasize its distinct cultural identity. We attended a *Catholic* boarding school. Symbols were ubiquitous. The chapel dominated the campus, and its walls contained beautiful stained glass and murals celebrating the "one true faith." Crucifixes adorned every public wall and blessed every student's room. Statues of Jesus, Mary, and a multitude of saints, if not huge and imposing in courtyards, were insinuated into nooks and crannies throughout the campus. Libraries held Catholic books and magazines. History courses were Catholic history courses. Prayers (usually the Hail Mary) began and ended every meal, class session, and sporting event.

Time spent in chapel set the tone for seminary life – prayer, mass, more prayer; morning, noon, evening, after dinner, before lights out. Each seminarian had his own prayer book, hymnal, and, prior to and for a few years after Vatican II, bible-sized book of Latin liturgical chant (the *Liber Usualis*) at his assigned place in his assigned pew. Every day honored a particular Catholic saint or major event. Sunday masses were extravagant in their length, pageantry, and centrality to the remainder of the day and our reason for being in the seminary. Advent and Lent – periods of abstinence, penance, and contemplation of the birth, death, and resurrection of Christ – were exceptional in their focus. Their capstone events, Christmas, Good Friday, and Easter, were celebrated with particular fervor. *Veni, Veni Emanuel, Jesu Redemptor, O Sacrum Convivium, Terra Tremuit.* We'd sing our hearts out in Latin polyphonic. We were *Catholic.*

Catholic, yes, but with a wrinkle in the cultural canvas. *White,* Western European Catholic. While we would encounter kids of Dutch, French, Polish, Portuguese, Swedish, and Spanish heritage in the seminary, seminarians of the 1950s and 1960s came in the main from Irish, German, and Italian stock. They were a step removed from the immigrant, urban and rural enclaves of their grandparents, but they had grown up celebrating their old-country heritage. Good-natured joking and competition prevailed. "Dago" was thrown about freely on campus, as were "Mick" and "Kraut" – even by some of the priests. St. Patrick's Day brought green shirts and a much anticipated, annual "Irish vs. the World" basketball game. That was the shape of "diversity" and "inclusivity" in Catholic seminaries.[25]

---

[25] I recall only two students at St. Pius X Seminary who were born abroad, one from the Azores (thus, Western European) and the other from the Philippines. Regarding the latter, a classmate remembers:

In our senior year at Pius, there was a Filipino kid, Danny, who joined our class – actually he had graduated from a public high school but was held back for Latin and other "deficits." He was shy and unsure of himself but a very nice guy. His English was good but seemed weak when he was nervous, which was mostly in class. It was clear that [Father] Anthony [our Latin teacher] thought him unsuited for Pius; or maybe the whole faculty did and sent Anthony after him. At any rate, Anthony would dismantle the kid day after day until one day he just said in front of the whole class that Danny did not belong at Pius and asked Danny if he did not agree. The kid just nodded and cried. We all just sat there stunned and angry at Anthony for the way he did it, but we said nothing (as usual). Danny was gone the next day. It's funny – there were lots of white kids who did not belong or perform so well, but they were counseled out of Pius quietly and more gently.

As noted in Chapter Two, the Catholic Church failed to grasp the possibility of vocations, and, thus, the potential sustainability of endangered, under-enrolled seminaries, among minority faithful. Chief among those generally ignored were persons of Hispanic origin, a very high percentage of whom was Catholic, in the Southwest and West and within large cities throughout the rest of the United States. Under assumptions of the day regarding who should be the shepherd and who the flock, the possibility of a Mexican American priest in a parish of Western European-American Catholics was barely imagined much less debated. Reflecting this, a hand-count of Hispanic-surnamed seminarians from my own era (1961-1967) at St. Pius X Seminary produced only 14 names among the 377 boys (i.e., about 3.5 percent) with whom I was schooled. When I asked several former schoolmates to name ten, they were unable.

Mexican American boys who did enter St. Pius X flew under the radar after arrival. Little reference was made to their heritage in the sense that it was for boys of Irish, Italian, or German descent. And they certainly did not participate in the banter about cultural lineage that students of Western European descent shared (though one interviewee remembered being called a "Spic" by another seminarian who did not employ the term good-naturedly). Outside of Spanish class, there was scant talk of Our Lady of Guadalupe, for instance. One Mexican American former student at a Claretian seminary near Los Angeles noted that there was little consciousness one way or another regarding ethnicity, because, he speculated, the students were drawn nationally rather than locally and the focus was more upon the priesthood than upon characteristics of the students themselves. Cultural background was acknowledged little:

There were only a few Mexican kids there, and we ate white-people food all the time. When my mother would bring homemade tostadas on visiting day, we'd share them and everyone loved them. Then we'd go back to white-people food.

Another Mexican American former seminarian considered his heritage neither a problem nor an asset, though his memories of "white-people food" also remained prominent. He was careful to place the ethnicity issue in perspective:

You have to remember that the early 1960s were years of assimilation for people of Mexican heritage. We did not want to stand out, we wanted to blend in. Our parents wanted us to merge well into traditional American middle-class culture. My folks spoke English around us and Spanish to each other. They anglicized the pronunciation of our name. And there were not many Mexican American kids in the pipeline. The key was Catholic elementary school, and most Mexican families could not afford that. The few of us that got recruited to [the seminary] actually found it easy to blend in. No one resented us even if they didn't recognize our ethnic heritage.

During the same years that I attended St. Pius X, there were three black seminarians. I could find no record of students of African American descent before my time, and I have been told that another two attended the school in the ten years it remained open after I left. Civil-rights sensitivities of the era meant that these students generally were watched with interest but interacted with as if they possessed neither color nor cultural history, though that was not the case in all seminaries. Supreme Court Justice and former seminarian Clarence Thomas (2007: 43) recalls the death knell sounding for his vocation when some of his schoolmates at Immaculate Conception Seminary in Missouri celebrated the shooting of Dr. Martin Luther King: "That's good.... I hope the son of a bitch dies."

Walled In

To shape its charges toward desired ends, the total institution controls the exposure of those charges to the outside world and governs their movements within the twenty-four-hour day. Thus, minor seminaries most often were set in isolated rural areas; if not, they were fenced to accomplish the same end. After a short time, the seminarian's family increasingly grew distant in the rearview mirror, and his social world was little more than the sum of his peers and the people who governed him or provided necessary services.

In most seminaries of the 1950s and early 1960s, a student saw his family once a month for six to eight hours on "Visiting Sundays."[26] If you were fortunate enough to live in a nearby town, and the institution permitted it (many did not), you could go home with your folks right after high mass (about noon), have an early (non-institutional) dinner, and be driven back by 7:00 for night study hall. Families that lived further away generally were left to picnic or wander the grounds for most of the day or perhaps to drive into the nearby burg for a meal at a diner. Seminarians whose parents lived truly far away (often the case for boys who attended the seminaries of religious orders) would not see them until a major holiday trip home.

We lived about seven hours from the sem. My folks brought me down from temperate Northern California to a place that was burning hot in September. We walked around for an hour

---

[26] Visiting Sundays evolved into Visiting Weekends in the mid-1960s as seminaries began to loosen their reins in the face of enrollment declines. This did not help those whose families lived far away, for if the families visited, they needed to find hotel accommodations. Most families could not afford to do so very often.

looking at the place, and then a priest suggested that I might like to go swimming. I said fine and went to the pool which felt weird because I didn't know any of the other kids. After about half an hour, my folks suddenly appeared by the pool and said they're leaving. I'm looking up at them, a fourteen-year-old boy, dripping wet, not really knowing what was happening. I suppose they wanted to avoid a sad-goodbye scene. But wow. I did not see them again for almost four months. (Alumnus, St. Pius X Seminary)

I remember my first Visiting Sunday. My family came for mass and then we drove home for the afternoon. Thinking they were doing a good thing, a neighbor family had us over for dinner about three. I was being celebrated. Then we went back to our house and suddenly it was after six and time to hit the road. It was as if I never went home. I waved to a few kids on the block. I barely talked to my parents. I wonder what it was like for them. (Former seminarian from Los Angeles)

The whole school went into the city for this big religious event where grade-school kids marched all around a stadium singing and praying. Parents and families were in the stands listening to the speakers yammer on about communists and Jesus and Mary. We [freshmen] had been in the sem about a month, and we had not seen our parents since they dropped us off. A lot of them were at this rally. I could see mine looking for me in the seminary section. All of a sudden, [the rector] said: "Don't leave the group. We are here representing the seminary, and we'll stay together." Some kids defied him, but most of us just sat there with a weak wave to our folks. It was painful. It was also clear who owned us now. Not our parents. (Alumnus, St. Pius X Seminary)

Getting outside the walls, any way you could, became the dream if not the outright objective of most students (Hendrickson, 1983: 142). Anything to break the routine and taste, if only for a moment, the world out there: the choir sent by bus to perform in town, the basketball team playing some small rural school, the graduating seniors or college men spending (with permission) most of the day at a nearby lake or getting to go into the city – always in a group and in their suits – to see Richard Burton in *Hamlet* or Peter, Paul, and Mary or Simon and Garfunkel in concert.

> *It's hard to believe looking back, but everyone was genuinely envious of [a classmate] who would be driven weekly into Galt [the neighboring town] for an allergy shot. He got out! And whenever there was a call for volunteers to go with a priest or brother on an off-campus errand – like picking left-over grapes in vineyards or the pumpkins remaining in patches after Halloween – guys would kill for the chance.* (Alumnus, St. Pius X Seminary)

> *Guys would sneak off campus at night. They had no place to go. It was just an adventure to walk along the quiet roads though you worried that a priest would drive by coming back from someplace. I remember once sneaking out into a field to have a beer with another guy when I was in college. While we were sitting there – about 10:30 at night – we saw movement up by the building. It was about five high-school kids, rookies, who had snuck away for a smoke and BAM! There was a priest waiting by the door. They were dead ducks and in big trouble. We just pinned ourselves to the ground and later snuck way around the back and into our rooms.* (Former seminarian from Seattle)

The social isolation of seminarians was reinforced by the institution's control of their communication with the outside world. At most seminaries, personal radios were not permitted, and the few communal radios available were monitored to prevent "abuse."[27] Most also had but one television for students, accessible in the student lounge during afternoon free time; in those days, there was little to watch in the afternoon on the few channels available.[28] Newspapers were banned in some seminaries; others permitted copies in the recreation rooms though it was not uncommon to find holes in pages from which stories had been clipped. The result, obviously, was little sense of what was occurring in the world. A former student in the Archdiocese of San Francisco's minor seminary recalled that his classmates and he knew nothing of Russia's launch of the Sputnik satellite in 1957 until a week after it had happened (Wall, 1999). Another seminarian from Sacramento remembered learning about the 1962 Cuban missile crisis two weeks after it had occurred.[29]

Magazines such as *Time* and *Newsweek* were permitted because they arrived through the mail. A faculty member (usually the "Dean

---

[27] The irony of radio-containment was that it did little to halt our exposure to potentially "problematic" music, e.g., the Shirelles' *Will You Love Me Tomorrow?* For we had the radio at home! We would return after holidays and summer breaks with all the new songs to talk about, especially those by groups that we could imitate while walking. Like Mick Jagger, we could get no satisfaction, and we were certain that Simon and Garfunkel were talking about us when they sang, "I am a rock. I am an island." Denied immediate access to the world and a sense of what normality entailed, the songs we had memorized held us until the next home visit.

[28] Filmmaker Michael Moore apparently dropped out of a minor seminary in 1968 after his high-school freshman year in part because of restrictions on television viewing (Schultz, 2005:8).

[29] The exception to this delay in news of world events, not surprisingly, was word of the assassination of John F. Kennedy in November of 1963. We heard about it within minutes in part because it was simply that important an event and in part because, as the first Catholic president, Kennedy was revered as the man whose election meant that Catholics finally had arrived.

of Students" or "Prefect of Discipline") could then peruse them for problematic stories just as he inspected incoming and outgoing letters to and from family and friends. In some institutions, censorship of mail was highly formal. Students often were called into the dean's office to explain segments of letters from friends or to be told that they should rethink what they had just written their parents – "We would not want to worry them, you know." Books were another matter: brought from home, always subject to examination if found, always subject to seizure if "problematic," always indicative of an attitudinal problem if seized.

> *If you wanted to bring a book from the outside, you needed to get a stamp on that book and there needed to be a priest's signature on that stamp to make it valid. This was referred to as an "Approved Book." Unapproved books were a no-no.* (Wall, 1999)

> *I was put on probation (the worst punishment available short of expulsion…) in my senior year for being caught with an unapproved copy of* The Diary of Anne Frank *on my desk (there was an approved copy in the school library).* (Hedin, 2003: 14)

Some seminaries permitted students to go in groups into town to see movies, as long as approval for the viewing was obtained beforehand. More often, however, movies were shown on campus; in our school, they were viewed monthly on Saturday nights in the refectory with its hard-backed chairs. The films were dated since older movies had cheaper rental fees. They also were "safe" movies for the most part though not necessarily soft. I remember good films such as *Twelve Angry Men, Bigger than Life, Shane, Marty, The Diary of Ann Frank*. (Then again, I also recall *Stars and Stripes Forever*, the 1952 John Philip Sousa story.) "Less-safe" movies (*The*

Pawnbroker, for example) were left to vacations at home for those who dared deceive their parents.

Engaged and Quiet

Seclusion did not mean lock-down or time on one's hands, as so often is the case in total institutions designed solely to contain or punish. Quite the opposite. The whole point of seminaries for boys and young men was to hold them safe from worldly distractions and focused on the future (even if that future was, for freshmen, twelve years distant). The formula was obvious: keep those kids so busy that they have little time to think, and don't let them talk too much.

We were busy, and we were regimented. We attended classes even on Saturday mornings. Class preparation and homework assignments seemed always on our minds, and it was not uncommon to find boys studying by flashlight in the shower or under blanket-tents during the night. If the objective of our curriculum was to occupy our time, it was accomplished. However, the purpose was grander. The seminary's overall goal had become a broad liberal-arts education, the equal of that offered in most Catholic high schools and, where pertinent, Catholic colleges (see Chapter Two). Religion courses were taken every semester for six years, as were Latin courses (in addition, at St. Pius X, to two years of Spanish in high school and another in college and two years of Greek in college). Offerings and requirements otherwise essentially mimicked those of any accredited educational institution of the day: math and science (fairly weak in rigor and quality), physical education and civics (of unremarkable rigor and quality), and the ever-challenging English, literature, history, speech, and music (all of substantial rigor and quality). We wrote, and we read, and then we wrote and read some more – classical literature, short papers, essays, book reports, poetry, and term papers. Our work almost always was returned with comments. Weaker students bit the dust; better students worked harder to maintain the distinction.

No event or obligation was left to individuals to recall; everything happened in response to a bell. We heard the bell; we moved to the next item on the schedule. We were in the chapel, refectory, classroom, or residence hall most hours of the day and night. We rose at 5:50 each morning (except on Sundays when we were permitted the luxury of a 6:30 awakening). We were in chapel for morning prayers and mass twenty minutes after climbing out of bed. Breakfast was quick, and we were in class at 7:55. Mandatory study hall sessions occurred at 9:30 AM, 4:45 PM, and 7:30 PM – the latter two followed by a trip to the chapel for prayer and thence to a meal or to bed. Lights out came at 9:30 PM.

Lights out brought an additional obligation: the Grand Silence. To the extent that we were not sleeping, we were to be meditating or contemplating, never talking. Officially, the Grand Silence commenced with the conclusion of night prayers at 9:10 PM and ended with morning prayers at 6:10 AM, nine hours later. Yet, the sum of time spent in mass, classes, study hall, prayer, and rosary – activities in which social conversation was not permitted – effectively added nine more hours of silence to the standard weekday. Further, since the possibility of conversation during meals rested exclusively with the priest at the head table, the silence may have been extended still further. Indeed, the high-school seminarian on any given weekday was "guaranteed" the ability to converse socially about three and a half hours per day.

Free time was precious and rarely wasted by the student or the institution. It occurred most weekdays between 3:00 and 4:45 though Wednesday, Saturday, and Sunday afternoons provided freedom from 12:45 until 4:45. Some of that precious time was poached by the institution because seminarians also were responsible for a portion of the upkeep of the campus; we were assigned work duties such as building maintenance, and these could occur only when we were not in class, chapel, or dining hall.

Free periods brought involvement primarily in organized activities, not the least of which was athletic competition (Bazzett, 2010; Carnevale, 2014; Cornwell, 2006; Fausel, 2003; Hedin, 2003; Hendrickson, 1983; Howard, 2013; Miles, 2012; Murray, 2018; Thomas, 2007; Vautier, 2013; Wall, 1999).[30] There were many outstanding athletes in the seminary; pursuit of the priesthood did not signal lack of heart and hand-eye coordination. We would spend hours on the field or court. Shorter free periods would bring pick-up games and practice. Every game spurred thoughts of the next game. Every spring brought the long-awaited "Track and Field Day" that pitted seminarian against seminarian in contests of speed, strength, and stamina. These were not simply distractions that soaked time; they became activities and objectives for which we had far too little time.

Competition made seminarians feel "normal." A letter in basketball sewed onto your school sweater by your mom meant that you could walk with your head high not only within the seminary but among outside high-school contemporaries. When we beat an outside team in basketball (the only varsity, extramural sport at St. Pius X in my day), we exulted in demonstrating that "holy boys" could walk and chew gum simultaneously. And nothing topped a high-school class team beating the college team in any sport. I can still see classmates crying when as juniors we beat the college men on the gridiron; David had slain Goliath.

Music and theater played the same role for many seminarians (and it was common in such small schools to find students engaged

---

[30] Free time also brought involvement in campus organizations (e.g., the Sodality of the Blessed Virgin Mary), student government, and clubs. (St. Pius X Seminary even had a gun club.) These, in turn, spawned events such as carnivals to raise funds for the organization's use.

in athletics, music, and theater). A music letter distinguished a student as more than a member of a choir or band; he was devoted to music. A theater award, including one earned by a stagehand or set designer who had spent hours behind the scenes, conveyed a passion for and a sense of the power in the arts:

> *When I was a sophomore at St. Pius, we put on T.S. Eliot's play, "Murder in the Cathedral," and I won the role of Archbishop Thomas Beckett. We had the opportunity to do the play in the cathedral in downtown Sacramento. At the beginning of the second act, I started Tom's sermon by saying, "In nomine Patris et Filii et Spiritus Sancti." And all the people in the audience made the sign of the cross. That's when I thought, 'Wow. This is the power of performance.'* (Corcoran, 2017, quoting actor LeVar Burton).

Behaved

If control of time and talk did not subdue the adolescent spirit, discipline was meant to. We were watched constantly. The majority of seminarians were "good boys" who were unaccustomed to getting into serious trouble.[31] Few did. Yet, as Durkheim (1958 [1883]: 67) noted more than a century ago,

> *Imagine a society of saints, a perfect cloister of exemplary individuals. Crimes properly so called, will there be unknown; but*

---

[31] This is not to suggest that the seminary did not contain some troubled young men. For example, a former seminarian from San Diego had not forgotten: *A classmate and I were standing in the doorway of our study hall one afternoon, and he pointed to a workman on his knees on a nearby lawn fixing a sprinkler. He had his back to us. This guy says, "I could walk up behind him and hit him in the back of the neck and kill him, and he'd never know what hit him." He wasn't kidding. He actually was playing this scene in his head.*

faults which appear venial to the layman will create there the same scandal that the ordinary offence does in ordinary conscious- ness. If, then, this society has the power to judge and punish, it will define these acts as criminal and will treat them as such.

Infractions in the seminary were acts of little consequence on the outside. Theft was rare.[32] Boys got into fights, but no one ever was seriously injured. Instead, kids were punished for the transgressions of speaking during the Grand Silence or in study hall, arriving late (i.e., after the bell had rung) to an obligatory event, reading a book surreptitiously during a lecture, sleeping in, running where forbidden, being in the wrong place at the wrong time, breaking a window while goofing around. Length of sentence was determined by seriousness of infraction, and the penalty generally was predictable: writing papers, kneeling at your desk, forfeiture of free time, assignment to a "work crew," "paint crew," or "dish crew." More serious infractions – cheating on tests, smoking, leaving campus without permission, dating during summer – occasioned heavier doses of the same punishments and per- haps probation. Very serious acts or frequently repeated transgressions brought the hammer: dismissal from the seminary.

Dismissal from the seminary was no small matter even for those who were unhappy in it. As a threat, it was a very blunt instrument, often employed by less-mature priests on the faculty to gain the upper hand over a student: "I could have you thrown out of here right now if I wanted to." There was no way that it did not produce a degree of shame, for the seminary was a school for exemplary boys who might someday hold among the highest of statuses in

---

[32] Thefts did occur occasionally. A St. Pius X Seminary alumnus recalled: *One evening after we finished dinner, we had to line up as we left the refectory and place our hands under an ultraviolet lamp. That night, a freshman – from my own parish! – was sent packing. Someone had been stealing money from gym lockers. They put some kind of dye on some bills and left them in a locker for the thief to find.*

the Catholic Church. Getting booted brought a sense of "complete failure" (Vautier, 2013). Neither the boy nor his family could pretend that he had sought clarity from God about his vocation and chose to leave; the choice was not his; he was not worthy. This so stuck in one dismissed interviewee's craw that his entry into a second seminary after high school was "partly to stick it to [his former seminary]."

Institutional stances on punishment hardened or softened with the times and with admission and attrition fluctuations. During the heyday era, when seminaries possessed the luxury of more applicants than they could absorb, faculties could turn brutal:

> ...[F]our members of my Third High class were caught down on the playing field after Lights Out. They had a portable radio and they wanted in the worst way to listen to a key Ohio State basketball game on the radio. It was a playoff game. For this double infraction of the seminary rules, the four of them were thrown out of St Joseph's and they were class leaders. The two infractions were: caught with a radio and caught outside your room at night. (Wall, 1999)

> One soon-to-be ex-seminarian had forgotten this principle [of keeping one's mouth shut] and returned to his room after Night Prayer to find everything he owned piled high on the disassembled bed. On top he found the four pieces of his transistor radio and a note [from the Prefect of Discipline] that read "Come to my room".... (Hinsvark, nd)

> We came back from Christmas break in our freshman year and found out that four seniors, big-deal guys, had been kicked out for "bad attitude." It scared the hell out of us. I went around

for years worried about getting kicked out. (Priest interviewee from San Francisco)

Fairly universally, interviewees and authors reflect with awe upon the Dean of Student's or Master of Discipline's seeming omnipresence and capacity to know of every wrongdoing:

Every priest had a nickname there. Cat Canfield was the Prefect of Discipline at the seminary, which was a pretty important job back then. Well, Cat was suited to this job, maybe too well suited. The poor man had insomnia and he only slept two or three hours a night. So he was a natural for catching guys joking around in the hallways after Lights Out. He wore these shoes that had some special soles on them and you couldn't hear him when he walked up behind you. Hence the name "Cat". This man had an incredible ability to appear out of nowhere when something was going on. (Wall, 1999)

The priest who presided over the schedule... was Father Constantine Doole, Prefect of Discipline ... [who] did not use a switch; he did it all with his grimaces.... Mostly I saw him as enforcer. What he could not abide, I think, was someone attempting to get away with something under his nose. The issue was control.... (Hendrickson, 1983:73-75)

I was dozing off when I was surprised by the sight of a black figure in the darkness moving silently along the dormitory. ...[I]t was Father McCartie [Prefect of Discipline]. For an age, it seemed, I could see his black figure standing in silence at the doorway halfway down the dormitory. (Cornwell, 2006: 55)

There was a lighter side to misbehavior and discipline; even the offenders often laughed and shrugged when they learned that their antics had earned an afternoon "work crew" assignment. But there was a darker side too:

You'd hear [Dean of Students] Father Charles's door close further up the corridor, and the guys in the back of the study hall with the good sightline would watch for his shadow. If they saw it they'd whisper, "Chuck," and the room would go very still. He had vowed to crack down on comportment and attitude problems. And here he was again, filling the doorway with his huge frame, Brando to whip James Dean. He wore his pants below his waist. His T-shirt had tiny burn holes, and he had rolled up its sleeves an inch. Maybe he was a little drunk, or just worried that he was not winning his battle with us. He held a sneaker in his hand. Left beneath a bed, if no one's, it was all of ours, as likely he hoped.

"It's mine." And we all gaped at John LeBlonde. A quiet guy, a renowned sneak-out smoker, a year older than we, he could drive.

Chuck struck LeBlonde's face with the sole of that sneaker about eight times on each cheek. We shook and squirmed like adolescent baboons, paws over incisors, but we did not shriek. We took it like John took it, even though we knew we should be chasing that priest to a monastery to drown in altar wine.

Another true story, scary and sad as it is. Fortunately, I was not the victim in question, though I was in the adjacent desk, and that was far too close. I'll always admire John LeBlonde – shed not a tear, said not a word, just took it while a six-foot-four, 225-pound, thirty-seven-year-old man with a boom-box voice snapped John's head to and fro.

Though I have encountered references to corporal punishment in the literature on seminary life (Hendrickson, 1983:93; Cornwell, 2006:62, 78; Miles, 2012), I do not wish to suggest that Father Charles McDermott was in any sense prototypical. Most disciplinarians did not beat up kids.[33] Rather, they assigned traditional punishments that generally fit the severity of the infraction, sometimes chastised a transgressor publicly, and were the offense sufficiently severe, brought the problem to the rector and the faculty for discussion of the boy's fit and fate within the seminary. That said, what Charles did was but a step removed from the norm in a total institution such as a seminary. He encountered little in the way of external oversight of his actions; only the rector imposed internal accountability (if he was aware of the problem or considered it a problem in the first place); few victims ever would consider complaining to an adult. Ultimately, then, the behavior in question was determined by the presence or absence of a propensity for physical discipline. Most deans stayed south of center on the propensity scale; Charles sat decidedly north of center.

To this day, none of us who experienced Charles's three-year reign (1962-1965, my class's sophomore, junior, and senior years) as Dean of Students at St. Pius X Seminary knows whether his appearance on our campus was pure happenstance, the result of problems in his former assignment as disciplinarian in a Salvatorian, inner-city Catholic high school, or requested by our rector

---

[33] Times changed, and what was a disputed practice became a legal issue. A former seminarian at St. Pius X Preparatory School a decade later recalled that police were called by the principal when a lay teacher gave a student a black eye during an argument. Then again, he also recalled the school principal slapping a "knucklehead" who got in his face. No call to the police was made.

who perhaps felt that our seminary lacked appropriate order.[34] His initial arrival sparked much discussion, mostly positive. Charles had attended a Salvatorian minor seminary but had left and joined the Army. As a twenty-year-old paratrooper, he had jumped into the Battle of Bastogne. He went to college after the war and then reentered the Salvatorian order. He was a man's man, a tough guy, less detached than most of the priests on the faculty. He spoke his mind.

Charles employed carrots as well as sticks. He was high-energy, engaging, and could make a kid feel important. He did everything the "Army way" – dressings down of groups at attention, calisthenics, and midnight runs and duck walks to break the rebellious spirit of an entire class or dorm. He pushed the basketball team to excel and helped us build a hardball diamond. He loved folk music, established student folk groups (that included him as bass), and would build bonfires on weekend nights for campus "hootenannies." He would often cancel Saturday afternoon study halls in warm weather and permit an outdoor dinner. He taught us how to write well and to engage an audience in public speaking. With a faculty colleague, he established the seminary's annual, well-received play, *Passion of the Savior*. And he took small groups of students to the rural south during the summer to minister to Catholics and to champion social justice.

---

[34] The previous Dean of Students had been old-school, ineffective, and accorded little respect throughout the school. Part of his problem stemmed from eyesight so poor that, when he removed his glasses while sitting at the raised prefect's table in the refectory, upper-classmen at the back of the room would wave their white napkins as if they were stranded on a desert island and a ship was passing. He looked straight at them and saw none of it. He once warned that if students did not behave during study hall, he would "swoop down" on them. Every effort he made to maintain order and discipline thereafter garnered catcalls of "SWOOP!" whose authors he could not see. He was transferred to a mission parish at the close of our freshman year.

But good deeds went only so far. Upon arrival, Charles had told the upperclassmen that, if they behaved themselves, he'd leave them alone. He set his sights upon the first- and second-year classes which he intended to mold as he saw fit. This inequity did not sit well with the sophomores who just the year before had been typical seminarians and were now labeled the "bad class." He had his favorites and, as an interviewee termed them, his "smoking buddies" (in an institution that forbade smoking by high-school students) to whom he dispensed privileges. And it soon became clear that the source of his seemingly other-worldly awareness of transgressions was informants, usually upperclassmen with whom younger admirers had shared secrets.

Charles's rages grew more frequent, as did the number of times he lifted students to their toes or even off the ground with his hand at their throats. Calling offenders to the middle of the refectory at dinner's end and driving them to the floor with slaps to the side of the head did not engender good will. And the beating administered with a tennis shoe was never forgotten:

I really loved the guy at first. I mean, he was a paratrooper during the war! In the Battle of Bastogne! And he was cool. But after a while, especially after he beat up LeBlonde, I started to see him as unhealthy, definitely not a good guy. (Alumnus, St. Pius X Seminary)

He was an asshole, a drill instructor without a troop. (Alumnus, St. Pius X Seminary)

Among interviewees who had experienced the Charles era, none had spoken a word of these events to his parents while at St. Pius. We were able to navigate through such difficulties by walking with our eyes fixed straight ahead. Would we have been believed had we outed him? Perhaps. Many parents seemed genuinely shocked and angry years later when we told them almost matter-of-factly. But our seminary years occurred when priests still were revered; "If Father did it, he must have had a good reason." The fact remains that we spoke not a word. We honored Charles's oft-repeated mantra: everything that happens within these walls stays within these walls. Indeed, it seems that the mandate was countered only once by a sophomore whom Charles had struck. Over the victim's protestations, his mother complained to the rector. There is no record or memory of anything in particular done in response, but the following summer Father Charles moved elsewhere. The next dean did not hit people as often or as hard.

References

Anello, Robert L. 2018. *Minor Setback or Major Disaster? The Rise and Demise of Minor Seminaries in the United States, 1958-1983.* St. Louis MO: EnRoute Books.

Appleby, R. Scott. 1990. "Part I: The Transformation of the Roman Catholic Parish Priesthood." In Jay P. Dolan et al., eds. *Transforming Parish Ministry.* New York: Crossroad. P. 3-107.

Bazzett, Timothy. 2010. *Reed City Boy.* Reed City MI: Rathole Books.

Carnevale, Rick. 2014. *When Pigs Fly.* Bloomington IN: Author House.

Corcoran, Betsy. 2017. "LeVar Burton to Educators: 'I See You.'" *EdSurge* (April 27).

Cornwell, John. 2006. *Seminary Boy: A Memoir.* New York: Doubleday.

Durkheim, Emil. 1958 [1883]. *The Rules of Sociological Method.* (Translated by S.A. Soloway and J. H. Mueller.) Glencoe IL: Free Press.

Fausel, Donald F. 2010. *From Blind Obedience to a Responsible Faith.* Bloomington IN: iUniverse.

Hedin, Raymond. 2003. *Married to the Church (Updated Edition).* Bloomington: Indiana University Press.

Hendrickson, Paul. 1983. *Seminary: A Search.* New York: Summit Books.

_____. 2002. "Altar-Boy Innocence; A Former Seminarian Reflects on Moral Ambivalence." *New York Times* (https://www.nytimes.com/2002/04/28/weekinreview/the-nation).

Hinsvark, John. Nd. *Remembering St. Joseph Seminary.* www.stjosephscollege .org/memoirs.

Hoge, Dean R. and Jacqueline Wenger. 2003. *Evolving Visions of the Priesthood.* Collegeville MN: Liturgical Press.

Howard, Ted. 2013. *Our Seminary Years: 1956–1964.* https://www.mixbook.com/photo-books/family/our-seminary-years-1956-1964-9395897.

Ingleby, Ewan. 2006. "Reinventing Melchizedek: Interpretations of Traditional Religious Texts in the Seminary Context." In Elizabeth Arweck and Peter Collins, (eds.), *Reading Religion in Text and Context.* Burlington VT: Ashgate. Pp. 120-136.

Miles, Vincent J. 2012. *Boys of the Cloth: The Accidental Role of Church Reforms in Causing and Curbing Abuse by Priests.* Lanham, MD: Hamilton Books.

Murray, Joseph C. 2018. *Ex-Seminarian Guy: A Memoir.* Exsegu Publishing.

Pissardo, Giuseppe. 1961. *Message of Congratulations to the Bishop of the Diocese of Sacramento upon the Dedication of St. Pius X Seminary* (February 28th). Rome: Sacred Congregation of Seminaries and Universities.

Schultz, Emily. 2005. *Michael Moore: A Biography.* Toronto: ewc Press.

Sipe, A.W. Richard. 2007. *The Serpent and the Dove: Celibacy in Literature and Life.* Westport CN: Praeger.

St. Pius X Seminary. 1962. *General Bulletin.* Galt CA: St. Pius X Seminary.

Thomas, Clarence. 2007. *My Grandfather's Son: A Memoir.* New York: HarperCollins.

Vautier, Dominic. 2014. "Seminary Memories – 1956-57." *www. ses4legacyfullessays, wordpress.com* .

Wall, Bill. 1999. *A Day in My Life at St. Joseph's College (Seminary), 1958.* www.stjosephscollege.org/memoirs_bill-wall-day.html.

CHAPTER SEVEN

Survival Skills

*N*early to a person, former minor seminarians remember walks. Two or three guys shooting the breeze, gossiping, nodding to others doing the same. Walks generally occurred in the evening – after dinner and before rosary and study hall. They provided a getaway, forty five minutes breathing a bit differently from the way we did inside. Things could be said that would not be spoken in the dorms or hallways. Rock songs could be sung aloud. Or, maybe, little was said. We just walked unwatched and therefore free – sort of. We almost always stopped right at the seminary's perimeter, maybe a step further in daring or protest. The boundary was easy enough to decipher. It was marked by the path worn into the soil by the walks taken by seminarians long before we got there.

It is clear in retrospect that, while some growth was expected of us, the main objective of the minor seminary was to isolate us from worldly influences until we were ready to be advanced to the big leagues, the major seminary. It was purely a game of odds. Some percentage of those recruited would leave early and some later, but the survivors – those who might well persevere all the way to the priesthood – would be greater in number than were the church to leave their fate to chance (i.e., vulnerable to distraction). The late Bishop Emeritus of the Diocese of Sacramento, Francis Quinn, looking back upon his ninety-four years of life, made exactly this point regarding his own vocation, which he regretted not at all (Bretón, 2016):

When asked how Quinn's life might have been different had he gone into the seminary when he was older than 13, he paused. His eyes welled up. His voice dropped to barely above a whisper. "If I hadn't gone to the seminary at 13, I would have never gone in," he said. "Once I was in high school, I think I would have met a nice girl. I think God thought, 'If I'm going to get this guy, I better get him now.'"

In this same spirit, we were housed for the better part of the calendar year in a social world reduced to those residing with us and those "protecting" and "forming" our vocations. Each of us recognized and appreciated this to some extent – we were not fools or oblivious to the dangers of the world into which we were allowed only during summers and holidays. And, despite our protests, few of us truly objected to the structure to which we were subjected; adolescents may hate structure but generally do not appreciate its absence. Yet, most of us never were entirely happy. Though kept occupied to an incredible degree, our minds wandered. Even the most vocation-focused among us was susceptible to rejection of the seminary's stifling routine, seclusion, and discipline. Further, in truth, we *were* attracted by the "bright lights" of the world about which our seminary's spiritual director warned us at the close of each school year. And every kid who failed to return from that world each fall made us wonder why we were still in the seminary.

On the outside, most kids our age could seek at least some relief and comfort from their families when they felt unhappy or adrift. We could do so too, but to a considerably lesser degree. For our families had surrendered us such that we never again could or wanted to recapture the traditional parent-child relationship. We were not going to high school; we were pursuing a (holy) career. We felt it the very first time we returned home (Vautier, 2013). Our parents would ask for details about our life away, and we would hold back or answer vaguely, as if they could not understand and appreciate our world fully. They seemed to accept this and to trust us out of their sight to an extent not granted our siblings. When we were with family, we were "on leave," independent, just passing through.

During summers and holidays, seminarians often spent time with each other. (One interviewee noted that his seminary mandated the contact and assigned a fellow seminarian from the same hometown the task of "summer prefect.") Sometimes classmates from another town would stay for a few days at a student's home, and the two connected with other seminarians. They would shoot a few hoops, then pile into a car and drive around aimlessly, trying their best to emulate their secular contemporaries... until a car full of girls asked them where they went to school. Most interviewees reported being excruciatingly bored over the summer, sitting around, out of the mainstream. Some were fortunate to find summer employment and, in some cases, to get a look at life otherwise unexperienced; tire shop employees did not censor their conversations and modes of expression in the presence of a kid who planned to be a priest.

Seminarians also reunited with childhood friends, but this often was not as rewarding as in younger days. The friends now were maturing, dating, and talking about college just around the bend. The gap in worlds was glaring:

HomeKid: *Our high school team just beat last year's city champs. What a game!*

SemKid: *Must have been exciting. Our varsity just beat St. Rose Parish's CYO [Catholic Youth Organization] team in overtime.*

HomeKid: *Remember Jimmy Drake? He just starred in his school play and got to make out with a gorgeous girl in one scene.*

SemKid: *I had the Judas role in the Passion Play and got kissed by Jesus.*

HomeKid: *I'm going on the tour of colleges this semester. Wonder where I'll end up.*

SemKid: *I'll spend my first two years of college in the same place I'm now going to high school. I'll have eleven classmates.*

HomeKid: *Whoa! Did you see the curves on that sweet young thing?*

SemKid: *Um, uh, yeah, yeah, I did. Wow.*

More to the point, there was no way that seminarians were going to share their vocation angst with guys from the old neighborhood. The sadder fact was that they rarely talked much about that angst with their peers within the seminary. The seminarian had many friends but relatively few friendships. At least in small to medium-size institutions, everyone knew everyone. Boys and young men participated in every kind of activity – sports, theater, music, clean-up crew. A seminarian would play football with a kid and then find the same kid standing next to him in glee-club practice an hour later. There were Big Men on Campus, to be sure, but few non-BMOCs felt ignored or identified by number only. There was a closeness especially among boys who persevered into the third year and beyond. By that time, the herd had been thinned dramatically – more than half of the boys in my freshmen class were gone by junior year; one author noted three-fourths of his freshman classmates gone by the close of his senior year (Carnevale, 2014). For many seminarians, this meant that "the ones who had given me trouble, were gone as well" (Thomas, 2007:37). For the most part, the remaining students liked or respected each other or at least appreciated the fact of their shared circumstance.

Nearly every interviewee had a close friend in the seminary with whom he spoke of classes, teachers, classmates, sports, cars, music, and girls (imagined). They often got in trouble together. They likely broke rules, snuck out at night, played jokes on class-mates, covered for one another, whispered or tapped an answer to a test question. One might tell the other that he was thinking about leaving but rarely explained why. For to venture there was to tread forbidden ground: abandoning one's vocation, disappointing the folks (or going home to an alcoholic dad), acknowledging inade-quacies. And, deep down, every seminarian feared that stating his doubts to anyone left him open for "trouble" with the priests:

> *I was a good boy. Always kept myself busy. I never confided in the priests. In the six years [in the minor seminary], I only saw my spiritual director once – in my senior year. He called me in because I had said something to my parents about feeling like I did not have an identity, that I was doing something mainly because people wanted me to do it. My dad got worried and said something to the spiritual director. We had a twenty-minute talk. I talked around it. After that, I stayed under the radar at home and at school.* (Former priest from Chicago)

I avoided the priests like the plague. I never went to their offices or rooms. If I needed to talk to them, I did it after class in the classroom. When I decided to leave, I did not tell anyone, except maybe my best friend – and I'm not sure I did that. (Former seminarian from Texas)

But lifelines often were lost. It was common to return from summer vacation or the Christmas holiday season and find that a friend – often your major confidant – had gone:

I called up my best friend ... and told him I would not be returning after the Christmas Break. We said our good byes over the phone, and that conversation was punctuated with some tears. ...Later, I heard from some of my friends that, when class resumed after the Christmas Break, my classmates were surprised that I left the seminary. I really didn't give any outward indication or any hints that I was going to leave. I kept it all inside myself.... (Wall, 1999)

Finally, one would assume that a seminarian's best friend was The One around whom both vocation and angst revolved. Yet, few minor seminarians with whom I spoke felt close to God (or certainly any closer than did the average Catholic) during and even years after adolescent pursuit of the priesthood. The seminary's curriculum focused little attention upon spirituality.[35] Its religion classes (called, in some schools, "theology" classes) were little different from those offered students in most Catholic high schools – a review of the rules by which to live within the faith, their history,

---

[35] Spirituality in this context refers to maintaining a closer relationship with God, knowing what he wishes for and from the individual, and gaining a better sense of God's presence in the world. This is accomplished, in the Catholic tradition, by prayer and contemplation.

and their application to "real-life" hypotheticals (e.g., "How starving do you have to be before stealing bread is not a sin?"). Spirituality for most young priests-in-training was a matter of formulaic prayer and liturgy, some of which was splendorous and inspiring but had little to do with a closer walk with Jesus. This should come as no surprise given the lifelong ebb and flow of most ordained priests' effort to develop and maintain a spiritual bond with God; it is exceptionally hard work (Hedin, 2003: 86-87; McDonough and Bianchi, 2002:132-159).

The above notwithstanding, I am struck by accounts of former seminarians who ventured into the chapel to seek God's (or the Blessed Virgin's or a saint's) counsel or intercession concerning elements of their vocation. They prayed for guidance and strength (Cornwell, 2006; Thomas, 2007). I always had problems doing this. On those few occasions on which I went privately to the chapel (for reasons that now escape me but that surely did not include asking God to guide me in my vocational pursuit), I saw few peers. In fact, I did not pray much outside of common recitation, nor did many of my interviewees no matter the seminary they attended, unless our prayer was primarily of the type we employed most often: petition[36] – "Please, can you help me, God, to [*choose as many as apply*: make my mom well, pass that test, get that teacher off my back]? If you do, I promise to [*choose as many*

---

[36] The other types of prayer prescribed by the Catholic Church were adoration (recognizing God's awesome power and his love for us), penance (recognizing the need to seek God's forgiveness for our breeching of his moral codes), and thanksgiving (recognizing the need to thank God generally for all he has bestowed upon us and particularly for his responses to our petitions). Most of these matters were addressed liturgically in the mass or common prayer (i.e., they were scripted) or in the confessional (also scripted). That these were a package for the individual petitioner – it was hard to seek help or a favor if adoration, penance, and thanksgiving were not addressed first or at least simultaneously – was given relatively little attention in our training.

as apply: be good, work harder, treat people better, visit chapel more often]."

> *In my four years there, I remember going into the chapel by myself maybe twice.* (Alumnus, St. Pius X Preparatory School)

> *Whatever was there, was there before I entered Pius. I realized later that it was fear of God. You know, God is love but before that he is an exacting God. I guess I lost that in the sem because I have no memory of anything spiritual during my time there.* (Alumnus, St. Pius X Seminary)

> *Not so much prayer.... But I did, on my own, begin to explore spirituality. I liked the retreats where you did not talk but just focused all day on a theme. I meditated. I read Aquinas and Augustine and Merton. But prayer, no. Spiritual conversation, no.* (Former seminarian from Texas)

For most of us, the minor seminary was not conducive to development of any sense of personal relationship with God. While we coped with the day-to-day monotony, crises, and pressures that made us struggle with staying or leaving, that larger cloud was always there when the curricular and extracurricular distractions abated: "Why am I here to begin with?" It is difficult to imagine a young teenager answering that question easily or channeling God sufficiently to permit a meaningful discussion of the matter.

Humor, Infraction, and Small Victories

> *I remember being punished, a long work-crew assignment, for filling the coffee cups on the college table with water. Coffee cups were always placed upside down on the saucer; I guess it*

was supposed to keep them clean. So, you'd turn them right-side up, fill them with water, and put the saucer on top to form a seal. Then you'd flip them back the way they were supposed to be so that the water stayed there all night and came pouring out when the person picked up his cup in the morning at breakfast. It was a riot, except they didn't think so. (Alumnus, St. Pius X Seminary)

Elements of resident culture in total institutions often include shared ways of withstanding or even of circumventing the institution's rules. Some of these infractions are performed purely for the fun of it or to offset the monotony within the occupants' routine. Others reflect students' need occasionally to feel that they have some say in what happens in their lives.

The fun part usually is talked about first by one-time residents. Place any two former boarding-school students together, and their discussion likely will turn quickly to tales of pranks and adventures. The "good memories" capture the positive side of social bonding and peer support but also disclose mechanisms by which to cope with difficulties of life in a contained world, to control the immediate social environment, perhaps even to survive within it.

Seminarians' escapades most often occurred during the pranksters' favorite venue, night; sleep was traded for "danger." Balls (including oranges and shots used in track and field events) were rolled down dormitory hallways to the priest-prefect's door. Kitchens were raided at midnight. Adhesive tape was placed on the inside of an unsuspecting boy's white BVDs while he slept. A priest's VW bug was lugged upstairs and planted outside his door (Hinsvark, nd.). Daytime brought tricks too: loosened rolls of toilet paper tossed into showers filled with bathers, toilet bowls covered in plastic wrap, rags burned in coffee cans in upperclassmen's rooms, iodine injected into Dixie Peach hair wax.

Many pranks involved the feature of seminary life that truly provided the seminarian with a sense of individuality and ownership – his bed and the space it occupied. Hiding his bed elsewhere, for example, left the kid standing as if without a home while his chums entered theirs. The quicker gag was to short-sheet the bed or put worms under the covers; one interviewee recalled placing the leg of a road-kill rabbit under a dorm mate's pillow. Or fill the bed with everything from baseball bats to bricks. You could flip a boy out of bed if you wished to teach him a lesson. Or tie him down while he slept. If you desired to look elsewhere for fun, you could steal a kid's clothes from his locker or place something awful in his bed stand. A million laughs, goofin', boys being boys ... at least as recounted years later over scotch at class reunions.

After the happy tales at seminary reunions, other tales typically emerge. Some are decidedly not humorous:

When I was a sophomore, I was assigned to be a [supervisor] in a freshman dorm. A kid comes up to me and says that someone has smeared shit on the walls of one of the toilet stalls. Sure enough. He says that he thinks Morton did it. So I ask Morton if that was true. He says, yeah, he did it. Why? He says he doesn't know. I told him to go clean it off and not to do it again. He didn't do it again. But can you believe that? And he went on to finish high school at Pius. Go figure. (Alumnus, St. Pius X Seminary)

There was this fad going on for a month or so when we were sophomores. The trick was to snap a guy with the back of your hand right in the nuts when he wasn't looking or suspecting it. Best time to do it was just as the teacher walked into the class-room or just as we all were going into the chapel. Then there was nothing he could do but take it – usually he'd laugh because he knew he had let his guard down. It was hilarious. Everybody was walking around doing the swimming-hole pose. (Alumnus, St. Pius X Seminary)

We called it flushing. This involved grabbing the offender, and transporting him to the toilets. After properly and legally advising the offender why this was happening to him, we'd dangle him by his feet and dunk his head into the bowl. We always finished the dunking with a nice clean flush to tidy the offender up a bit prior to release. (Carnevale, 2014)

Ron and I had a summer job at the diocese's camp for kids right after our junior year. Ron came up with the idea to make the kids believe that if they lay down flat on their backs with their eyes scrunched closed while we counted to twelve and then they sat up real fast, they would feel like they were flying. While I counted, Ron would pull down his pants and squat over the boy so that, when he sat up fast, he'd jam his face right up into Ron's barn mm. It was pretty funny, but sometimes the kid would cry. (Former seminarian from Montana)

Clearly, the minor seminary was not inhabited by juveniles walking around in Vienna Boys Choir robes, hands folded in prayer and eyes cast down. While seminarians were "good boys," as both the selection process and the seminary's mission and culture made fairly inevitable, they nonetheless were adolescent boys. They behaved as did most adolescents, the more so when confined together twenty-four hours a day. And their keepers, the priests who taught and supervised them, organized their regimen around the fact of their charges' lesser-maturity status or, in the case of college seminarians who had risen through the ranks, the nascent adulthood of young men whose adolescence had been spent in the same total institution.

Not all humor was meant to be fun. Tricks instilled fear; gags could unite or could isolate and exclude. Pecking orders were established by seminary boys just as they were by boys on the outside. Sometimes best friends turned on each other to clarify who was above whom or to ingratiate themselves with observers of a higher order. Hendrickson (1983: 125; 130-31) referred to the practice in his seminary as "knifing," and he pointed to *Lord of the Flies*-like episodes whereby bullying became collective and excessive. It may have been directed at a bed-wetter or at the new kid who was embarrassed to shower in front of others. Or it simply may have been aimed at the oddball. In any case, posing as humor, it was always targeted toward weakness, always reaffirmed a social hierarchy, and always struck fear into the student performing it lest he become the next victim.

Most seminarians learned quickly how to survive life in a boarding school. A few hid – in the piano-practice room or the stage workroom – busy to the point of invisibility. Some victims sought bonds with their tormentors by consistently being good sports. Others seemingly begged for more abuse; abuse was attention. Some seminarians stood above it all. A few developed a defensive posture and hit back even in a losing effort.

Only as an adult have I come to understand the source of my own survival strategy. I became my dad – the same guy who failed to protect his son from his wife's dream for him. (Other former seminarians have made similar observations about their fathers, usually in reference to the stoicism necessary to grinding it out day to day.) My father was like most men in post-World War II America: tough, serious, removed. We loved and feared him equally. He was a good man who worked very hard. He often was distant, as if in another room. He was an athlete and passed to me his love of sport and competition. He laughed a lot and liked telling jokes. But Dad had a temper and did not suffer fools easily, and he could cut you in an instant with a remark or a glare.

I had some of my dad's temperament (and some of my mom's) and much of his temper, as well as his physique, his manner, his drive, his humor. I was a very small kid when I first arrived at St. Pius, barely five feet tall, one of those kids who had been made by his grade-school teachers to stand at the front of every processional line. In elementary school, I had been a good student, industrious, altar boy, choir boy, nice kid who laughed a lot and had few enemies. I avoided bullies and stayed out of fights because I knew I'd lose them. I was fast and coordinated, loved sports. I tried out for every school team and usually made the roster, though as bench-rider, just too small and not part of the cool crowd. The kiss of death was that I also was a "nun's favorite" because – this is easy – I was going to be a priest!

The seminary offered a new lease on life. I had not entered it with the goal of "personal development" in mind, but small ponds promote notice. I quickly became visible among peers, so much so that a former grade-school chum who entered with me asked at the end of freshman year how I'd gone from nobody to somebody. (He meant it as a compliment.)

Besides working hard on grades and sports, I had decided early on that I would not be pushed around by bullies, towel-snappers, and kings-of-the-hill who buoyed their buddies' status by telling lesser beings to get lost. (Truth be told, the worst of bad seminary boys, with few exceptions, would have rated as good boys outside.) I did it just as my dad would have: a sharp tongue put folks on notice not to mess with me. The approach succeeded, so well in fact that, even after I no longer needed that tool – most of the "difficult" kids were long gone – I remained known for it. By junior year, I had grown to nearly six feet, was a strong student and athlete, and was willing to push back physically if challenged. But fists no longer were necessary among upperclassmen, except perhaps in sports contests. One classmate-interviewee wondered, "Did you ever play in a ball game without getting into a fight?" (Actually, yes, a few times. And they were not fights. Fighting was against the rules. They were spirited disagreements.)

Humor and wit were not the only tools minor seminarians utilized to soften the effects of monotony and constraint. As adolescents, they tested the waters through violation of rules small and large. Infractions conveyed a sense of victory over an institution that defined success in terms of behaving well within the rules, simple compliance. Many boys chafed under the yoke and acted out so often in the first two years of seminary that they were asked to leave; such, apparently, was the outcome of actor Tom Cruise's two-year stint in a minor seminary (White, 2013). Others so feared being tossed that they became slaves to the rules. But most of us by the junior year of high school found ways to violate norms and not (or rarely) be caught; indeed, some were masters of deception.

The great feats of infraction were, not surprisingly, fairly ordinary acts that would seem to outsiders a bit childish – some variant of the water pail above the door (Carnevale, 2014). Yet, at base, the rule violations were efforts to seize the gold at the top of the hill and have no one notice that it was gone. To behave so was risky, especially during the seminary heyday when those who failed to toe the line would be asked to leave if for no other reason than to deter those left behind. But that was the point: to watch the Dean of Students search fruitlessly for the culprit. Radios were hidden in ceiling compartments. Food was brought from home or pilfered from the seminary kitchen, stashed in residence halls, and shared with buddies in the middle of the night. Students would sleep in and skip morning mass only to blend expertly into the crowd as it moved toward breakfast. Statues were relocated. College men's lounges were violated. College men themselves snuck into town for a beer or a movie. And, as if mimes, students silently practiced baseball double plays behind the gym during retreats when quiet contemplation was the order of the hour.

On a Saturday night, small red dots blinked far out on dark seminary grounds where a smoker could drop his cigarette and distance himself quickly from the discarded butt were someone to approach. Many seminarians were revered for their ability to smoke multiple times daily, never to be caught even though both peers and faculty knew what they were up to. Years after seminary days, one such artist revealed that he smoked high in the rear chapel wall, by the organ pipes, in a space accessible only through the back panel of a confessional. Heavy doses (perhaps even a small swig) of aftershave helped to keep the cops at bay.

Drinking at St. Pius X Seminary was not uncommon for seniors and college men. Beer was the drink of choice of my classmates, cans hidden deep within boxes of clothes in our rooms and then snuck onto campus grounds on Saturday nights and drunk warm. (A classmate and I, each with a can of beer in his jacket pocket, were stopped one night by Father Anthony who admired and felt my friend's jacket; fortunately, he did not ask if he could try it on.) Others brought wine from home and tippled in their rooms. We thought we were very daring until we learned that younger students not only were drinking harder stuff but were obtaining it from the priests' own lounge – the same sin that led to Tom Cruise's exit from the minor seminary (White, 2013). To label drinking in the seminary during those years a problem would overstate the matter vastly. The amount consumed and the frequency of drinking were quite small. But the risk seemed huge to us. The thrill of infraction was greater still.

Variations on a Theme: 1970s

By the 1970s, minor seminary enrollment was plummeting. Fewer students were moving on to major seminaries. Vatican II had redirected the attention of the faithful worldwide toward ecumenism and lay involvement in matters Catholic. Large numbers of men were leaving the priesthood, many for married life. Issues of civil rights, social justice, and war (including draft deferments) increasingly informed societal debates and individual decisions.

On the one hand, life in minor seminaries (high schools and colleges) was easier for students. Smaller numbers meant more concessions and less structure. Students had cars on campus. Their school day started later. They also had more freedom regarding study practices and social life. For those in transformed "preparatory schools," seminarians likely were in the minority within the student body, and young women now visited campus as non-seminarians' interests (including dances) were accommodated. Religious obligations decreased; "We had mandatory mass only two days a week," one interviewee noted, "late in the morning so the commuter students could go." Interest in off-campus social-justice activities increased. The blending of non-seminary and seminary curricula and social life spawned a broader educational culture. Students now focused upon college readiness, making it considerably easier for a seminarian to change course midstream, from priestly to secular aspirations, without leaving the school.

On the other hand, for seminarians who entered with traditionally "conservative" leanings, the transitioning minor seminary could be a tough place. Seminary goals had blurred in the wake of Vatican II, and Catholics and seminaries were working (some struggling) to rethink themselves and their church. Rose (2002: 160-61), for example, writes of a new freshman accosted by a faculty priest who had heard that he opposed the notion of ordination of women. "I was just fourteen years old," the student recalled, and the priest warned that "I'd better get those 'old' and 'outmoded' ideas out of my head." Another priest told the same boy that he should not be reading anything in Latin and should be reading instead "*Playboys* like the other guys."

College years (i.e., pre-theology studies in philosophy) in the seminary changed too during the crash era. Indeed the change had begun in the mid-1960s. Within the six-six minor seminary model that characterized the heyday years (see Chapter Two), continuing students remained in the minor seminary for two years of college before moving on to two more years of college in the major seminary and thereafter to major-seminary curricula. The quality of the education received by those college students was suspect; looking back, most remember it as another two years of high school (again with strong emphasis on English, literature, writing, and history). In most seminaries, college men were kept distinctly separate from high school boys; they had their own residence hall, classrooms, dining room, and lounge – and the privilege of smoking within it.

The dwindling numbers of the late heyday era became obvious first in the college-enrollment figures of the minor seminary. These were addressed by the active recruitment of men with "belated vocations," many with prior service in the military. In the fall of 1965, for example, seven new students entered the college program at St. Pius X Seminary, increasing the size of the college first-year class by 50 percent. Their entry changed the numbers but also the culture of the college (indeed of the entire institution which now mixed fourteen-year-olds with grown men).

Four of the newcomers were in their mid-twenties and had served in the military. They were more mature, which meant little tolerance for our still-adolescent views of the world; they also were too mature to tolerate the "rules" that defined seminary life for us. Drinking violations transitioned from beer to vodka gimlets. Practical jokes were ramped up a notch. Sneaking off campus became fairly obvious forays into town. Sexual conversation moved quickly beyond adolescent foci. Traditional college seminarians suddenly became more daring; three historically "good boys," for example, "appropriated" a car from the priests' fleet after dark to meet high school girls for pizza in town. A college-student outing to a local lake became a daylong beer bust when the "older guys" stopped to buy cases of Pabst Blue Ribbon.

More important was the new breed's impact on the classroom and study habits. Questions by veterans asked of professors regarding the morality of "shacking up" overseas took a few of those teachers aback. Study hours and assignments were taken more seriously. Belated-vocation students saw their work as remedial and themselves as short-termers doing what was necessary for movement into the major seminary. Unlike the rest of us, they did not simply go with the flow; theirs had been a far more conscious and adult decision to pursue the priesthood (though not a single one of them in my class ultimately was ordained).

The newer model of seminary-college (institutions offering four integrated years of college classes) also was gaining momentum in the late-1960s, though the cost of the model already was viewed as likely unsustainable. Now set apart from traditional, minor-seminary "kids" and not yet theology "men," students taking classes in the four-year college behaved as other college students of the time did. They questioned authority. They left campus routinely both to play and to engage in internships and social-justice projects. They partied much harder. More important, they attended college during the years following Vatican II. Their sense of the church's place in the world was newer, their orthodoxy shakier, their notion of governance-by-conscience much more compelling.

Life in a college seminary was a challenge for a traditional Catholic college seminarian post-Vatican II. Fellow seminarians were less pious. Drinking, drug experimentation, and partying mimicked that of college students outside; marijuana was grown on campus, and seminarians and priests drank together on some campuses (Flannery, 2002). Little about religion was left unquestioned. The sacred often was scorned; anti-Marian sentiment was prevalent; motorcycles were ridden into chapel (Schorsch, 2012); Dylan's "Lay Lady Lay" was played during mass (Carnevale, 2014). Relationships with women were more common among seminarians, as was increasing tolerance of the concept (if not the behavior) of homosexuality.

In short, the college seminary was what the church was: an institution in flux in a decade of larger social flux. Seminarians left in greater numbers (and seminaries folded as they did). Yet, as was the case in the traditional minor seminary, many students stayed in the box, floating through and even mocking curricular and liturgical change without seriously questioning why they were there (Carnevale, 2014). They were kept busy until age and degree – and, perhaps, draft status – forced them out of the minor seminary and into a decision about movement into the major seminary and, finally, an actual decision about becoming a priest. Much had changed about life in the seminary; much had not.

Remaining in the Box

Years after we had left the minor seminary, a classmate wrote that, "Unlike many 'ex' seminarians, I have little or no bitterness about 'those years.' It was a different world in a far distant place." He is a bit more forgiving than I, but I cannot quarrel with the sentiment. It is easy to paint a difficult time as a foot in hell. Life in the seminary decidedly was not hell though I have trouble with the notion of minor seminary as a "camp," as one of Hedin's (2003:22) research subjects suggested, and cannot but wonder how any former seminarian could describe his two and a half years in the minor seminary as "the best of my life" (Wall, 1999).

In fact, while few former minor seminarians, including those ultimately ordained, would repeat their pursuit of "God's call" at so young an age and surely would not wish the journey upon anyone's son (Hendrickson, 2002), fewer still gaze upon their own journey with overt contempt and anger. Interviewees, none of whom favored the concept of minor seminary, told me consistently:

I found my community in the [minor] seminary. Really, it's the first time I received emotional support. I came from a cold family. I had no siblings. (Former priest from Chicago)

I loved St. Ben's. *It was caring, intellectual.* (Former priest from New Orleans)

I had a great time at Pius. I remember fun times. The guys. Never bored. Being that close was like a family. (Alumnus, St. Pius X Seminary)

The friendships are my best memory. And the religious stuff, the ritual, the liturgy. (Alumnus, St. Pius X Seminary)

Were I interviewed about the same topic, my response would be similar:

I did not feel that I should be there. Something was wrong. I should have gotten out sooner. But I had a good time, and I can't deny it even with some of the bad memories. I had friends, some of whom I still hold dear. They made me feel that I mattered. I have fond memories of the most trivial of our adventures and some of the characters we knew. And many of the challenges I encountered taught me that I need not panic in the face of new ones.

Why did we stay, especially those of us who remained for more than a year or two? Part of the answer lies in the "heavy stuff" noted in Chapter Three. Most of us possessed a sense of obligation, usually associated with a parent or parents but sometimes even with an entire parish, and we definitely did not wish to disappoint. Others of us could not go home; home was not a nice place. Most of us had little *real* sense of vocation and priests' work and thus did not burden ourselves daily with worry about God's design for us. Instead, being in the seminary with our friends – camaraderie was a persistent theme among those who stayed – became our vocation. To some extent, the seminary, to borrow from Hedin (2003: 28), "suited us"; we *wanted* to be there; we *liked* it at the same time that we wanted out. We knew our role, and we understood that we shared a goal. And that goal was nested within a set of rules and beliefs, Catholicism pre-Vatican II, that was already decided and, thus, predictable. No questions necessary; just learn the answers. Seminary regimentation freed us from even the ordinary decisions with which kids on the outside had to contend. To consider leaving was to imagine loss of friends and stability. What we knew afforded more security than what we did not.

Yet, there was more to our persistence than the hook set prior to our entry into the seminary (the "heavy stuff") and the camaraderie and rules that framed our everyday life there. Prisoners do not turn down parole to remain with their buddies in stir. We must concede, in all candor, that the church's formula for us was spot on: separate those boys (and college men) from worldly influences (including their parents), keep them occupied, quiet, and concerned about getting into trouble, and you've got them or, at least, more of them than otherwise would be the case. No matter why we entered, the seminary distracted us with academics, play, and problems sufficient to hold some of us in the traces longer; what we thought of as staying equated to moving forward instead of out. Ironically, as we blunted the sharper edges of life in our total institution with humor and small acts of rebellion, we actually strengthened the social bonds and personal satisfaction that coaxed many of us into remaining in the box, some of us far longer than we should have. As one classmate put it: "You were always trying to wriggle off the hook, but, a lot of the time, most days even, you didn't even remember that there was a hook."

References

Bretón, Marcos. 2016. "Bishop Quinn Looks Back, Questions Celibacy for Priests." *Sacramento Bee* (https://www.sacbee.com /news/local/ news-columns-blogs/marcos-breton/ article55104045.html) (January 17).

Carnevale, Rick. 2014. *When Pigs Fly*. Bloomington IN: Author House.

Cornwell, John. 2006. *Seminary Boy: A Memoir*. New York: Doubleday.

Flannery, Gregory. 2002. "Confessions of an Ex-Seminarian." *Killing the Buddha (www.killingthebuddha.com/mag)* (August 15).

Hedin, Raymond. 2003. *Married to the Church (Updated Edition)*. Bloomington: Indiana University Press.

Hendrickson, Paul. 1983. *Seminary: A Search*. New York: Summit Books.

————. 2002. "Altar-Boy Innocence; A Former Seminarian Reflects on Moral Ambivalence." *New York Times* (https:// www. nytimes.com/ 2002/04/28/ weekinreview/the-nation).

Hinsvark, John. Nd. "Remembering St. Joseph Seminary." www. *stjosephscollege.org/memoirs*.

McDonough, Peter and Eugene Bianchi. 2002. *Passionate Uncertainty: Inside the American Jesuits*. Berkeley CA: University of California Press.

Rose, Michael. 2002. *Goodbye, Good Men: How Liberals Brought Corruption into the Catholic Church*. Washington DC: Regnery.

Schorsch III, Albert. 2012, "A Day of Atonement for Blasphemy in the Seminary, 40 Years Later." *Sanity and Social Justice.net* (December).

Thomas, Clarence. 2007. *My Grandfather's Son: A Memoir*. New York: HarperCollins.

Vautier, Dominic. 2014. "Seminary Memories – 1956-57." *www. ses4leg-acyfullessays, wordpress.com* .

Wall, Bill. 1999. *A Day in My Life at St. Joseph's College (Seminary), 1958.* www.stjosephscollege.org/memoirs_bill-wall-day.html.

White, Chris. 2013. "Tom Cruise Started Religious Journey with Catholic Church." *New York Daily News* (https://www.nydailynews.com / entertainment/gossip/ cruise-considered-catholic-priesthood-kicked -seminary-article-1.1278436) (March 4).

CHAPTER EIGHT

Behind the Blinds

*R*emember *when we were on the bottom floor of the college dorm in our last year at Pius? You had the room next to mine. Our beds were about a foot apart, just on the other side of the wall from each other. Well, I'm sleeping one night, and all of a sudden someone jumps in my bed and starts kissing me and feeling me up. He's laughing and whispering in my ear. I'm in a panic because I'm sure you'll hear it through the wall. I kept shushing him. It was Bailey [in the class behind us]. I had been messing around with Jan [also a student in the class behind us], and he and Bailey were playing around too. He told Bailey that he should pay me a visit.*

My jaw dropped when my classmate from St. Pius X Seminary, Gene, told me this story. Gene, who had attended both minor and major seminaries, had come out publicly years later, so his sexual orientation was not the news here. But, at Pius? With Jan? And *Bailey*? I was not wholly surprised to learn about Jan; I had heard that he had been discovered in bed with another student the year after I had left the seminary. (Neither student had been expelled.) However, I had had no inkling that he was gay, let alone sexually active, at the time I was there, and no sense at all that Gene and he had been an item. Bailey I had not regarded as any but an ordinary, straight seminarian. That's what I was having trouble with: how could I not have suspected any of this?

"Any of this" covers a lot of ground. Most of us who attended seminaries had little sense until recently that there were institutional blinds to look behind. The past four decades have placed the Catholic Church under a microscope as case after case of sexual abuse of minors (and sometimes of young adults) by members of the clergy has come to light and as the church's efforts to sweep the problem under the rug have demoralized its membership. Fingers are being pointed at seminaries of the past alleged to have arrested the emotional growth of young men such that some became unable later to resist their basest sexual urges. The wisdom of celibacy within the priesthood (i.e., foregoing the only sex permitted, heterosexual activity, within the only setting in which it is allowed by the church, marriage) is debated constantly – as if sexual abuse of minors is a reasonably-expected outcome of depriving men of the chance to marry women. Many argue too that the church has undermined its standard of priestly celibacy and put young Catholic boys at risk by softening its stance on homosexuality and permitting elements of gay culture in its (primarily major) seminaries – as if "gay" and "sexual abuse" were synonymous or, at least, highly correlated.

In the coming pages, we first will examine sexuality and sexual activity among students within minor seminaries of the 1950s, 1960s, and 1970s. We will follow this in Chapter Nine with a look at the truly serious problem of sexual abuse of seminarians by the priests assigned the task of "forming" their vocations. To the extent that there exists a link between the two topics – sexual activity among youths and sexual exploitation of youths by adult guardians

– it rests within the concept of the minor seminary as a total institution (see Chapter Six). The setting itself made possible, or was unable completely to deter, covert activity of many kinds while enabling the institution to hide most such activity once detected. The same setting made understandable the shared ignorance of most attendees of minor seminaries regarding both activity and ensuing cover-up.

Who Knew?

Naïvete about matters sexual appears to have been the norm in the seminary of my day. Of the 24 former minor seminarians whom I interviewed extensively, only three had any notion that there was sexual activity occurring among students within the institution. One was Gene, quoted at the onset of this chapter. One was a priest who, as a seminary college student in the Midwest, also was awakened one night by a visitor in his bed,[37] and the third was a St. Pius X Seminary alumnus whose close friend in high school told him later that he had been active sexually with other high school seminarians ("including jocks!"). The remainder of the interviewees had no clue that sexual relationships were occurring in their schools:

> I was really naïve, I guess, but I never saw anything that made me suspect that students were sexually involved… and I sure wasn't. (Former seminarian from San Diego)

---

[37] "I said, 'What the hell? And I told him to get off of me and out of my room or I would start screaming for help at the top of my lungs.' He got out of there fast." Cornwell (2006:255) similarly notes a nighttime visit from a peer during his days in the seminary, and Miles (2012) reports an attempted sexual molestation by an older student.

No, I did not even suspect it though, looking back, I am not surprised. I know no one ever hit on me. …Maybe that's an insult, huh? (Former seminarian from San Francisco)

We knew zippo about sex and zippo about anyone we knew having sex. And if anyone was caught having sex with another kid while I was in the seminary, I sure never heard about it. (Former seminarian from New Orleans)

It's all hindsight. I didn't suspect anything, though years later I figured out that this one guy who confided in me in high school that he was having trouble fitting in was gay. I don't know if he was having trouble coming to terms with his feelings or if he was actively doing homosexual things with other guys. (Former seminarian from Texas)

Had I interviewed legally-incarcerated young adults (male or female) of the same era, I would have found that homosexual relationships were common and commonly known in their total institutions (Hensley and Tewksbury, 2002). Tales of (and jokes about) such relationships among shipmates at sea and soldiers far from home are legend, and books have been written about homosexual activity even among pirates (Burg, 1995; Turley, 1999). Relationships among boarding-school students in England (and elsewhere) for decades have been grist for works of fiction and nonfiction (*The Guardian*, 2005; Gathorne-Hardy, 1978; Waugh, 1917).

Most of these peeks behind the curtain have treated homosexual relationships among peers as situational, i.e., inevitable, hormonally- and emotionally-driven behavior by wards in custodial organizations without normally-accepted sexual outlets. The "situational" take considerably underestimates both homosexual and bisexual numbers and culture within total institutions, to be sure, but the point is made nonetheless: why would we *not* expect sexual interest and behavior among young people (at least some of whom, in fact, are homosexual or bisexual in orientation) housed together day and night?[38] We certainly expect it among adolescents in standard heterosexual settings in spite of warnings and surveillance designed to discourage it. Kids find ways.

Sexual Identity

As did their contemporaries on the outside, many seminarians – especially younger ones – worried about their sexual identity (Hendrickson, 1983:161). A former St. Pius X seminarian recalled this brief exchange with a classmate:

Roger says, "Wagner, you're a homo." I say, "You're the homo." And you know what he says, seriously? "Wait. I was only kidding. You don't really think I'm a homo, do you?"

Sexual identity was critical to survival within the seminary. Boys and young men, including those with gay tendencies, worked hard to avoid being branded homosexual (Dias and Demczuk, 2019). The tag affected in large part one's place in the class's pecking order, and it dictated ostracism of sorts – certainly ridicule and bullying. Interviews of former seminarians from the 1950s and early 1960s produced themes revolving around the "real man" (see Chapter Five):

I liked sports, and I liked music. But I made sure to get myself recognized as a jock before I joined any of the choirs or bands at Pius. (Alumnus, St. Pius X Seminary)

---

[38] One interviewee reported that, years after he had left the institution, his mother confided that she had wondered, when he first entered the seminary, whether he might be gay. (He was not.)

It was all about sports. Being a jock was a social statement, not just about who you were but who you weren't. (Former priest from New Orleans)

The big deal was not to be "effeminate" or not to be identified with those who were "effeminate." You stayed away from those guys. They were different from you. And you did not want to be thought of as with them. (Former seminarian from Cincinnati)

As they were on the outside during the heyday era, "fruit," "homo," and "queer" were standard derisive terms employed within seminaries, frequently in jest or in anger, sometimes as a tool to secure control over another student, and most often as a shield by which to ward off the very label in question. The seriousness of the context and the label is captured in this anecdote from an interviewee:

I was walking with another guy after dinner along the edge of the sem when this guy, Trainer, from our class, steps out from behind a tree. Without a word, Trainer slugs the guy with me right in the mouth and yells out, "You faggot!" The guy told me that Trainer had been threatening him for some time. (Former seminarian from Milwaukee)

The seminary worried about homosexuality too. Some schools were particularly strict; never was a student allowed in another's room, for example. But the primary indicator of trouble was choice of friends — better put, number of friends chosen. Nearly every interviewee recalled some variant of the Latin admonition, "*Numquam duo, raro solus, semper tres*" ("Never just the two of you, rarely by yourself, always in groups of [at least] three"). The directive was aimed at what were called "particular friendships," and the assumption underlying the concern was that, if the institution permitted too close a bond between two young men, the odds of sexual activity between them increased.

Particular friendships were not assumed automatically to involve sex. Some, in fact, were simply close and supportive relationships. Others involved psychological dominance or exploitation of one seminarian's labor by another. However, some relationships definitely involved sexual attraction – small, fair boys ogled and touched by older students (called "chessies" in the seminary of one interviewee and "swishers" in another's) and often wooed into what at least resembled ongoing sexual dyads (Moody, 2014; see also *The Guardian*, 2014). Other special friendships involved boys who became so enamored of each other that others could not help but notice; these grew especially intense if the boys were of the same age (Cornwell, 2006: 49, 53). Little attempt was made to disguise the activity other than to avoid its engagement directly in front of a priest on the faculty.

More common, however, were relationships that were reminiscent of those in the outside world featuring younger, worshipful, high-school girls and strutting, more senior, high-school boys. In the seminary, these were not explicitly sexual in nature; instead they produced "status points" for the younger student who attracted the sought-after school hero and reification of Big-Man-on-Campus (BMOC) status for the older student. Indeed, many freshmen and sophomores (usually well-respected members of their own classes) worked, in some ways competitively, in the first months of each school year to attract the attention of given BMOCs, some of whom trolled the competitors (Hendrickson, 1983; 165). Winners emerged, and the new "couple" then walked slowly about campus during free time deep in conversation. On occasion, a relationship became so prominent that something was said by a faculty member to the BMOC about spending too much time with one person, an "unhealthy social practice." Sometimes, one or both students would be pressured by classmates to spend more time with peers, in the spirit of "class unity." And, not dissimilar to romances in the outside world, on occasion the BMOC would throw over the younger boy for another; in turn, the younger student might shift allegiance to a different BMOC.

> *I was in one of those relationships – I was the older guy. It wasn't sexual or anything like that, but it was a very emotional relationship. It worried me because I'd heard so many things about the dangers of particular relationships. I went to talk to my spiritual director about it. It was as close to a crisis as I can remember. The power of the relationship is what I'm talking about.* (Former priest from Chicago)

Self-Control

Sex, for seminarians, was framed always as a matter of self-control. We felt ourselves obliged to be exceptional in attitude and conduct, aspiring someday to be men of virtue who made principled decisions to walk the straight and narrow. Every day brought new tests; every failure brought new guilt. According to one interviewee, the specter of such a lifelong contest drove his college classmate, Angelo, from a seminary in Milwaukee in the middle of the night. He packed his bag and hitchhiked home, telling his best friend that he realized that he never would be able to resist his sexual urges sufficiently to honor the priesthood.

Masturbation (not to mention the "impure thoughts" that accompanied it) was the bane of the minor seminarian's efforts at self-control, an ongoing struggle for nearly everyone (Bazzett, 2010; Hendrickson, 1983; Miles, 2012). Cornwell (2006: 118), for instance, tied his hands at night in an effort to avoid self-gratification. More than his secular counterpart who had not chosen so holy a vocation and likely encountered a variety of opinions about masturbation's suitability, the seminarian lived in a world undivided in its stance against it. It was a standard topic in meetings between seminarians and their spiritual directors.

On the one hand, masturbation was sufficiently common that it spawned jokes (e.g., the double entendre, "How many ejaculations[39] did the priest give you in confession today?"). On the other, it presented a special dilemma for the seminarian beyond his effort at self-control. Whereas few boys on the outside attended mass daily, seminarians were expected to attend daily and to receive communion. To the extent the average Catholic boy living in the world could tolerate mortal sin on his soul – the sin assured passage to hell should one "die in an accident" before gaining absolution in the confessional – he had until the next Sunday to redeem himself as a worthy recipient of the communion host. Seminarian-sinners, on the other hand, were less fortunate; they had only until the next morning when, again, they would attend mass with their peers.

Thus, each dawn found seminarians lined up outside the confessional at the back of the chapel, hoping for a hospitable priest in the box, desperate to avoid the ignominy of stepping aside during the mass to let pew-mates march forward to receive Christ's body and blood. Stepping aside effectively signaled to all that the

---

[39] A reviewer of this chapter suggested that many non-Catholics and perhaps even younger Catholics would not know what "ejaculation" means in this context. Ejaculations were (are still) short prayers uttered quickly: "Jesus have mercy," "Mother Mary, guide me please," "Sacred Heart of Jesus, I Trust in Thee." These were commonly assigned by priests during confession as a portion of one's penance, as in, "Say five Our Fathers and fifty ejaculations."

individual was in the "state of mortal sin"[40]; receipt of the eucharist in such a state would compound the offense. The particular sin in question was not difficult to discern. It was highly unlikely that a seminarian had violated the Ten Commandments through murder, rape, robbery, or serious assault, theft, or falsehood. It was similarly difficult to dishonor parents who now played a less significant role in one's life. Coveting one's neighbor's wife hardly applied, and few of one's neighbors in the seminary had goods worth coveting. There was but *one* reason for foregoing the trip to the communion rail: "All right! Yes, last night I choked the bishop!"[41]

Alone or With Others?

Context matters. The Catholic Church of the heyday era was anything but tolerant of sexual activity outside of marriage, thus demanding abstinence from all forms of sexual behavior (and thought) from its seminarians. Every former seminarian remembers the standard query from the priest in the confessional, especially regarding sins of the flesh: "Did you do this alone or with others?" An affirmative response to "others?" brought a second question and

---

[40] On top of this, the church had relaxed its rules regarding fasting as a prerequisite to communion and, thus, had removed the potentially handy justification for declining it: "I forgot and ate (or drank) during the night." Prior to 1953, Catholics were required to fast from midnight until receipt of communion, and the fast applied to water and medicine as well as to food. In 1953, the prohibition against water and medicine was lifted and, in 1957, the fasting period was reduced to three hours before communion. In 1964, the period of fasting was altered again, this time to one hour before communion.

[41] The reviewer mentioned in Note 39 also suggested that readers might not understand the meaning of "choking the bishop." The term commonly refers to masturbation, and the reference is to the resemblance of the bishop piece in the game of chess to a penis.

then a third: "Is this a one-time or an ongoing activity? If ongoing, how many others are involved?" In short, a temporary lapse in moral judgment or self-discipline was one thing; a pattern of moral turpitude and contagion was quite another. Above all else, seminarians were expected to resist sinning with others.

Given the seminary's goal to hold its wards well within the fold for as long as possible, its primary focus was upon external dangers, and almost always was expressed through general warnings to avoid contact with girls during school breaks. As it happened, a few (literally, just a few) heyday-era seminarians dated girls casually during the summer – usually without their parents' knowledge – going to movies, perhaps holding hands. Each year, an even smaller number of students in most seminaries would become romantically involved with girls to the extent that their decision to return at summer's end was difficult. (Once back in school, these boys often assumed celebrity status within their classes when other seminarians from the same neighborhood or small town gossiped at the start of the school year. This was huge news, a match in dry grass! "He could be booted for this if the priests find out, but what a lucky bum!")

Judging from interview data and first-person accounts, interaction of any kind between minor seminarians and young women other than their sisters was fairly rare. The seminary forbade such activity generally and threatened dismissal of students who violated the rule. A classmate from Sacramento recalled that his mother was contacted by the seminary rector and warned not to repeat a party she had given during the summer to celebrate her son's sixteenth birthday. She had invited to the event seminarians and non-seminarians, including a few daughters of relatives and family friends. A seminary classmate in attendance had become anxious about violating seminary rules and had approached the Dean of Students begging for mercy. That same summer, a student at St.

Pius X attended, with permission and with other seminarians, a religious conference at a Catholic college. The conference included both young men and young women and ended with a dance in which the seminarian chose to participate. A chaperoning Jesuit from the college took umbrage and alerted the seminary rector who promptly informed the seminarian that his presence at the seminary no longer was desired.

Most seminarians actually had few opportunities to interact with young women, and when they did, they possessed little in the way of intuition, prior instruction, and role modeling to pursue them:

My only contact with sex — not sex, but interaction with girls — came when the seminary brought high school girls into the passion play in the women's roles. Three or four of us got to talking with three of them and, before you knew it, we'd snuck away in one of the seminary vehicles and met them in [town] for pizza at 10:30 at night. We actually did it four or five times. Nothing happened, of course, but it was great just to talk to girls — and one of the guys actually ended up marrying one of those girls. (Alumnus, St. Pius X Seminary)

I was absolutely petrified of girls. I did not know how to talk to them or what I was supposed to do when I met them. They must have been able to tell that I was weird too, because they never came near me. This happened way into my college years after I had left the sem. (Former seminarian from San Francisco)

When I'd go home for the summer, I would walk around the neighborhood in the evening hoping to meet a girl. I don't know how I thought that would happen — that they'd just stop me and say, "Hi, wanna talk or go to a movie with me?" No luck. Ever.

So one time I finally get up the nerve to approach a teenage girl standing in her front yard. I say "Hi." And she turns and runs in the house. I ran home so fast I could have won the Olympics, and the whole way I could see my face on a front-page story about the cops catching a rapist. That ended my walks. (Redemptorist priest from St. Louis)

Indeed, priests-to-be entered the minor seminary quite naïve generally, and many were considerably behind the maturity curve, still speaking in the sophomore year, for example, in Donald Duck voice and giggling when someone said "organism."[42] Once in, others pushed boundaries a bit, at least in the context of the seminary. An interviewee remembered a classmate who "after his showers would look at you from between his legs, you know, giving you the red eye, and say, 'Think about Maria [the seminary cook].'" Hendrickson (1983: 164) similarly recalled a student who routinely would pull down his pajamas after lights out and moon everyone while his dorm mates shone their flashlights on his "huge, creamy, red rear."

The average seminarian, especially one in the first two years of school, engaged not so much in sexual practice as in sexual conversation. Thus were spawned the tales of "Boner Barry" who could not walk the length of the chapel without "saluting," late nights with

---

[42] Some clearly were operating in junior high-level mode. Hendrickson (1983:151) recalls classmates late at night chasing a priest's dog within a dark gym, firing starting guns at him and frightening him nearly to death. Carnevale (2014) writes of classmates staging "turd races" through water pipes to the septic tank. An alumnus of St. Pius X Seminary offered a particularly illustrative episode: *I was standing in my dorm when Crockett [another freshman] started yelling from in the john to get in there quick. I go dashing in there thinking he has a snake or something. Instead, he is standing on the toilet seat with the stall door open, squatting above the toilet. And he lets loose with this huge stream of diarrhea, and he's laughing his head off.*

forbidden novels such as *Candy* smuggled in and shared among buddies, and the embarrassing interruption of boys in solitary *flagrante delicto* in the shower. Seminarians' sisters, who often visited campus with their parents on Visiting Sundays, became, in the absence of females more generally, nearly an obsession within banter sessions.[43]

Sex was something in which someone else, out there in the bigger world, participated. Most sexually-oriented conversation followed the common lead-in, "What would you do if…,"and "reliable information" was the coin of the realm. The talk was similar to that occurring among contemporaries in the outside world but was considerably less informed (and sadder) given the seminarians' isolation from that world:

> *A group of us [sophomores] were talking at breakfast, and one guy says, "Have you guys heard of Spanish fly?" Another guy says, "What is it?" "It's a powder, and you give it to a girl, and it makes her go crazy to have sex." Someone says "I wonder where I can get some." And a guy pipes up, "Girls, you mean?"* (Former seminarian from Chicago)

Most seminaries offered little guidance.[44] One interviewee described the totality of sex education at his institution as:

> *… stern warnings from the spiritual director to "watch out" for temptation, a chapter in our sophomore biology text that the*

---

[43] In fact, eventual marriage of former seminarians to the sisters of schoolmates was not uncommon, as one interviewee noted, naming four such nuptials among alumni of three successive classes in his seminary.

[44] The extent and quality of sex education across minor seminaries actually is unclear in the literature. Hendrickson (1983:76) suggests fairly thorough attention at least to the biological elements of reproduction. Cornwell (2006:104) recalls considerably less attention to detail.

*teacher did not discuss in class, and a few words from our soph-
omore guidance-class teacher about a problem among soldiers
called "lack-a-nookie" and the need to understand that sex is
really powerful. "Otherwise," he said, "why would two people
want to roll around together in bed and get all sweaty?"* (Former seminarian from Oregon)

Having lived in such a closed world, no interviewee reported
engaging in heterosexual activity (beyond the occasional social
interaction and the rare date during the summer) or credible
knowledge of such activity among schoolmates; nor do first-person accounts in the literature reference physical relationships with
females. To the extent that sexual activity occurred among students
in the minor seminary, it was homosexual in nature and fairly rare.
Given the close eye kept upon students and the fact that nearly
every student began his seminary career as a sexually and socially
immature freshman in high school, these findings should not surprise. Heterosexual activity may have been talked about, but par-
ticipation in it while physically at the seminary was accomplished
vicariously.[45] Homosexual activity was available by definition but
culturally prohibited by the institution and among seminarians
themselves.

Gene, the classmate who, many years later, told me of his own
involvement in sexual activity with other seminarians at St. Pius X

---

[45] Multiple interviewees from one seminary independently recalled a possible exception, a story they'd each heard. Darrell, a college student, had access
to the school's old pickup. He would drive it down a fairly untraveled road at
night and would meet a young woman who was employed by the seminary
during the day to handle clerical duties. Schoolmates who also were sneaking
out late apparently came upon them more than once. Exactly what or how
much transpired during those late-night rendezvous was known only to the
two in the truck. But the story gave legs to the seminary's greatest worry:
exposure of its residents to members of the opposite sex.

Seminary, was careful to qualify the notions of frequency and type of his experience:

> *Don't let your imagination go nuts here. Really only a few guys were involved as far as I know. Most of it was sneaking around and quick stuff. Everyone was afraid of getting caught – how would we explain that one to our families? And most of it was just touching and mutual masturbation. It was definitely not affairs and orgies on campus. …I did not even think of myself as a homosexual in that period, just a guy enjoying a little adventure and daring, I guess. … I didn't even do anything in my first year of college. And I think I wouldn't have done anything in my second year if Jan hadn't shown up [in the class behind us]. He was definitely more aggressive and less afraid of risk.*

The sexual culture of minor seminaries changed somewhat during the late 1960s and early 1970s as many six-year minor seminaries and four-year college seminaries began to recruit persons with "belated vocations" – older students with a bit more experience in the world and a bit less fear of authority. At St. Pius, few of those new students had much interaction with younger high-school students.[46] Sexual banter among high-school upperclassmen and college students, on the other hand, grew somewhat more sophisticated and graphic though still focused upon "What if …?" We traditional seminarians – and even some members of the faculty – were awed and sometimes embarrassed by the sexually

---

[46] The exception was a man in his late twenties with considerable prior gay sexual experience. He lasted but a year and was remembered for having "very close" conversations with students more than a decade younger. Whether or not this eventuated in actual sexual activity was never known among his classmates.

explicit stories (never told in the first-person) of the new students who had served in the military.

At the same time, Catholicism's positions on homosexuality and exposure of candidates for the priesthood to women before ordination were softening, in part due to cultural changes in the larger world and in part to the willingness of Vatican II to enjoin discussions of "modern" social issues. Distinctions between the state of being homosexual and engaging in homosexual activity began to occupy discussions in college- and theology-level seminary courses. Gay men began to feel somewhat more welcome in seminaries. As a prelude to ordination, seminarians also were being encouraged to pursue public ministries that coincidentally involved members of the opposite sex. This inevitably resulted in many young men entering into heterosexual relationships and leaving the seminary rather than living with celibacy:

This was the 1960s, and guys were really struggling with this. They were interacting with women and did not know how to deal with the feelings. I interacted but kept my distance. Some guys left. Others developed very involved relationships with multiple women. (Former seminarian from Sacramento)

In July before we moved up to [our second two years of college at the major seminary], a bunch of us were invited by a classmate's family to a weekend at Lake George. The classmate had brothers and sisters, and they had friends, so there were plenty of girls at the house all weekend. One guy, Walter, really shy, seemed to be talking a lot to one girl, a little shy herself. I did not think a lot about it. When we showed up for classes in the fall, I did not see Walter. When I asked where he was, I found out that less than a month after meeting, Walter and the girl from the weekend at Lake George got married. Jesus.... (Former seminarian from New York)

In the summer between minor and major seminary, I worked in a factory in the city and had my own apartment in the sub-urbs. I was making plenty of money working overtime. Next door was a woman about my age – mid-twenties [his was a "late vocation"]. *Good looking, smart. We hit it off. I didn't hide the fact that I was studying to be a priest. We talked about it a lot. But she had me over for dinner after work a bunch of times, and one thing led to another, just like in the movies. I was a virgin, and she had to teach me everything. It was really nice. It was hard for me to leave for the sem at the end of the summer, and I know it was really hard for her. But I knew I had to stick with my vocation* [which he did for another year before leaving the seminary]. (Former seminarian from Miami)

College seminary philosophy and theology curricula of the late 1960s and early 1970s also featured a change in the notion of relationship of individual to God: was the relationship to be primarily one of following divine dicta (i.e., what the church said we should do) or of being sufficiently close to God to determine within conscience one's moral obligations? In this vein, many sem-inarians grappled less than previously with the moral implications, for example, of a heterosexual affair. The issue instead was framed as a matter of reconciling conscience with church rules (to break them was not necessarily to break with the church), for God him-self permitted the seminarian to act in good faith.

Seminarians who engaged in homosexual activity were in a similar moral position. On the one hand, the church forbade the practice. On the other, the church also posited that ultimately one's position in the eyes of God was determined by one's intent and one's conscience. Gene captured the essence of the dilemma well:

Talk about a ticket out of jail. I went from worrying about not being able to be a priest because I was a queer to worrying about not being able to be a priest because I was a queer who couldn't keep his pants zipped, to just having to ask God if it was okay if I played around with someone and no one was hurt by it. And God said, "Go for it, and you can still be a priest!"

Gene found the freedom to explore sexual intimacy within his seminary, but freedom did not lead to the priesthood:

I fell in love with Doug. People who paid attention — and that wasn't very many people — began to treat us as a couple. And it became clear that, once we were ordained, we would not have the life that we were having together in the sem. So, midway through theology studies, we left [the seminary], rented a house, and moved in together. We stayed together for another ten years.

Looking Back

From the distance afforded by time and judging from interview data and the literature, there is little actually to report about boys, young men, and sex in the minor seminary during both the heyday and the crash eras. Involvement in heterosexual activity was very rare. That homosexual activity occurred is indisputable but hardly unexpected given research regarding total institutions and young people. To the degree that it happened within the high school sector, it involved relatively few boys and, according to one interviewee, was always "quick and dirty." On occasion it was discovered, in some instances leading to dismissal of students (Rohde, 2011) and, even though it was assumed to trigger automatic expulsion, in other instances not. What is abundantly clear is that the vast majority of high school-level minor seminarians were unaware of sexual activity among peers.

Greater levels of sexual activity and awareness of it occurred among college men in the minor seminary, particularly in the 1970s. Yet, even here, estimates of prevalence at the average seminary were not of a level that astounds, and the activity that occurred largely was surreptitious. (There were definite exceptions; prevalence at some college seminaries was much higher and much more visible [Flannery, 2002; Pringle, 2005; Schorsch, 2012].) While it was clear to the average seminarian of the day that a new culture of openness about things sexual had developed in the seminary, direct knowledge of sexual relations among peers was limited even if suspected. Graduates of one West Coast seminary, for example, differed in their recollection; some recalled rampant licentiousness while others had witnessed nothing of the kind (Pringle, 2005).

Was sex among students in the seminary a problem? That would seem a matter of the glasses you choose to wear. Those familiar with the structure and culture of total institutions likely see sex in the seminary less as problematic than as "normal" within an environment bent on thwarting a basic human need. Those who hold to a vision of seminarians as necessarily "holier" than most or as "early celibates" would view sex at any prevalence level among boys and young men as unacceptable. Through the prohibition lenses, the failure to dismiss students discovered in sexual activity could only be regarded as highly problematic. Finally, some view "liberal excesses" in the seminary (and the Catholic Church) in the 1970s as the beginning of the end of priests as "real men" – traditional heterosexual males who had made a serious choice to live a celibate life and to model restraint and pursuit of holiness (Mason, 2015; Rose, 2002). Indeed, some see Catholicism's "moral ambivalence" toward homosexuality – especially within the ranks of seminarians – as the root of the sexual abuse scandal that has drained respect for the church among the faithful since the 1980s. It is to that scandal that we turn in the next chapter.

References

Bazzett, Timothy. 2010. *Reed City Boy*. Reed City MI: Rathole Books.

Burg, B. R. 1995. *Sodomy and the Pirate Tradition*. New York: New York University Press.

Carnevale, Rick. 2014. *When Pigs Fly*. Bloomington IN: Author House.

Cornwell, John. 2006. *Seminary Boy: A Memoir*. New York: Doubleday.

Dias, Elizabeth and Gabriella Demczuk, 2019. "'It Is Not a Closet. It Is a Cage.' Gay Catholic Priests Speak Out." *New York Times* (https:// www.nytimes .com/2019/02/17/us/it-is-not-a-closet-it-is-a-cage-gay -catholic-priests-speak-out.html).

Flannery, Gregory. 2002. "Confessions of an Ex-Seminarian." *Killing the Buddha (www.killingthebuddha.com/mag)* (August 15).

Gathorne-Hardy, Jonathan. 1978. *The Old School Tie: The Phenomenon of the English Public School* New York: Viking Adult.

Hendrickson, Paul. 1983. *Seminary: A Search*. New York: Summit Books.

Hensley, Christopher and Richard Tewksbury. 2002. "Inmate-to-Inmate Prison Sexuality: A Review of Empirical Studies." *Trauma, Violence, & Abuse* 3:226-243.

Mason, James. 2015. "The Forgotten Vice in Seminary Formation." *Homiletic and Pastoral Review* (https://www.hprweb.com/2015/07/ the-forgotten-vice-in-seminary-formation/).

Miles, Vincent J. 2012. *Boys of the Cloth: The Accidental Role of Church Reforms in Causing and Curbing Abuse by Priests*. Lanham, MD: Hamilton Books.

Moody, Fred. 2014. "The Secret life of a Seminary." *Pacific NW Magazine/ The Seattle Times* (https://www.seattletimes.com/pacific-nw-maga- zine/the-secret-life-of-a-seminary/ (March 4).

Pringle, Paul. 2005. "Trail of Abuse Leads to Seminary." *Los Angeles Times* (https://www.latimes.com/archives/la-xpm-2005-nov-17-me -stjohns17-story.html).

Rohde, Marie. 2011. "The Prophet." *Inside Milwaukee* (http://www.insidemilwaukee.com/Article/9192011-TheProphet).

Rose, Michael. 2002. *Goodbye, Good Men: How Liberals Brought Corruption into the Catholic Church.* Washington DC: Regnery.

Schorsch III, Albert. 2012, "A Day of Atonement for Blasphemy in the Seminary, 40 Years Later." *Sanity and Social Justice.net* (December).

The Guardian. 2005. "When I Was at School." *The Guardian* (https:// www.theguardian.com/education/2005/oct/12/publicschools.schools).

Turley, Hans. 1999. *Rum, Sodomy and the Lash.* New York: New York University Press.

Waugh, Alec. 1917. *The Loom of Youth.* London: Bloomsbury.

CHAPTER NINE

Betrayal

I am the sister of three brothers who attended [St. Lawrence Seminary] during the sex abuse years. Although I love my Catholic faith, I am painfully aware that my brothers suffered deeply trying to be good Catholic teens. I am continually confronted with the brokenness of my brothers.... None of the three who attended are practicing their faith, in fact, one of them has determined there is no God. Alcoholism and dangerous behaviors define their lives. ... [They are] boys turned men who are living in broken, fragmented, pain-filled lives because of their experience at St. Lawrence Seminary. (Anonymous [blogger], 2011)

For any number of reasons (see Chapter Five), many Catholic families entrusted their sons to minor seminaries in the Mid-Twentieth Century. They did so with no sense that those sons might be harmed. Quite the reverse; they placed them under the protection of men of God and within environments that limited their exposure to trouble. The worry, perhaps, was that they might not mature fully away from the experiences of secular life. Never was it that the men of God who were to care for their sons would betray the trust of the families and their sons. But that is what happened more frequently than we would care to believe … many times in some seminaries.

Sins of the Fathers

Like many such men, [Father] Tom Adamson was himself molested for more than two years, by a hired hand on his parents' farm, starting when he was fifteen. In 1961, as a young priest and assistant principal in the town of Adrian [Minnesota], he molested a boy on the school basketball team. The liaison would continue for twelve years, as the boy moved through seminary and became a priest himself. (Berry, 1992: 282-83)

Over my shoulder, the priest, who had sexually assaulted me in the confessional during college and exploited me for two years after, clapped away. During the Mass [of Thanksgiving, celebrated by a new priest in his local parish], he'd said the homily. I hadn't wanted him anywhere near the celebration, but his absence would have raised questions. An unwritten tradition held that the pastor of the parish "honor" his priestly protégé by preaching at the special Mass. My Franciscan counselor had encouraged me to let my perpetrator preach, as an exercise in forgiveness and letting go. (Rastrelli, 2012)

The notion of members of the Catholic clergy preying upon their charges in the seminary once was unimaginable, or certainly not imagined widely. That is not the case today. What began as anger and disgust over the discovery in the late 1980s of a history of sexual abuse of children by a few parish priests has evolved presently into global outrage over the pervasiveness of such predation and, especially, the scope of the church's attempt to cover it up. A 2018 Pennsylvania grand jury report (Pennsylvania Attorney General, 2018) put the matter front and center once more. It cited (conservatively) 1,000 victims of sexual abuse by at least 300 priests in six of the state's eight dioceses since the 1940s. It further accused church officials not only of a massive failure to address the problem but also of a massive effort to hide it.

The financial cost since the 1990s of legal settlements between the church and victims of sexual predation by its priests has been enormous, estimated at over $3 billion. The demoralization of Catholics (and of truly good priests, the majority) around the world has been unprecedented. In the wake of the re-explosion of attention to the problem, Pope Francis (2018) wrote in a letter to the "People of God":

With shame and repentance, we acknowledge as an ecclesial community that we were not where we should have been, that we did not act in a timely manner, realizing the magnitude and the gravity of the damage done to so many lives. We showed no care for the little ones; we abandoned them. [In the words of then-Cardinal Ratzinger], "How much filth there is in the Church, and even among those who, in the priesthood, ought to belong entirely to [Christ]! ...[I]t pierces his heart."

If in the parish, why not in the seminary? Should we not have sensed that a sacred trust was being (or certainly could have been) violated in minor seminaries during (and before) the heyday and crash eras? The setting itself begs for a closer look. To the extent that tendencies or temptation existed for seminary priests, what better environment to act upon them than a physically and socially isolated institution with little oversight of its individual faculty members. What better opportunity structure than a system that affects "care" of students through the placement of priests' inviolable personal space – offices and rooms – in close proximity to their charges day and night? What better chance first to offend and then to deflect blame than within a culture of automatic trust of and respect for priests? And how much more freedom could have been afforded priest-perpetrators than within a seminary and a larger Catholic Church willing to protect the institution before the seminarian?

To be clear, none of my interviewees and the many other former seminarians with whom I spoke less formally recalled hearing about or sensing, let alone being the victim of, obvious sexual *crimes* by priests while they were in the minor seminary. One interviewee recalled being "creeped out" by the way a priest kept touching him. Another knew of a classmate in college who was visited routinely in the middle of the night by a religious brother who worked in the seminary; he presumed the sexual activity involved was consensual though decidedly inappropriate. A third interviewee described his loathing, during his college years in the late 1960s, of a seminary rector who repeatedly sought to kiss him:

> *When I would speak to him about my sexual concerns, he would always seem to understand and would always say I needed to stay vigilant. Then, as soon as we were done with that, he'd come over and sit next to me and put his arm around me and start hugging me and giggling. He'd say, "Come on, relax." And then he'd go for the old lip lock. God, I hated that. I'd squirm every time, but I also didn't want to piss off the rector.*

Only one of the authors of the major first-person accounts of minor seminary life relied upon in this study referred to an explicit episode of overt sexual contact with a faculty priest, in this case a thwarted effort by the cleric to examine the student's penis to assure that he was developing appropriately (Cornwell, 2006:273). Indeed, the literature on sexual abuse within seminaries, though limited, finds the offer of "education," "medical instruction" or "intervention" – checking for hernias or scabies, bringing down fevers – in numerous accounts and complaints by seminarians (usually years later) against their seminaries and the priests within them (Howard, 2013).

Hendrickson (1983: 167-174) offers an account of his spiritual director, rather than touching him directly, "helping" him (and other boys in his class) overcome impure thoughts and a tendency to masturbate. Under the spiritual director's guidance, he would drop his trousers, masturbate, and recite his sexual fantasies and why he wished to overcome them; just short of ejaculation, the priest would hand him a crucifix, and Hendrickson would walk himself back from the precipice. Notably, the priest seemed uninterested in the sexual aspect of the activity, rarely looking and apparently focused on other business during the ritual. The more stunning aspect of this practice was that it occurred at least *biweekly for nearly six years* when Hendrickson, at twenty years of age, finally said, deferentially and diplomatically, "no more." Some years later, he wrote the priest for an explanation and was told that, yes, in retrospect, the counsel in question probably was not wise in light of contemporary standards regarding appropriate spiritual guidance within the seminary. No harm had been intended.

In the same vein, three interviewees from St. Pius X Seminary related a highly similar story concerning a priest who "helped" freshmen understand their reproductive organs and capacity:

He would invite me into his office after lights out to put ben gay on my lower back which was sore from some sports injury

– it was really nothing; the attention was what I liked, and I think he knew it. My pajamas were always down to my knees. Somehow he always managed to rub around toward the front and brush against my dick enough to give me an erection. Then he'd tell me not to worry about it – it was normal and no big deal. Then he'd explain how reproduction works by physically touching me and indicating where everything started and came out. Very clinical. Nothing more ... he never massaged me or behaved sexually or even looked like anything sexual was happening. He always seemed like a doctor.

Interviewees remembering less extreme accounts from years past – of, for example, the young priest so smitten with a fifteen-year-old that he coincidentally appeared in the vicinity of the student at every possible study break and ball game, the priest who sat distraught freshmen on his lap or hugged them at every opportunity, or the old priest who would ask a seminarian to give him a massage to soothe his aching lower back – tended to forgive if not to excuse, to see "both a Christ figure and an ill man" (Hendrickson, 2002):

Even then, I think I got it. I certainly do now. I did not see these priests as perverts or dangerous. I probably would have hit them if I did. They were creepy, for sure. But they were so incredibly isolated! Even more than we were. They had to be circumspect. They could not share a worry or show an emotion other than anger when we screwed up or calm when we were upset. Almost all of them had gone to minor seminaries and then into the priesthood. From the time they were fourteen, they had no normal contact with anyone – just like would have happened to us if we stayed. Never mind sex. No intimacy. No touching.

Always on guard. I mean, what do you expect in that situation?
(Alumnus, St. Pius X Seminary)

Criminal Behavior

The situations and events recalled by seminarians to this point (inappropriate acts by isolated, lonely, immature men) pale in comparison to those that occurred when entire institutions, rather than a few faculty members within them, seemingly slipped off the moral rails. No better examples of faculty members' ongoing and ignored sexual exploitation of boys and young men exist than those of St. Lawrence Seminary, a Capuchin institution in Wisconsin, and St. Anthony's Seminary, a Franciscan institution in California. An independent investigation commissioned by the Capuchin order found that, based on *known* accounts, 28 minors in St. Lawrence Seminary were subjected to sexually inappropriate or criminal actions between 1964 and 1986 by eight different Capuchin friars (priests and religious brothers), including the seminary's dean of studies and eventual rector (Burnett et al., 2013). A similar investigation commissioned by the Franciscan order concluded that, between 1964 and 1987, 11 members of the faculty and staff, including the prefect of discipline, at St. Anthony's Seminary abused 34 seminarians (and other vulnerable minors) (Stearns et al., 1993).

The abuses in question included rape, fellatio performed by and upon the abusers, masturbation by and of the abusers, persistent fondling of students' genitals, and corporal punishment of a sexual nature (Isley, 2004). Some episodes involved supplying students with alcohol and pornography. Some students were seduced, others capitulated to "authority" or "trust," and others simply were physically overpowered. All were left confused and disheartened, many for life (Finley, 2003: 36-37). These were not isolated incidents; their frequency was as horrific as their content. One seminarian reported being molested fifty times by one friar, as well as by others. In many instances, the abuse of victims continued for years. Some victims were abused multiple times by multiple offenders. The St. Lawrence Seminary rector in question was estimated to have molested dozens of minors during his career as a priest in and out of the seminary. The St. Anthony's Seminary disciplinarian in question may have molested as many as 250 minors during his career as a priest.

Did anyone tell? Relatively few and generally with unimpressive results. On occasion, a seminarian told his closest friend. Rarer still, parents were informed, complained to the rector, and withdrew their son from the school. This brought at least superficial attention to the perpetrator, but the accusation almost never became public. Some victims reported the activity to a trusted member of the faculty only to find that little came of the report or that word got back quickly to the offender (Elbagir et al., 2019b). Or, worse, the trusted faculty member to whom the offense was reported was himself a sexual predator, often colluding with the original offender.

By and large, however, victimized boys and young men kept the abuse a secret (and often were stunned years later to learn how many others had been violated). Their reasons are familiar to anyone who has been sexually abused: *I didn't think anyone would believe me. I was too ashamed. He threatened me, saying he'd deny it and would get me expelled. I knew that homosexual activity got guys thrown out of school. He warned that it would kill my mother to learn of it. I liked him; he had always been nice to me, and I did not want to get him in trouble. After each time, he'd put on his stole and hear my confession. He told me not to worry about it, that it was not really wrong. I was confused. He was a priest – how could he be doing something that was wrong? I worried that it was my fault.*

Did other seminarians know? Often someone did, at least to a degree. A victim might share it with a trusted friend who might tell others, or a failed attempt at seduction might precipitate warnings among students to steer clear of a certain priest. In the end though, if seminarians suspected that something was going on, even *knew* that it was, they likely kept their thoughts to themselves. Moody (2014) recalls coming upon a group of students at St. Anthony's Seminary looking up at an open window, listening to screams coming from within the room of the dean of students. They did not stay long. Wanting not to get in trouble, they hustled away with "blinders firmly in place."

The St. Lawrence and St. Anthony's scandals opened the floodgates for allegations and investigations of similar levels and types of abuse within seminaries throughout the nation primarily in the heyday and crash eras but often extending well into the 1980s.[47] Most could not be pursued as criminal acts because statutes of limitation precluded prosecution. Some allegations resulted in legal settlements. Many complaints remain unresolved, in large part because so many of the minor seminaries in question have closed and so many of the alleged offenders have died over the years.

A new wave of allegations and lawsuits followed the 2018 release of the Pennsylvania Grand Jury report. Most differed from those of the past many years in that they involved college-level seminaries and students who had reached the age of majority. Here the prey was not defenseless minors. Instead, the accusations reflected the vulnerability of persons placed in the position of having to choose between principle and career goals – the classic dilemma of victims

---

[47] Among notables brought down by the scandal was Father Marcial Maciel, founder of the Legion of Christ, a global conservative religious order with an estimated 2,000 seminarians at its height in the 1980s and 1990s. Maciel was accused by nine seminarians of sexual abuse when they were ten to sixteen years of age (Berry and Renner, 2004; Berry, 2011).

of workplace sexual harassment in which superiors pressure and exploit subordinates, oftentimes very subtly and over a long stretch of time, sometimes more directly.

The prototypical offender in this newer seminary-harassment scenario, by all accounts, is Cardinal Theodore McCarrick, former Archbishop of Washington D.C. McCarrick resigned his position as an active priest and cardinal of the church in 2018 amid allegations of prior sexual abuse of minors. However, that scandal brought further accusations against him of sexual exploitation of college seminarians during the 1980s and 1990s. The seminarians, mindful of the power of the bishop to determine both ordination and career prospects, chose to live with sexual harassment. As one college seminarian noted in recalling the bishop's hand inside his bathing suit at a beach gathering, "Seminarians were very much under the gun, always being evaluated. They knew the score: if the archbishop asks you, you just do it" (Bruenig, 2018; see also Rohde, 1993).

What Happened?

The problem of sexual abuse by priests in the Twentieth Century was neither limited nor isolated. Sexual exploitation of minor seminarians existed within a much broader set of violations of children by members of the Catholic clergy. Through various investigative lenses, here is what researchers ultimately are trying to explain: thousands of allegations, seemingly highly credible, of sexual abuse of minors by priests from the late 1940s forward. (Data of reasonable quality pertinent to activity before the late 1940s are lacking in most investigations.) The 1,000 cases reported by the Pennsylvania Grand Jury alone grabbed headlines. More stunning are the nearly 11,000 allegations of sexual abuse of minors in multiple settings across the nation by 4,392 priests (four percent of all priests) between 1950 and

2002 (John Jay College, 2011).[48] Nor is the problem confined to this country (Elbagir et al., 2019a). In 2018, for instance, the German Bishops Conference released a report alleging 3,677 victims, mostly young boys, of sexual abuse by 1,670 priests between 1946 and 2014 (Connolly, 2018). Australia's Royal Commission into Institutional Responses to Child Sex Abuse (2017) found that as many as 20 percent of the members of some Catholic religious orders (priests and brothers) and 40 percent of one particular order had been accused of sexual abuse between 1950 and 2010. It also found 1,870 clergy allegedly responsible for the molestation of 4,440 young males and females between 1980 and 2015.

Educational institutions – boarding schools, residential industrial schools, orphanages – have produced among the worst allegations of sexual abuse of children. Ireland's 2009 *Ryan Report*, for example, labeled rape and molestation of children *endemic* to Catholic children's residential institutions administered by clergy (primarily religious brothers) between 1930 and 1999 (Commission to Inquire into Child Abuse, 2009). Of similar import, a single priest in a Wisconsin Catholic school for the deaf was alleged to have sexually abused as many as 200 students over many years (Goodstein and Callender, 2010). Allegations of this type also have been leveled against teachers and administrators in schools for the deaf in Italy and Argentina (Nadeau, 2018). The dozens of cases in St. Lawrence Seminary and St. Anthony's Seminary discussed earlier, as well as related allegations from students in other seminaries

---

[48] Most studies of the incidence and prevalence of sexual abuse by Catholic clergy in the United States rely in the main upon files supplied by or subpoenaed from the Catholic Church. Considering the widespread and credible belief that the church has hidden abuse cases for decades, estimates based upon these data likely are conservative. Further, the files and supplementary data provided by victims (long considered reluctant to report abuse by priests) leave open the possibility of differences between reported and unreported cases.

of the same era, make clear the vulnerability of residents of total institutions and the potential for violation of trust within them (Chinnici, 2010).

No report on sexual abuse of minors by priests fails to note that more allegations pertinent to the period of study can be expected as victims who have been quiet are encouraged now to come forward. The sheer magnitude of settlement payouts by Catholic dioceses and religious orders globally and the enormous number of priests whose names are listed as alleged or documented offenders by sexual-abuse victims' advocacy- and support-organizations suggest easily that we have seen only the iceberg's tip. How did this happen?

Explanations of the incidence and prevalence of sexual abuse of minors, including minor seminarians, by Catholic priests vary considerably but generally reduce to three types: those that focus upon abusive priests, those that focus on cultural change within the Catholic Church that might have affected rates of sexual abuse, and those that focus less on cause than upon the failure of the church to police its priests and to protect its young people. Research into these three types typically relies upon one or a combination of historical case studies, reviews of allegations of victimization, and clinical-treatment studies. None is without methodological weaknesses. Historical studies by definition are time-bound and require replication in multiple eras to establish patterns. Allegations by victims, even when verified, involve *reported* offenses and offenders and leave unanswered the question of similarity to unreported offenses and offenders. Clinical studies are limited in generalizability by sample size and selectivity (including self-selectivity) biases.

Priests as Criminal Sex Offenders

In February of 2018, former priest Dino Cinel, 76, was stabbed to death in Medellin, Colombia by an eighteen-year-old male with whom he was having a relationship. Cinel once was an acquaintance of mine, an affable and talented cleric-historian on the faculty of Tulane University. That was before he was unmasked in 1988 as a priest who brought troubled teenagers into the parish rectory in which he lived and engaged in sexual relations with them. Some of the episodes were filmed and found their way into pornographic outlets in Denmark. When the case appeared in New Orleans media, Cinel revealed that he too had been the victim of sexual abuse by a priest, the headmaster of his boarding school, as a thirteen-year-old. A skeptical university colleague noted sarcastically, "Oh, sure." "No," I recall replying, "for sure." I knew that the odds of being right favored me.

What do we know about priests who sexually abuse minors? The only non-clinical study that offers profiles of any breadth of priests as sex-abuse offenders – the John Jay College (2011) investigation, a review of allegation data for the years 1950 to 2002 – indicates that close to two-thirds of offenders were between thirty and forty-nine years of age; those under thirty and over fifty accounted for smaller, nearly equal amounts of offending. Fifty-six percent of the offenders had only a single allegation lodged against them; 41 percent were accused of between two and nine offenses; only three percent were the subject of 10 or more allegations. Twenty-six percent of abuse allegations traced to 3.5 percent of the accused priests. Four in five of the victims of abuse by priests were male (and male victims tended to be older minors than were female victims).

Beyond these basic characteristics of sexually abusive priests, we know fairly little. (For summaries of what is known, see John Jay College, 2004: 207-285; John Jay College, 2011: 103-117; Miles, 2012; Sipe, 2007.) We have learned that "causes" are very difficult to pinpoint, thus making screening of prospective priests for indications of eventual abuse exceptionally difficult. We know too that correlates of abusive behavior are distributed at sufficiently high levels within non-offending populations as to make meaningful predictions problematic. For instance, we understand that abusive priests may display higher levels of childhood physical, emotional, or sexual abuse (often by a priest) than do non-abusive priests, but we also know that many abusive priests were not themselves abused as children.

We know that heterosexual and homosexual orientations – central to so many discussions of sex abuse by priests – are not themselves causes of sexually abusive behavior. Involvement in sexual activity before entry into the seminary or while in the seminary predicts sexual activity after ordination, but with other adults rather than with minors. Indeed, sex abuse appears to be much more a matter of availability of vulnerable targets than of sexual preference or prior sexual activity. Thus, the abhorrent priest-villain in the 2017 documentary, *The Keepers*, abused adolescent boys while a parish priest and then shifted to adolescent girls when appointed chaplain at a girls' high school. Similarly, a California priest involved in among "the worst Catholic Church sex abuse cases" in the San Francisco Bay Area (*Mercury News*, 2018), molested school girls in the late 1960s (while still in the seminary) and early 1970s and school boys in the late 1970s.

The stunted social and sexual development wrought by minor seminaries upon their adolescent charges (and reinforced later in major seminaries) by itself does not account for the church's sexual abuse problem (Dias and Demczuk, 2019). However, we now better understand that "vocation formation" in the 1940s, 1950s, and 1960s ignored issues of sex and sexuality (in some sense thought irrelevant to a celibate life) and interpersonal relations generally. This, in turn, produced in some individuals serious problems with personal intimacy, social integration, and substance abuse, all somewhat predictive of sexual predation (Sipe, 1999, 2003). Yet, we know too that that far more priests exhibit intimacy, isolation, and alcohol-dependency problems than engage in sexual abuse. Miles (2012) argues persuasively that the key to the puzzle is the interaction of social isolation that the seminary mandates and prior abuse-related events and variables (e.g., sexual molestation as a child). In short, we cannot isolate youngsters who have problems, fail to address those problems, and then not expect to see those problems appear later as abusive behavior and, in some cases, serial predation. The standard victim: a child, since arrested development within the seminary would produce an adult more comfortable socially with children than with adults. And a boy, since the abusive priest has greater access to young boys than to young girls.

Given the above, we are left with considerable evidence and insight concerning clerical sexual abuse but simultaneously with a science of explanation and prediction that has not yet caught up with the abuse problem. And we know far more about clerical abuse generally than about abuse within seminaries with their captive populations. Were seminary priests who abused their students similar to abusive priests in parishes? Sexual abuse within minor seminaries has garnered little research attention.[49] Practically speaking, there are little data concerning such abuse in large part because most of those institutions disappeared after 1980. We can surmise that screening of seminary faculty members by dioceses and religious orders during the middle third of the Twentieth Century likely would not have produced a high batting average;

---

[49] The John Jay College study, for example, was not directly aimed at assessing abuse in seminaries. Only 187 allegations, 1.8 percent of the total cases in that study, pointed to seminary personnel as offenders (though not necessarily with seminarian victims) between 1950 and 2002. In the way of perspective, St. Lawrence Seminary and St. Anthony's Seminary, though not specifically identified as sites of offending in the study, by themselves produced 62 credible allegations during the period in question.

neither knowledge base nor technology was up to the task. The fact remains, however, that dioceses and orders did *not* screen at anywhere close to a level that reflected good faith or even interest, and that inaction came with significant and painful costs. We know too that had the church been forthcoming about abuse in its seminaries when it occurred, we likely would know more about both offenders and victims. We shift our attention then from predators to the church's role in the sexual abuse of minor seminarians.

Church Culture and Abuse

We may not understand fully an individual's motivation concerning, and certainly cannot predict with any certainty, which individuals will engage in sexual abuse within an institution (beyond the obvious, a known record of abuse). But we can understand another piece of the puzzle: cultural elements and practices of the Catholic Church, and changes within them, that might have encouraged or permitted sexual offending (Hidalgo, 2007; Miles, 2012). Stated differently, did the church act in ways that directly or indirectly produced higher levels of sexual abuse during the late Twentieth Century?

For some, the answer is no. They view the explosions of allegations and outrage since the late 1980s concerning sexual abuse by priests as simply a matter of centuries-old chickens coming home to roost; the only change has been in the church's ability in recent decades to ignore or hide the problem (De Boer, 2019). Indeed, historical studies point to serious sexual exploitation of boys and girls in religious schools (including seminaries) and parishes, unacknowledged or hidden by the church over many centuries (Doyle, 2003; Isely, 1997; Liebreich, 2004).

Others point out that, though the sexual-abuse problem within the church may not be new, its incidence and prevalence seem to have spiked considerably in the 1960s through the 1980s. John Jay College researchers, in fact, found via their survey of allegations a) increases during the 1960s in sexual abuse by priests, b) the highest volume of abuse in the 1970s, and c) a marked decrease in allegations pertaining to sexual abuse during the 1990s (John Jay College, 2011; Miles, 2012; Pringle, 2005). These trends correlate well with another well-documented trend: the rapid decline of minor seminary enrollment during the crash era, the late-1960s and 1970s. It is at least theoretically plausible that enrollment pressure brought weaker attempts at screening candidates, both students and faculty members, for entrance into seminaries and kept in minor (and major) seminaries students who otherwise would not have persisted. That particular subgroup of seminarians may have contained greater numbers of potential sexual predators (assuming the necessary conditions later in life). In this light, the decrease in incidents alleged to have occurred in Catholic parishes during the 1990s would seem to reflect the church's effort during that decade better to screen and to educate candidates for and within college-level and major seminaries and to put in place other impediments to abuse.

Setting aside matters of screening and educating seminarians concerning sexual abuse, what else might have led to the spike in offending in the 1960s and 1970s? As they did regarding the downward spiral in seminary enrollment beginning in the mid-to-late 1960s, some argue that the real culprit in the abuse scenario – that which turned potential into actual offenders – was the Second Vatican Council. Critics argue that Vatican II introduced liberalism into Catholicism to such an extent that it drove away spiritually and emotionally healthier priests and candidates for the priesthood (Rose, 2002). Further, Vatican II allegedly fostered among the faithful a moral ambivalence regarding sexual activity once considered wrong: heterosexual activity outside of marriage and homosexual activity involving consenting adults. This, it is posited, encouraged a libertine culture, especially regarding homosexuality, within seminaries and ultimately exported into the Catholic world by a small but impactful group of morally bankrupt clergy (Berry and Renner, 2004).

Miles (2012) turns the Vatican II-argument on its head. He believes that, rather than creating a culture that either produced or failed to spot potential sexual predators, Vatican II, with its emphasis on modernity and change, reversed (by design or effect) the centuries-old practice of isolating boys in minor seminaries and young men in major seminaries that were mere cultural extensions of minor seminaries. The result may have been a greater openness toward gays within seminaries (problematic or not) but also greater exposure of seminarians to the social world. Further, as minor seminaries decreased in number, the average seminarian's age increased. In short, the cycle of arrested social development and ensuing problematic behavior was itself arrested.

Moral ambivalence regarding consensual sex between adults (heterosexual or homosexual), whether or not a product of Vatican II, is in no sense the equal of a green light for sexual abuse of minors. To the extent it has posed a problem for the church, it has not been the *cause* of the predation-problem in question. Further weighing against the Vatican II-thesis is substantial evidence that sexual abuse was occurring in seminaries of the 1950s and that one in five abusive priests outside the seminary was ordained in the 1950s, i.e., well before Vatican II when seminaries were filled with "real men." Priests ordained before 1960 (1930s through 1950s) accounted for 44 percent of the alleged sexual abuses occurring between 1950 and 2002 (John Jay College, 2011: 37; Miles 2012). Within this same context, Gale Leifeld, the rector of St. Lawrence Seminary who ultimately was accused of serial sexual abuse of his students, attended St. Lawrence as a high school seminarian in the

1940s and was ordained in 1955. Mario Cimmarrusti, the prefect of discipline at St. Anthony's Seminary accused of serial abuse of students, himself was educated at St. Anthony's during the 1940s and ordained in 1957.

Required celibacy within the priesthood also has come under fire, though from different directions, as a "likely cause" of sexual exploitation of minors by clergy (Berry and Renner, 2004). From some commentators: if the church and its priests took celibacy seriously, there would be fewer cases of abuse within priestly ranks. From others: were the celibacy requirement lifted, less abuse would occur within priestly ranks. Celibacy (including among homosexual priests) may or may not be reason for ongoing worry within the church.[50] Obviously, to strengthen commitment to it might well attract a different type of person into the ministry, as would to decrease commitment to it. In either case, however, there is neither logic nor a research foundation to the premise that were priests permitted adult sexual partners, women or men, abuse of minors (including nominarians) would decrease accordingly (Wills, 2019). Celibacy within the notion of the priesthood entails an informed avoidance of legitimate and normally-encouraged behavior, while sexual abuse entails the reprehensible and criminal exploitation of children and vulnerable adults. They are not two sides of the same coin.

In sum, we can conclude reasonably that "something happened" during the seminary heyday and crash eras to produce a spike in

---

[50] Celibacy is an ideological issue (Wills, 2002) but also a financial one. The labor- (i.e., priest-) cost now incurred by the church would increase dramatically were celibacy abandoned and priests were to marry. Wages sufficient to contribute to the welfare of an entire family would vastly exceed what now is spent on the welfare of a single person. Further, attention to the needs of that family would reduce the extent to which priests could be on call around the clock, thus necessitating an increase in the number of priests required simply to keep pace with the current status quo.

sexual abuse of seminarians by their teachers, though we remain mindful that abundant abuse was occurring previously. That said, no one has been able to identify adequately the "something" in question. Vatican II-liberalism and traditional priestly celibacy (either insufficiently enforced or too-well enforced) are common targets of criticism in the era of sexual abuse, but neither functions well as a direct "cause." What is clear is that the church failed to *discourage* priests who preyed sexually upon youths, minor seminarians included. We turn now to that failure.

A Failure of Guardianship

We have looked for answers for the "causes" (individual-pathological and cultural) of sexual abuse of minors by priests and have found little presently that satisfies either as a full explanation of abuse or as the basis for policy. By itself, motivation to abuse someone sexually does not explain the abuse. It must coincide with the freedom to abuse (the belief that the behavior is not morally wrong[51] and/ or the sense that it will not be detected and punished), the opportunity to act on this freedom (placement within the proximity of potential victims), and the skill, likely honed progressively, to convince a victim to capitulate and remain quiet about the abuse (Sheley, 1983). Effectively, potential and actual abusers of vulnerable people in institutions act on their impulses when nothing stands in the way, whether the institution in question is an orphanage, a nursing home, a school for the deaf, a camp for gymnasts, a day care

---

[51] Some abusive priests are without moral conscience and, therefore, wholly free to abuse. Most, however, gain the freedom by rationalizing their behavior to the extent that they can convince themselves that they are causing no real harm or that their victim desired the sexual encounter (Thomson et al., 1998; Sheley, 1980).

center, a mental hospital, a prison, or a minor seminary – each of these types of institution has experienced significant allegations of sexual abuse. Serial predators succeed when organizations do not provide adequate guardianship of their wards.

In this light, here is what is indisputable: Boys and young men, often emotionally immature, were placed in or attracted into total-institution seminaries. Contact with the external world was limited, and few outsiders looked behind the seminary's walls at its inner workings. What occurred inside was determined by the priests and religious brothers who staffed the school, and few of these men were monitored to any great degree by their colleagues. No systematic mechanisms to report abuse were available within seminaries of the day. No education or warnings concerning abuse were provided students or priests. No external audits of possible abuse occurred. The ensuing vacuum meant that predators, a minority of priests and religious brothers (though, in retrospect, perhaps a larger minority than one would have assumed at the time), easily could prey sexually upon seminarians, particularly younger ones. Victims typically told no one. If a victim did report the incident, or if a perpetrator otherwise was discovered, the incident was covered up or certainly addressed very quietly. The victim's psychological damage generally was ignored or underestimated. The perpetrator himself suffered relatively little damage.

In short, we may not know why a decided minority of seminary priests and brothers abused seminarians, but we do know how they were able to do so. For all intents and purposes, the door to the minor-seminary vault was left open, no guards were posted, and bad guys who worked at the institution stole what was most valued, innocence. Such was life in the minor seminary, an obscene piece of which was neither observed nor even sensed by most of us. That obscenity could have been prevented, or at least diminished, had the Catholic Church exercised appropriate leadership

227

and acted upon the knowledge that it had at the time. Instead, seminaries, the dioceses and religious orders that administered them, and the church more generally, placed the reputational and economic interests of the organization above the seminarian, often not only failing to penalize offenders but also placing them again into environments containing minors (Elbagir et al., 2019a). The cycle continued until someone finally said "enough," and the truth began to emerge (Berry and Renner, 2004; Chinnici, 2010). It was a very ugly truth.

Behind Seminary Blinds

Our look behind the seminary's blinds in this and the previous chapter produced one very clear finding: the vast majority of boys and young men in minor seminaries were *not* involved sexually with other persons except perhaps in their dreams and fantasies (which usually engendered strong feelings of guilt). A small percentage of students, most often in college-level seminaries, was involved in homosexual activity. But our look through the blinds into a dark corner of the seminary, not easily seen and clearly not meant to be, also turned up something very disturbing: a number of the boys and young men (a minority, to be sure; no one knows exactly how many) in minor seminaries lost their virginity – and their trust, optimism, sense of faith, and self-confidence – to adults, sometimes to serial, sexual predators who took them because they could and because potential victims were handy and abundant.

I am left wondering whether any of my classmates was a victim of sexual abuse – no interviewee has suggested anything like this about himself, a fellow student, or any of the priests who taught us at St. Pius X Seminary. That said, in recent years, Catholic dioceses have made public lists of priests accused "credibly" of having engaged in sexual abuse of minors. On one such list provided by the Diocese of Sacramento resides the name of a priest who taught us at St. Pius X Seminary in the 1960s. The priest in question was accused in 1986 of "sexual touching and fondling" of a male minor in 1962 – sometime during my class's freshman or sophomore year, though there is nothing to indicate the age of the alleged victim or even of the place the act occurred. The name prompted considerable conversation among St. Pius alumni, including a revelation by a former seminarian of physically staving off the priest's advances.

I understand well that, notwithstanding the crimes visited upon many seminarians, the odds of the average seminarian in my day being sexually abused were low. Still, in light of what has been revealed about so many minor seminaries (and any of us could have attended one of those seminaries, as some of our transfer-school-mates did), I feel fortunate not to have endured the pain, humiliation, confusion, and disillusionment that sexual-abuse victims experienced. For I possessed the features of the typical prey when I entered the minor seminary at thirteen: small, naïve, good boy, lonely and desiring attention, and very respectful of priests. This much I know: had I been sexually abused by the men I looked up to and admired, I almost certainly would not have told a soul, definitely not anyone on the outside. Our institutional culture encouraged us to bury such things deep; what went on within the seminary stayed within the seminary. I would have been one of those boys-turned-men who bore his wound for life, repressing the memory, pocketing the rage and shame.

I was just plain lucky.

References

Anonymous (Blogger). 2011. "St. Lawrence Seminary Celebrates 150 years of Education." *www.badgercatholic.blogspot.com/2010/06/st-lawrence-seminary-high-school.html#comment-form/* (February 22).

Berry, Jason. 1992. *Lead Us Not Into Temptation: Catholic Priests and the Sexual Abuse of Children*. New York: Doubleday.

_____. 2011. *Render Unto Rome: The Secret Life of Money in the Catholic Church*. New York: Crown.

Berry, Jason and Gerald A. Renner. 2004. *Vows of Silence: The Abuse of Power in the Papacy of John Paul II*. New York: Free Press.

Bruenig, Elizabeth. 2018. "He Wanted to Be a Priest. He says Archbishop McCarrick Used That to Abuse Him." *Washington Post (https://www. washingtonpost.com/he-wanted-to-be-a-priest/eff6e/726)* (September 12).

Burnett, Michael, Thomas Doyle, and James Freiburger. 2013. *Report of the Audit and Review of the Files of the Capuchin Province of St. Joseph*. (www.docplayer.net/70128)

Joseph P. Chinnici, 2010. *When Values Collide: The Catholic Church, Sexual Abuse, and the Challenges of Leadership*. Maryknoll NY: Orbis Books.

Commission to Inquire into Child Abuse. 2009. *Report of the Commission to Inquire into Child Abuse. Volumes 1-5*. Dublin: The Stationary Office.

Connolly, Kate. 2018. "'Shocking' Sexual Abuse of Children by German Clergy Detailed in Report." *The Guardian* (https://www.theguardian. com/world/2018/sep/25/report-details-sexual-abuse-german-catholic -church).

Cornwell, John. 2006. *Seminary Boy: A Memoir*. New York: Doubleday.

De Boer, Wietse. 2019. "The Catholic Church and Sexual Abuse, Then and Now." *Origins* (https://www.origins.osu.edu/article).

Dias, Elizabeth and Gabriella Demczuk. 2019. "It Is Not a Closet. It Is a Cage.' Gay Catholic Priests Speak Out." *New York Times* (https:// www.nytimes. com/2019/02/17/us/it-is-not-a-closet-it-is-a-cage-gay -catholic-priests-speak-out.html).

Doyle, Thomas P. 2003. "Roman Catholic Clericalism, Religious Distress, and Clergy Sexual Abuse." *Pastoral Psychology* 51: 189-231.

Elbagir, Nima, Barbara Arvanitidis, Katie Polgase, Bryony Jones, and Alex Platt. 2019a. "How a Catholic Order Dedicated to Protecting Children Failed Them." *Cable News Network* (cnn.com/interactive/2019/11/ Africa/luk-delft-intl/).

_____. 2019b. "Pedophile Priests Operated at This California School for Decades." *Cable News Network* (cnn.com/interactive/2019/us/salesians-of-don-bosco-intl/).

Finley, Mitch. 2003. *It's Not the Same Without You: Coming Home to the Catholic Church.* New York: Doubleday.

Goodstein, Laurie and David Callender. 2010. "For Years, Deaf Boys Tried to Tell of Priest's Abuse." *New York Times* (https://www.nytimes. com/2010/03/27 /us/27wisconsin.html).

Hendrickson, Paul. 1983. *Seminary: A Search.* New York: Summit Books.

_____. 2002. "Altar-Boy Innocence; A Former Seminarian Reflects on Moral Ambivalence." *New York Times* (https://www.nytimes.com/2002/04/28/weekinreview/the-nation-altar-boy-inno-cents-a-former-seminarian-reflects-on-moral-ambivalence.html).

Hidalgo, Myra L. 2007. *Sexual Abuse and the Culture of Catholicism: How Priests and Nuns Became Perpetrators.* New York: Haworth.

Howard, Ted. 2013. *Our Seminary Years: 1956–1964.* https://www.mixbook. com/photo-books/family/our-seminary-years-1956-1964-9395897.

Isley, Peter J. 1997 "Child Sexual Abuse and the Catholic Church: An Historical and Contemporary Review." *Pastoral Psychology* 45: 277-299.

_____2004. "2004 Report: St. Lawrence Seminary, Capuchin Sex Offenders, Court Documents, Victim Testimony." *www.bishop-accounability.org/reports.*

John Jay College. 2004. *The Nature and Scope of Sexual Abuse of Minors by Catholic Priests and Deacons, 1950-2002.* Washington D.C.: United States Conference of Catholic Bishops.

_____. 2011. *The Causes and Context of Sexual Abuse of Minors by Catholic Priests in The United States: 1950-2010.* Washington D.C.: United States Conference of Catholic Bishops.

Liebach, Karen. 2004. *Fallen Order.* New York: Grove Press.

Mercury News. 2018. "The Worst Catholic Church Sex Abuse Cases in the Bay Area History." *Https://www.mercurynews.com/2018/08/15/the-worst-catholic-church-sex-abuse-cases-in-bay-area-history/.*

Miles, Vincent J. 2012. *Boys of the Cloth: The Accidental Role of Church Reforms in Causing and Curbing Abuse by Priests.* Lanham, MD: Hamilton Books.

Moody, Fred. 2014. "The Secret life of a Seminary." *Pacific NW Magazine/ The Seattle Times* (https://www.seattletimes.com/pacific-nw-magazine/the-secret-life-of-a-seminary/ (March 4).

Nadeau, Barbi L. 2018. "The Sex Abuse of Deaf Orphans in Pope Francis's Backyard." *The Daily Beast* (https://www.thedailybeast.com/the-sex-abuse-of-deaf-orphans-in-pope-francis-backyard) (September 29).

Pennsylvania Attorney General. 2018. *40th Statewide Investigating Grand Jury: REPORT 1 (Interim – Redacted).* Harrisburg PA: Office of the Attorney General, Commonwealth of Pennsylvania.

Pope Francis. 2018. *Letter of His Holiness to the People of God.* (August 20): Vatican City: Libreria Editrice Vaticana.

Pringle, Paul. 2005. "Trail of Abuse Leads to Seminary." *Los Angeles Times* (https://www.latimes.com/archives/la-xpm-2005-nov-17-me -stjohns17-story.html).

Rastrelli, Tom. 2012. "Confessions of an Ex-Priest: How Catholic Seminary Forms Victims and Forces False Forgiveness." *Huffington Post* (https://www.huffpost.com/entry/confessions-of-an-ex-priest-how-catholic-seminary-forms-victims-of-sexual-abuse-and-perpetrators-to-forgive)(October 19).

Rohde, Marie. 1993. "Seminary in the Eye of a New Sex Scandal Storm." *National Catholic Reporter* (https://www.questia.com/magazine/1G1-13685772/seminary-the-eye-of-new-sex-scandal-storm) (April 9).

_____ 2011. "The Prophet." *Inside Milwaukee* (http://www. insidemilwaukee.com/Article/9192011-TheProphet).

Royal Commission into Institutional Responses to Child Sexual Abuse. 2017. *Report of the Royal Commission into Institutional Responses to Child Sexual Abuse.* Sydney, Australia.

Sheley, Joseph. 1980. "Is Neutralization Necessary for Criminal Behavior?" *Deviant Behavior* 2: 49 – 72.

_____. 1983. "Critical Elements of Criminal Behavior Explanation." *The Sociological Quarterly* 24: 509-525.

Sipe, A.W. Richard. 1999. "The Sexual Abuse of Minors by Clergy: Problems of Prevention." In Thomas G. Plante, ed., *Bless Me Father for I Have Sinned.* Westport CN: Greenwood.

_____. 2003. *Celibacy in Crisis: A Secret World Revisited.* New York NY: Brunner-Routledge.

_____. 2007. *The Serpent and the Dove: Celibacy in Literature and Life.* Westport CN: Praeger.

Stearns, Geoffrey, Kathleen Baggarley Mar, Keith Mar, Eugene Merlin, et al. 1993. *Report to Father Joseph Chinnici, OFM: Independent Board of Inquiry Regarding St. Anthony's Seminary* (www.bishop-accountability.org/reports/1993).

Thomson, J.G., J.A. Marolla, and D.G. Bromley. 1998. "Disclaimers and Accounts of Catholic Priests Accused of Pedophilia." In A. Shup, ed., *Wolves within the Fold.* New Brunswick NJ: Rutgers University Press. Pp. 175-189.

Wills, Garry. 2002. "The Scourge of Celibacy," *Boston Globe Magazine* (http://archive.boston.com/globe/spotlight/abuse/stories/032402/magazine.htm).

_____. 2019. "Celibacy Isn't the Cause of the Church Sex Abuse Crisis; the Priesthood Is." *The Boston Globe* (www.bostonglobe.com/opinion, January 3).

PART IV

Flight

CHAPTER TEN

Unmarked Exit

We knew that the answer to the question, "Don't you want to marry and have a family someday?" was "I'm going to be married to the church." The path to the altar was long and narrow. The more time spent in the seminary, the harder it became to break the engagement. What had begun as an adolescent date (for many, a fix-up by a parent) had morphed into a betrothal between a teenager and a much older woman — centuries so.[52] With each passing year, people thought increasingly of church and seminarian as a couple. The irony, so apparent now, was lost on us then: the same seminary that denied us the

---

[52] That the polyandrous fiancée of the prospective priest was also "Holy Mother Church" was not lost upon boys and young men who progressed further into seminary years (Hedin, 2003: 164). Ordination (marriage) did not alter what was essentially a maternal relationship between female church and male priest. He would serve his spouse not on equal footing, as would a husband, but far more as the committed son would serve his mother.

tools necessary to develop and maintain meaningful personal relationships – especially with females – itself now was challenged with convincing us to embrace a monogamous, lifetime union with our decidedly polyg-amous bride-to-be. Those who stayed in the relation-ship beyond year two – and it only got tougher each year after – developed what gamblers and social scien-tists call side bets, related commitments that increase the likelihood that a line of activity will continue. To exit was to wound more than our fiancée. Our folks and lots of others were excited about our engagement, thrilled about the nuptials – a million years away. And now we were getting cold feet: "I don't know what love is, but I don't think I'm in love. Oh man, how do I get out of this?"

This chapter is about leaving a relationship entered into far too young and with so little sense of the attendant obligations that *naïve* barely describes the seminarian. What the average of my minor-seminarian interviewees knew for certain was that he was not happy and could not see how someday he would be. Time to look elsewhere, but no one made it easy for him.

Numbers

The minor seminary, in theory, was a place of personal discernment about one's future. In truth, the institution did not consider its ado-lescent wards capable of discernment (a correct assumption); the seminary faculty was responsible for such evaluations. Seminary faculties focused upon managing numbers. The idea was to attract boys and young men with cleric potential into seminaries, weed out quickly the "mistakes" (seminarians with poor academic performance, bad attitude, or problematic comportment) – those boys usually took care of that themselves – and preserve as many as possible of those with a "real chance" for movement into major seminaries. Beyond that, there was little science to the game. Seminary faculties knew from experience that they would end up sending to major seminaries only a portion of their wards though, beyond the obvious "write-offs," they could not predict exactly which ones. Buried in the perseverance-attrition process were surprises, both ways: boys who defied the stereotypes and hung on much longer than expected and boys with seemingly high potential who simply evaporated early.

The size of the fraction of minor seminarians ultimately sent to major seminaries varied across eras due in large part to cultural changes in the social value and encouragement of vocations and to the practical matter of seminary enrollments necessary to institutional sustainability (see Chapter Two). The fraction was larger from 1950 to 1965 than it became soon thereafter. The rector at St. Pius X Seminary during the 1960s, Father George Schuster, had attended minor seminary in the 1940s. He recalled that members of his freshman class were lined up and told to look right and then left and to understand that, when all was said and done, only one of every three students would move forward (see Anello, 2018: 53). By the late-1960s, as his ship clearly was listing, he likely wished for one in three. The best recruitment years (freshmen classes) of the heyday era at St. Pius, those of the early 1960s, produced very low yields (movement to the major seminary) during the later portion of the decade, in the neighborhood of 10 percent.

Again, these were the good years; perseverance within cohorts to follow went downhill after the mid-1960s. Seminaries once held the cards; seminarians now held them. Heyday-era seminarians "left" or "made it"; crash-era seminarians "left" or "failed to leave."[53] Era notwithstanding, students exited either because they were asked to or because they chose to. The former path out is much easier described than is the latter.

Booted

Seminarians were petrified of dismissal, for it always smacked of weakness and failure. Many students were asked to leave during the late 1950s and early 1960s. It went with the territory. During the 1950s, especially, when enrollment figures first began outpacing infrastructural capacity and old-school seminary culture still held sway, seminary faculties were quick to pull the trigger. A former priest among interviewees noted,

> *You had to be careful what you said back then. If you told your spiritual director that you were even thinking about girls, he would assume that you had no vocation. You were out of there quick, and another solid prospect took your place, and so many other prospects were lined up waiting to take his place.*

No matter the era, two types of students consistently were asked to leave, firmly but gently told that the faculty did not consider them "priestly material": those in academic difficulty and those

---

[53] Ironically, all these years later, many former seminarians, including ordained priests, refer to those who persisted as having "*failed* to make it… out." This is, of course, decidedly unfair to priests who believe that they have and always have had a true vocation and are glad to have been ordained and to have served. But the point is not lost; the average minor seminarian of the day felt trapped at least to some degree. As time has passed and the concept of minor seminary has been criticized, he cannot understand how any seminarian survived emotionally.

whose attitudes portended problems. Regarding the former, poor academic performance was a sure indicator of future challenges and, thus, a standard cause for dismissal in the first two years. More often than not, students performing poorly were warned first that they must improve (Cornwell, 2006; Thomas, 2003), and those who failed to do so were sent packing. By the junior year, the academic profile of the students was set; most survivors were considered solid in the classroom. But even here, the yardstick changed. Far from over, the competition remained pronounced, and boys who had been doing fine earlier sometimes found the contest overwhelming.

> *I became an avid reader, but never liked math and language, and I hated speech class. But I did not think of myself as a poor student in the first two years. My grades were okay, and there were lots of guys doing really badly. I did not stick out. But after those guys left, there I was, stuck with all the smart kids. What was B or C work became D work. It wasn't great for my ego. It was pretty much leave or get tossed.* (Former seminarian from Wisconsin)

The second type of student likely to be dismissed "had an attitude," and the attitudinal profile in question was that of either "wise ass" or "skeptic." Wise asses quickly shaped up or were shipped out; pretext was not a problem, for smart-mouthing a faculty member by definition was an offense. A 1961 freshman at St. Pius X who slouched and looked out the window during one of the rector's class lectures was asked if he wanted to be there. His sullen "no" earned him the gate, from the classroom *and* from the seminary, on the spot and none too gently. Students began sitting straighter in their chairs.

Skeptics were another matter. Too much questioning of authority, too many queries and critical comments in class, too much creativity in essays on doctrinal and social matters all pointed to the obvious: this kid is going to be trouble. Indeed, research into "leavers" and "persisters" in minor seminaries (high school and college) in the mid- to late-1960s found "leavers" as a group to operate at a more intellectual level (or to exhibit a greater balance of subjective and objective independence in thought and behavior) than did "persisters," also as a group, who operated at a more affective level (see, for example, Lee, 1969a, 1969b, 1970; Rachowski, 1965; Schlesinger, 1966).

In lay terms, that means that those who stayed were more social, socially submissive, trusting, sensitive, and anxious (not to mention more musical and literary) than were their departing classmates who were more assertive, independent, aloof, and introspective (not to mention more computational and scientific). "Persisters" were more likely to stay as a means of "pleasing their elders than as a personally rewarding goal" (Schlesinger, 1966:110). "Leavers," on the other hand, were less likely to conform and, therefore, more likely to exit or be asked to exit. Group profiles notwithstanding, it was very difficult to predict individual behavior and decisions, perhaps because the distinction references a continuum rather than a dichotomy. Most of us knew "leavers" who seemed like "persisters" and vice versa.

Judging from interviews and first-person accounts of seminarians in the 1950s and early 1960s, most students, even as freshmen, understood their options. They could leave (and many did early on), fail academically (and many did that too), be booted – even as an otherwise model seminarian – for a violation of rules (such as possession of a radio), or be found wanting as a prospect for the priesthood. It was the last of these that seemed most to terrify. Former seminarians of that era nearly always recalled the fear of being "blackballed." They remembered vividly their awareness of vocational progress being monitored, of meetings of the faculty at which their fates were determined, of spiritual directors who claimed that theirs were the only votes cast in favor of retention. They recalled too the tears of boys who got the bad news and who waited in the front lobby for their folks to arrive and drive them home (Hendrickson, 1983: 148). In some seminaries, a student who was being dismissed was not permitted to interact with his fellows (Wall, 1999).[54] Often the castaway's parents were informed during the day, and the student was picked up at night. The next morning, the young man simply was not there when his classmates headed to chapel (Hinsvark, nd). Students who lived far away were shipped home by bus or train.

For many, it was devastating news.

They called me in at the end of junior year and told me I was out. I was shocked. I had never gotten into trouble, and I had never gotten any direct negative feedback. But they did not like my ... I was a smart and rambunctious boy. The proud. I had influence. Leading other boys astray. They came up with phony stuff like they thought I had a girlfriend, which was completely untrue. Absolutely not. Some of the priests that I knew and cared about— I went to see them and cried – told me it was a railroad job. Plus, I had changed confessors – the first one was older and I could not relate to him (and later figured out he was a drunk) – and he, the older guy, is the one who did me in. (Former seminarian from Northern California)

---

[54] An interviewee who spent four months in a Jesuit novitiate similarly recalled that, whether or not the departure was voluntary, aside from quick goodbyes to a few close friends, most who left simply disappeared. A note was posted on a common message board the next day informing everyone that the young man had left and that he would remain in everyone's prayers. See also Bowman (2012), Murray (2012), and Treisman (2018).

At the end of the [freshman] year they asked me not to come back. After all, they had so many kids to pick from and could exercise a lot of judgment in this respect. The faculty thought something was wrong with me because I slept during math class (err—right), even though my grades were good. …My confessor advised me about the decision and he said that he really wanted me to stay because I was a good candidate for orders and he voted for me. This was not a lot of consolation to me because I felt like a complete failure. I wandered out by the statue of Mary in front and found several other kids who had likewise been asked not to come back and we commiserated together. (Vautier, 2014)

The late-1960s experience differed somewhat. The focus was upon academic performance and upon staying out of trouble (i.e., avoiding expulsion due to poor comportment). Attitude, unless it was expressed outrageously, was less a pressing matter; the seminary's enrollment numbers simply could not bear such proactive culling. The chips were left to fall where they may with students whose attitudes were not exactly what they needed ultimately to be. Most would find their way out anyway, and those who somehow persisted almost certainly would not persevere in the major seminary; that was the major seminary's problem to ponder.

By the 1970s, as enrollment plummeted, minor seminaries were practically begging – I exaggerate only slightly – traditional "leavers" to hang in. The rarer dismissal still did not sit well, and some dismissed students were devastated. They did not want to leave their friends, and their friends did not want them to go. In one extreme case, according to an interviewee of that era, a dismissed student in a combination seminary-preparatory school hid for days within a crawlspace in the chapel while friends brought him food and the staff frantically searched for him. But it was as likely that a booted student could frame dismissal as the seminary's problem, which is exactly what one interviewee, dismissed from his college program, did:

I was smart. I was active. I was president of my class, a leader. But it always seemed like they wanted to kick me out. For smoking or for things I said about social justice. They just did not like my attitude. So they did [kick me out]. It hurt because I knew that I could be a good priest, and others knew that too. But I also knew that I was not happy because all we did, really, is sit around and talk about catechism and that kind of bullshit. And I did not want to be part of that. We were college students, not kids! And my parents were fine with it. They had come to dislike [the seminary] and the priests who ran it. (Former seminarian from Buffalo)

Slipping Away Quietly

During both heyday and crash eras, freshman and sophomore years saw many young men leave the seminary. It was expected. A few were dismissed quickly and firmly, others more gently, usually at holiday breaks or at semester's end. But dismissal was not the exit path for the average seminarian. Most who left during those first two years did so of their own volition. They were not happy in the seminary. They were tired of the academic grind or chafed at the discipline. Some boys were unable to overcome their homesickness (Bazzett, 2010; Queenan, 2013) or the isolation. Some were runaways and found seminary life as problematic as had been their home life; they returned to hard times. Leaving was easier for those whose parents had said all along that they would support their sons no matter what they chose to do. Students who had entered or stayed more to please their parents than out of a true interest in the priesthood found departure harder. Thus, for both anointed boys and parental offerings (see Chapter Five), leaving reduced to degree of unhappiness in the seminary as against level (or duration) of parental unhappiness with the decision to leave.

I was not happy. I mean, I liked the other kids, but I did not like it there. When my older brother came to pick me up at the end of sophomore year, I told him that I could not imagine never getting married – like I even knew what that meant; I was trying out the line. But I did not say a word to my mom until just before it was time to go back for junior year. It was hard for her, but she got over it. (Alumnus, St. Pius X Seminary)

Toward the end of my first semester, when I went home at Christmas time, I realized that I did not want to be a priest. I went back, but when my folks visited a few months later, I told my mom. She then told my dad, and he was upset. He went to see the rector about how to keep his boy there. After a week or two and a couple of phone calls, they came back to get me. We had a family conference with the rector who told my dad, right in front of me, that I was stupid to quit. But I insisted and, I think, my mom took my side quietly, and they took me home. My dad was pissed for a while, but after a few months, things were okay. (Former seminarian from Los Angeles)

Runaways, on the other hand, often matured sufficiently physically and emotionally to enable a return to the home on sounder footing. A boy who entered the seminary physically dominated by his father, for example, might well have transformed into his father's match in strength and toughness. If not, he waited a few more years until he did.

I remember my dad being home sick one day during the summer when I was fifteen. I was on the front porch, and my brother was in the driveway. He and I got into a shouting match over something, and he threw a small rock at me, and it hit the door. I heard my dad get out of bed and head through the living room toward us. I stepped off the porch before he got there and moved to the side. He headed right for me and swung. I ducked and sort of flipped him over me. He went right over the top of me into a bush. I just turned and walked inside – waiting to get clobbered there or maybe to fight back – but that was the end of it. Nothing happened. My dad never tried to hit me again. (Former seminarian from San Francisco)

My dad, a bad alcoholic who used to hit us and ended every command with, "Or I'll kill you," pretty much stopped hitting me after I left the seminary. I was bigger then. But one day he hit my sister. I told him that if he ever did that again, I'd kill him – just like he would say it. I went out to the garage to put my golf clubs in the car and, sure enough, here he comes out of the house with a meat cleaver in his hand. I picked up a three-iron and said, "Come on. You want some of this?" Just then, my mother comes out of the house screaming and gets between us. I got out of there soon after. (Former seminarian from Idaho)

Runaways also were more likely than other seminarians to limit contact with their parents when they were home for breaks (i.e., to run away even while visiting home). They did not wish to be in the house, so they more actively sought out their old friends and, as they grew older, spent more time with them. They were less concerned about staying within the institution's guidelines. The outcome was a distancing from their problematic home but also a distancing from the seminary. The specter of leaving the seminary was less daunting for them.

There weren't many guys from school in the area where I lived. None that I wanted to hang out with anyway. I did not want to sit around the house. I worked a part-time job. Mainly I hung out with a few guys from town. One, in particular, Vince, was a big heartthrob in town – you know, good looking, muscles, cool ducktails. Girls loved him. Everybody knew him. Where he went, I went. So, everyone knew me too. (Alumnus, St. Pius X Seminary)

I knew that if I left, my parents might say, "I told you that you were not good enough to be a priest." So I was kind of trapped for a while. But after a while, hey, I just didn't care. (Former seminarian from San Diego)

Leaving the Group

By junior year, the notion of a true "class" took hold; poorer prospects and the unhappiest of students had left or been weeded out, and some better prospects had "rejected God's call." Continuing students no longer were "trying out" the seminary; they were, instead, *real seminarians* who had to answer "yes," not "maybe," to the question: "So, you're going to be a priest?" In theory, any and all of the remaining students could persevere to the major seminary and beyond. History indicated that not all would – we had only to look at the classes above us to see that – though history was not particularly adept at suggesting individual persistence outcomes. Students bonded and, though not everyone got along, tended to see themselves as invested in each other's wellbeing (Murray, 2012: 47). Departures rattled the group, produced an empty-chair feeling, and made everyone wonder if he would – or should – be next.

Our junior year at St. Pius X went well. We were truly in it now, for better or worse. We were viewed as a class, a cohort. We had our rhythm academically. We were strong athletically and took pride in fielding the best class teams. We were among the leaders within stage productions. Father Charles, the head-cracking Dean of Students, had turned his attention to classes behind us. We, in turn, knew fairly well the students in the three classes ahead of us, followed their progress, and could envision ourselves approaching the same milestones. Only one member of our class left during the academic year. June brought the obvious question; who would be back in September? No one signaled his impending exit to the group, but five did not return. Such decisions were never easy:

> I wrestled with it all summer. I was not doing well academically. I talked a lot about it with my best friend from school. He was saying he was leaving too. That made it easier for me – he was considered more serious and the smart one and, I figured, if I could point to him, no one could object. But I did not tell anyone else. I waited until the end of summer, when it was time to register for [the local high school], to tell my parents that I did not want to go back. I don't think they were surprised. They knew I was struggling academically, and maybe I had been giving off unhappy vibes. Anyway, they seemed okay with it. I don't remember any tears or big discussions. (Former seminarian from New Orleans)

> I wanted to leave after sophomore year, but my parents went and got the parish priest to do an "intervention." I went back. Nobody knew that I had tried to leave. But I was bored and wanted to try new things. After junior year, I tried again, and they brought in the parish priest again. It didn't work this time. I transferred to the local Catholic high school. It was part of the deal. It made it okay for my mom. (Former seminarian from San Francisco)

Some minor seminarians experienced emotional crises of sorts (trouble with a particular faculty member or doubts about academic ability, for example), though this was far more common among major seminarians who tended to leave the seminary because they suffered doubts about vocation or faith.[55] One former minor seminarian recalled a rebuke by a particular priest that pushed him over the edge and had him calling his folks to come and get him, not next week but right now. The question directed to a diocesan functionary by another former seminarian about why so many resources went to the missions rather than to the needy right down the block brought the response, "Why would you presume to think for the church?" and that, in turn, meant that "I was not coming back next year." A young man from San Diego, his dream of traveling down coastal highways with a surfboard strapped to the roof of his car and the Beach Boys on the radio growing dimmer, simply walked away in the middle of his senior year of high school.

By and large, however, most minor seminarians with more than two years in tended not to experience crises so much as periods of longer-term malaise. This may have prompted departure for the freshman and sophomore, but it did not suffice as the springboard out for the upperclassman with his need to please people. He looked instead for natural breaks. A variant of "leaving" was "not going back," and

---

[55] A former Jesuit seminarian, just two years from ordination in the mid-1960s, recalled his crisis:

> They had assigned me to teach and learn the ropes at [a Catholic university]. I was living in the priests' quarters. I had been troubled by what seemed to be a dead church – way out of step with the times. So, I come home one night and go into the kitchen to make myself a sandwich. One of the older priests comes in, grabs a beer, sits down, starts talking about his crisis of faith, how he has not believed in years. He drinks the beer, grabs another beer – he usually drank a six pack each night. I remember looking at him and thinking, "That's what I am going to be doing for the rest of my life. They are grooming me to end up like this." That's when I really started to think about leaving.

"not going back" happened over the Christmas holidays or over the summer. But the most natural of breaks for the heretofore continuing student came at the end of high school or college studies (two years of college in the traditional, six-year minor seminary, four years in the college seminary). Here, "leaving" became "not continuing." Yet, even that intention was insufficient sans an acceptable reason for abandoning a course of action in which you had invested time (i.e., a bet) and your parents' money (part of the bet), and leaving might break your mother's heart (side bet) and/or mean the loss of your closest friends, never mind abandoning your comrades in their parallel struggle (another side bet), and then there were your parish priests who had begun treating you like a member of the fraternity (still another side bet). "Unhappy" did not cut it.

For the most part, seminaries kept the vocabulary and the pressure soft. This was important for families as well as for seminarians. "Leaving" was the term of choice at most seminaries, for it afforded a certain dignity that did not attach to concepts reflecting failure or abandonment. The term also was employed at St. Pius X Seminary until the dean of students upped the ante in 1962. Upon his arrival at the seminary, Father Charles introduced the notion of "quit" into common parlance. One interviewee remarked that Charles "changed everything" by shifting the focus from trying to contain unnecessary attrition to trying to double the persistence rate. How? By eliciting worry and guilt within adolescents, already highly anxious, about letting God down: "God called you, and you are thinking of quitting on him?" It suddenly became much harder to leave/quit.

In the junior year and beyond (even to some degree in the freshman and sophomore years), leaving the seminary was far easier for the boy or young man who could frame the departure, for himself and others, as a matter of no longer wishing to become a priest. This moved the issue into the arena of discernment rather than unhappiness with the seminary experience.

I was worried about hurting my parents. So I told them that I had decided that another profession suited me better than being a priest. I wanted to be a lawyer. And I channeled JFK and said that maybe someday I could help people as a politician. I went from maybe being the pope to maybe being the president. They were fine with that, and I guess I said it as much for myself as for them. (Alumnus, St. Pius X Seminary)

Discernment that a calling to the priesthood did not exist also served to neutralize the suggestion that perhaps the seminarian might sample another institution and better assess his potential for the clergy. Though changing institutions was uncommon, most interviewees recalled people in their class who had transferred to or from another seminary. One interviewee who had done so and had decided after college to leave ultimately discerned both his interests and the potential of the priesthood to address them:

I realized that I wanted to pursue social justice, like Daniel Berrigan. But I also knew that the church did not want priests like Berrigan. And, forgetting about the sacraments and mass, I figured out that anything I wanted to do in the realm of social justice, I could do without being a priest. I didn't need to be a priest to do good things or help people or change society. (Former seminarian from New Orleans)

Seminarians who otherwise could not get off the dime regarding staying or leaving often invoked the possible-return option: "I need a time-out; I can always go back after I have had a chance to reflect and get my head clear." This tended to appease family members who were upset by the decision to leave (or to infuriate those who had not wanted their son in the seminary in the first place [Hendrickson, 1983:311]), but it also addressed a more personal need. We would expect time in the seminary to produce a sense of direction ("I've discerned that I do [or do not] want to become a priest.") and, thus, a sense of peace with a decision. In fact, the greater the time in, the higher the levels of indecision and anxiety and the more elusive the sense of peace. In part, this reflected the magnitude of the notion of being "called"; in part, it reflected risking investments (bets and side bets). The longer-term minor seminarian was apt to employ the "possible-return" crutch to ease his qualms about breaking his engagement to the church. And he could point to examples. Every seminary contained individuals (though not many) who had left and then returned for another shot (Howard, 2013). A trial separation, not a break up.

Novitiate Stress Test

During the minor-seminary boom years, lying between high-school and college seminaries, *novitiates* were employed by religious orders (though not by dioceses) to prepare and to evaluate the potential of young men beyond high-school age to join the sponsoring order (e.g., the Jesuits, the Franciscans). They still operate widely today as places and processes by which individual aspirants to the priesthood seek to discern whether or not a particular brand of religious life suits them, and religious orders, in turn, seek to discern whether particular aspirants suit them.[56] The novitiate experience normally lasts a year, perhaps two, before the individual is moved forward into more productive, though still evaluative, assignments and ultimately to final vows as a member of his religious order.

---

[56] Novitiate training also occurs within most women's religious orders as well those for men seeking to be brothers rather than priests. The structure and culture of the novitiate are highly similar to those of the religious orders of priests.

Novitiates during the boom era were icy ponds of sorts, and time spent in them was in many ways a dunking. Like the minor seminary, the novitiate sorted, tested, and cultivated young men – usually between eighteen and twenty-two years of age but sometimes older – for a religious order's college- and major-seminary experiences. They were far more intense than the minor seminary, they sped up what normally took years in a high-school seminary to accomplish, and they drove or kicked out a much higher percentage of their aspirants than did the standard seminary. To enter a novitiate was to enter a minor-seminary boot camp, and novitiate stories tended often to be stories of leaving the seminary.

"Boot camp" conveys notions of control, indoctrination, containment, segregation, objectification, survival, and stress-testing of individuals. It is designed to produce absolute commitment, loyalty, and responsiveness to the collectivity among those seeking membership. We know boot camps primarily as institutions of military induction and readiness-training structured to produce team-oriented soldiers prepared mentally and physically to respond immediately and positively to their superiors' commands, no questions asked and with pride in the organization and the endeavor.

Not all boot-camp inductees survive their test, even at the most basic levels. This is all-the-more true of those seeking to join more elite squadrons. The patch awarded to those who succeed announces to the world that these soldiers are special, individuals who can be counted on, members of a team who have excelled and will continue to excel no matter the level of pressure.

Four of this study's interviewees entered a novitiate immediately after high school; three sought to be Jesuits, one sought membership in the Redemptorist order. (Another interviewee entered the Claretian order as a freshman in high school but left the seminary long before proceeding to the novitiate.) Then, as now, members of religious orders, from novitiate onward, focused upon the order;

their notion of membership included priesthood but was more. As one former Jesuit novice put it:

> *The difference between being a priest and being a Jesuit is like the difference between having a doctorate and earning a Ph.D. from an elite university. The former is generic; the latter is special. Your identity rests with the order. No Jesuit says, "I am a priest." He says, I am a Jesuit priest." No former Jesuit says, "I used to be a priest." He always says, "I used to be a Jesuit."*
> (Former Jesuit seminarian from New Orleans)

The heart of a religious order is its sense of community, its particular value set, and its mission. Each has its own history, and each possesses its own vision of where it wants to be and to go. No religious order is wholly impractical – the compelling notions of both membership size and financial solvency demand attention and, often, adjustments. These factors (community spirit, values, mission, history, and practicality) comprise the fraternity that the priest-to-be novice aspires to join. Religious orders are highly selective. Most novitiates plunge the novice into a program that tests mental and even physical limits, one that demands ongoing and deep introspection and increasing movement toward and commitment to spirituality (see, for example, Capuchin Franciscans, 2018; Cistercian Abbey, 2018).

The product of the novitiate and the remaining elements of formation and discernment on the road to final vows, creates in the novice a sense of approach to all things spiritual and intellectual – the Dominican way, the Maryknoll way, the Franciscan way. It is a cultural and cognitive set that affects the novice, whether he remains or stays, for the rest of his life. A former novice-interviewee noted that, despite his relatively short tenure in the novitiate, "There will never be another way for me to define myself."

The novitiate of the era of the minor-seminary boom (heyday and crash, 1950-1980) differed from that of today. Some would describe yesterday's version as "tougher" while others would call today's "more sensitive and practical" than the traditional boot camp. Novices during the minor-seminary era also tended to be younger. Many orders had minor seminaries of their own that stewarded their wards toward the novitiate through their emphasis upon the history and culture of the order. Others contracted with dioceses to operate minor seminaries and thus intermingled aspirants to their order with diocesan seminarians; the mix provided further recruitment opportunities. Still others recruited only novices with high-school diplomas (minimally) and focused their seminary education, after novitiate, upon college and theology studies. The average novice was recruited directly out of high school (including diocesan minor seminaries) or soon thereafter.

Few who write or speak of the novitiate of past years have kind words, even when describing it reverentially and defining it as among the most important of their life's experiences.[57] It was a grueling test

---

[57] In the way of perspective, young men who attended major seminaries also rarely offer glowing reports of the experience. Greeley (1986) despised the institution. Fausel (2010) found it an exercise in memorization instead of critical thinking. Hedin (2003) experienced it as excessively rigid and impersonal. Cornwell (2006) felt as if he had been buried alive. Most of the interviewees in this study who progressed to major seminaries similarly found them stultifying and, as one put it, "something you knew you had to get through in order to be a priest; you just kept your head down and moved forward." Their remarks make even clearer the objective of the minor seminary as "containment" rather than "preparation." A St. Pius X Seminary alumnus noted that "The differences between St. Pius X and St. Patrick [major seminary] were startling. At St. Pius X Seminary, we seminarians had a good relationship with the Salvatorian priests and brothers and enjoyed some freedom. ... [At St. Patrick Seminary], I felt I had entered the monastic life. The Sulpician priests were our professors, not our friends. ... [T]he dynamic between students and faculty was neither positive nor helpful...." (Boll, 2017:19).

that included social isolation, no access to news or entertainment media, peer criticism, long silent retreats, physical labor, and complete subordination of every level of existence to the novice master's will. The novitiate sent young men like Paul Hendrickson (1983: 309) to the mines of sorts – with another novice, for a month, he literally was made to dig a trench beneath, and the length of, the chapel, so that it could accommodate the pest exterminator. The experience left him ill with serious digestive problems, and he (who already had spent six years of his adolescence within his order's minor seminary) departed after thirteen months, worrying about the pain his exit would cause his mother. One of this study's interviewees similarly became ill – severe insomnia and weeping sores on his arms and legs – and left after four months. He recalled being told by his novice master that he would face a lifetime of failure were he to depart so early: "I went back to my room and thought about that and went back a few hours later and told him, 'You guys are nuts; you don't know what you're talking about; I'm out of here.'" He had broken free, and that is the topic considered in the next chapter.

References

Anello, Robert L. 2018. *Minor Setback or Major Disaster? The Rise and Demise of Minor Seminaries in the United States, 1958-1983.* St. Louis MO: EnRoute Books.

Bazzett, Timothy. 2010. *Reed City Boy.* Reed City MI: Rathole Books.

Boll, John E. 2017. "Father John Eugene Boll." *Sacramento Diocesan Archives* (https://www.scd.org/sites/default/files/2017-06/Vol_3_No_18).

Bowman, Jim. 2012. *Company Man: My Jesuit Life, 1950 – 1968.* Chicago: Little Man Press.

Capuchin Franciscans. 2018. *www.capuchins.org/novitiate.*

Cistercian Abbey. 2018. *www.cistercian.org/abbey/vocations/novitiate.*

Cornwell, John. 2006. *Seminary Boy: A Memoir.* New York: Doubleday.

Fausel, Donald F. 2010. *From Blind Obedience to a Responsible Faith.* Bloomington IN: iUniverse.

Greeley, Andrew M. 1986. *Confessions of a Parish Priest: An Autobiography*. New York: Simon & Schuster.

Hedin, Raymond. 2003. *Married to the Church (Updated Edition)*. Bloomington: Indiana University Press.

Hendrickson, Paul. 1983. *Seminary: A Search*. New York: Summit Books.

Hinsvark, John. Nd. "Remembering St. Joseph's Seminary." www. *stjosephscollege.org/memoirs*.

Howard, Ted. 2013. *Our Seminary Years: 1956–1964*. https://www.mixbook. com/photo-books/family/our-seminary-years-1956-1964-9395897.

Lee, James L. 1969a. "Toward a Model of Vocational Persistence among Seminarians. Part I." *National Catholic Guidance Conference Journal* 13: 18-29.

_____1969b. "Toward a Model of Vocational Persistence among Seminarians. Part II." *National Catholic Guidance Conference Journal* 14: 33-43.

_____1970. "Toward a Model of Vocational Persistence among Seminarians. Part III." *National Catholic Guidance Conference Journal* 14: 104-111.

Murray, J. Richard. 2012. *Seen and Unseen Worlds: Private Memoirs of a Former Jesuit*. Lanham MD: Hamilton Books.

Queenan, Joe. 2013. "Homesickness: A Holiday Primer." *CNN (www. cnn.com/travel)* (December 22).

Rakowsky, Alex J. 1965. "Study of Junior College Seminarians on the Edwards Personal Preference Schedule." Masters Theses (Loyola University, Chicago). Paper 2029. *http:ecommons.luc.edu*.

Schlesinger, Susana J. 1966. "Motivational Patterns of Minor Seminarians." Masters Theses (Loyola University, Chicago). Paper 2205. *http:ecommons.luc.edu*.

Thomas, Clarence. 2007. *My Grandfather's Son: A Memoir*. New York: HarperCollins.

Treisman, Deborah. 2018. "John L'Heureux on his Time as a Jesuit Novice." *The New Yorker* (https://www.newyorker.com/books/this-week -in-fiction/fiction-this-week-john-lheureux-2018-05-21).

Vautier, Dominic. 2014. "Seminary Memories – 1956-57." *www. ses4legacyfullessays, wordpress.com*.

Wall, Bill. 1999. *A Day in My Life at St. Joseph's College (Seminary), 1958*. www.stjosephscollege.org/memoirs_bill-wall-day.html.

CHAPTER ELEVEN

Breaking Free

General patterns notwithstanding, every former student who left the minor seminary tells a somewhat different story about his decision, the process by which the departure was accomplished, the hurdles in its path. Parental sensibilities stood out as important among interviewees, and rarely was the potential defector ignorant of where a parent would stand on the notion of flight. Beyond that, the many variables in the mix were personally rooted, even more so than regarding entry into the seminary, and the way out was less through a door than through a tunnel filled with twists and switch-backs.

Searching for a Door

It was one thing to want to leave, and quite another to accomplish it. In some ways, parents always stood by the door of the seminary. The question was whether they would help or hinder the departure of the seminarian, hold the door open or press against it. Many parents had difficulty with their son's decision to leave, not unlike the parents of a son who had broken an engagement with a fiancé whom they had come to love. Paul Hendrickson (1983: 41), for example, returned to a mother who tried to be supportive but clearly was grieving. Clarence Thomas (2003: 44) found himself unwelcome in the home of his grandfather, the man who had reared him:

> *[H]e reminded me of my promise not to quit. I told him that he didn't understand what I was going through and that I simply could not stick it out. None of it meant a thing .... "You've let me down," he said.*

Some parents helped their sons identify a very clear path out:

When I finished high school, I wasn't sure about continuing. So my dad told me that it was time to get a job and earn some money. If I wanted to go on to college or stay in the seminary, I had to start paying my own way. That made the decision easier for me. I did not go to college or stay in the sem. I started working construction and made good money. (Former seminarian from Reno)

Supportive parents smoothed the transition immensely:

I took [my roman collar] off at home in the presence of Mum. ... [She said,] "It was never you." Standing in front of the mirror she tried the collar and black stock around her own neck. ... In a Dublin brogue she cried: "Y'are all sinners! And y'are all goin' ter hell!" We burst out laughing. (Cornwell, 2006: 306)

Sophomore year [of college], I discussed it with my family. I told them that I did not want to do it anymore. They were fine with it. They said that I could do whatever I liked. I said I wanted to explain, and they said, "You don't have to." One of the greatest

*gifts my parents ever gave me was that they respected my deci-
sion. They helped me out financially so that I could go to a Catholic university and not worry about losing any credits. They
were great.* (Former seminarian from San Diego)

*[My parents] were happy to have me home. They did not oppose
me going in. But, my mom, especially, maybe from day one,
maybe even before, she knew that I was miserable in the seminary, and she was just counting the days until I came home.*
(Former seminarian from Minnesota)

Yet, decisions to leave or to remain in the seminary were governed by more than degree of parental support. While it is true that
any of us simply could have walked away at any time, the fact is
that many of us did not, even those with supportive parents. Leaving was difficult and complicated for many reasons,[58] and this was
precisely what made each seminarian's struggle unique, personal,
and human. We conclude Part III of this book with a look at four
seminarians searching for a way out.

Trouble Dismounting

The number of times that Curt wanted to leave the minor seminary
equaled, minimally, the number of times that his parents drove him

---

[58] For many seminarians, finances entered the picture. On the one hand,
seminary tuition often stressed the family's economic situation, and the seminarian did not want to prolong this. On the other, leaving also raised the
specter of parents having wasted their money, and the seminarian thus did
not want to depart without a sense of certainty. Beyond this, two interviewees from the same diocese, one who left to join an order and another who left
after advancing to major seminary, recalled being asked by their bishop to
repay the diocese's financial investment in their education. (Neither did so.)

there (including the day he entered in 1965). His was the classic good-boy entry. He had made the mistake (if six-year-olds can make such mistakes) of telling his teacher and the other kids in the first grade that he was going to be a priest when he grew up. His mother was thrilled with the news. She saddled the horse and hopped on quickly, pulling Curt up behind her. She never took her eyes off the destination, and he never told her, or anyone else, that he did not want to reach it.

I met Curt for lunch in Sacramento and two times later to interview him. A former priest from Los Angeles now working for the State of California, he was soft-spoken. He recalled being frightened when he first went into the seminary.

> *I knew the whole year in eighth grade that I was not ready for this. The concept was overwhelming. The adjustment to living with a bunch of boys was overwhelming. The discipline was beyond overwhelming. And even though I got good grades, I felt overwhelmed there too. I just hated it there. I mean, I adjusted once I learned the ropes. Things got easier, especially in college when you got your own room to escape to. But I always hated it.*

Curt employed what he called "hiding mode." He stayed in the study hall after hours. He went for walks. He worked on theater projects and hid out in the auditorium work room. He started smoking so he had yet another reason to make himself go walking and even to feel a bit the rebel. What saved him, he believed, was the company of three friends much like him (a "forbidden clique" in the seminary's eyes) and his musical talent. "I played reed instruments and would spend hours, literally, each day practicing, mostly by myself."

Why did he not leave? Simply put, "I was too much a good boy." The first year in the seminary, Curt went as far as the dean's door, his hand raised to knock and to announce that he wanted to go home, but he turned and walked away. "I was afraid of him, and, I guess, even more afraid of disappointing everyone who expected me to become a priest." His mother had built her social identity around her son's vocation. During the summers, when Curt hoped to get a "normal job like a normal kid," she always managed to arrange work for him – at the Catholic hospital, at the offices of the diocese – that reinforced his future status.

> *The ladies there loved me. I was going to be a priest. And they became part of the group that I did not want to disappoint. Along with the people in my parish, the priests at my church, the priests in the seminary. Name it. Even in major seminary, other guys would say to me, "If you don't make it, I know I won't."*

Curt told me that when he finished his minor seminary studies, he obtained permission to pursue a college degree at a secular university, though, while in attendance, he lived at a nearby abbey. When he finished his degree two years later, he did not wish to go into the major seminary, but did so anyway, planning to stay for only about three months; "That way, no one could say I didn't try." Instead, he found that he liked the academic side of the institution, studies in philosophy and theology, the feeling that he was really doing graduate work. It was only when he faced the actual prospect of ordination as a deacon that he truly convinced himself to leave.

> *I was miserable and scared. I knew that someday I wanted a real relationship with another person, and I could not have that as a priest. Even my confessor saw how miserable I was and advised me to take some time off. So I left, but not before telling my mother. I remember driving to her house late one stormy night, with thunder, like in a movie. I rang the doorbell, and my*

*mother came to the door and said, "I was sort of expecting you."
When I told her what I was going to do, the first thing she said
was, "This has always been your decision, Curtis. Whatever you
want is what you should do."*

The escape lasted but a year. "I was lonely and just as miserable
outside. I had no friends and no social skills. I had no work skills.
Seminary training made you see yourself as unable to function as
anything but a priest." Twelve years down the seminary trail, his
fiancé said, "Okay, Curt, it's time to tie the knot for real." He was
ordained and married to the church. Ten years later, life in a love-
less marriage became unbearable, and Curt told his bishop that he
was filing for divorce. This time, he did not go back.

Confederates

Minor seminarians did not share their thoughts of leaving the
institution with many. Yet, when the possibility was broached, one
young man's less-than-clear intention to depart sometimes produced in his confidant not only understanding and support but
mutual consideration of flight (Miles, 2012). The two effectively
would prop each other up and provide the resolve necessary for
their departure. One of my interviewees was involved in just such
a dynamic.

A friend introduced me to Mark, a successful attorney living
in Chicago. Mark originally hailed from the far north of Wisconsin and entered a diocesan seminary in 1960. An only child, very
likeable, he was at once intense and good humored. He had never
been happy as a seminarian, at least outside the better moments.
But, as did most seminarians, he faced obstacles to departure, some
internal and others external. He came from a good Catholic family
and, by his own assessment, was a boy who sought to please. He

was also very aware of the cost of the seminary borne by his parents, and that the seminary tuition had worked a hardship on them. He did not want them to feel that they had spent their money unwisely though he believed they had.

Mark got on well with his classmates and was good friends especially with those who came from the same part of the state as he. He achieved academically and enjoyed sports and music. He was considered a leader of both his class and, as he grew older, the school more generally. Yet, as he put it, "Every time I returned from a break, every time we turned down the road to the seminary, I got this feeling in the pit of my stomach. I felt like a caged animal."

In his interview with me, Mark recalled sitting in the library with one of his closest friends, also from northern Wisconsin, midway through his junior year. No one else was in the room. "More or less out of nowhere, I said, 'I don't want to be here; I'm leaving.' And Bob looked right back at me and said, 'Me too.'" But the hook was deep in each of them. Mark especially felt ensnared by the seminary faculty's persistent appeal to heed God's call, to stay faithful to vocation, in many ways to frame a decision to leave as seriously consequential.

> We hated the notion of 'quitter.' You could leave any time, sure, but people would look at you like you were a quitter. We wanted to do things – leave – on our own terms. I also hated the unfairness of everything and being taken for granted. I played by all the rules and got little. Others with 'potential' broke the rules but got special treatment so they wouldn't leave.

The door to leaving was, for Mark and Bob, the natural break offered by high school completion which meant that they had a year and a half to ponder the decision. The same year and a half produced a sense of quiet conspiracy, the look exchanged when someone acted the fool or the seminary disciplinarian yelled at everyone yet again. Peer discussions of moving on to the major seminary brought the look, as did faculty warnings to resist temptation during the summer break. Both students became formal school leaders during their senior year, appointed by the administration to responsible student offices charged with maintenance of the campus and with assuring order among the students. Insider talk between faculty members and student leadership also evoked the look: "They haven't got a clue what we plan to do."

Seminarians rarely felt in control of anything. At some point during his senior year, Mark began formulating not simply an exit plan but a statement, *his* statement, of capacity to affect the very institution that had controlled him so extensively.

> *I thought, I'm doing this my way. I'm ... going to milk this for everything I can. Both of us – me and Bob – could tough it out no sweat. I mean, we were class prefects, class presidents, athletes. We did everything. We had the keys to the place. We became an internal gang, running the place. I had a prisoner mentality. I had to kiss up to the guards, but I was going to do things my way and make sure I took care of myself.*

He recruited into the intrigue two more classmates, both from the same part of the state as were Bob and he. These seminarians had told him that they also were fairly sure they would not continue on after senior year. Mark convinced them to hold the secret close (which meant not sharing it with the faculty members or any other students) and then to join Bob and him in revealing it during their final few days of school, when everyone's focus was upon graduation. With all conspirators on board, no individual could turn back; to reverse course was to reverse loyalties.

The four seminarians indeed stuck to the bargain and announced their intention to depart just days before graduation. Mark hoped the plan to leave jointly would shake up the seminary faculty as could little else: four well-known and respected students, each viewed as a credible candidate for the priesthood, suddenly gone. In his view, the message produced the desired effect: "When we told them at the end, they were shocked. We broke their hearts. They couldn't believe it. ...We left on our own terms." He said this with a certain teeth-clenched pride but also with a look of sadness, all these years later, still trying to figure out how and why any of this had happened.

Breaking Point

Another former seminarian introduced me to Stephen, in New Orleans for a business conference. We spent an afternoon together talking about our pasts and what created them. From Seattle, Stephen was an intense and politically conservative businessman, financially secure, crazy about football, politics, and history. He had entered the Jesuit novitiate in 1968 after spending his high school years in a diocesan minor seminary. He had grown up a good Catholic boy, originally attracted to the priesthood because, as he put it, "I bought the party line: people would be happy and be saved when they found God through Catholicism, and priests helped them do that." His mother gladly supported her son in his calling; his father was less enthused but did not openly oppose his decision.

Stephen had no regrets about his days in the minor seminary. He was "neither miserable nor happy." He enjoyed the camaraderie and, based on conversations during school breaks with friends in his old neighborhood, realized that he was receiving a good education. His primary difficulty rested with his "obsession" with members of the opposite sex, about whom he knew practically nothing.

I was prohibited from interacting with girls. I was petrified of them. I watched them in their bathing suits at the pool during the summer, and it made me crazy. My hormones had kicked in big time. I spent a lot of time in the confessional seeking forgiveness for my "impure thoughts."

During his senior year, Stephen began to consider joining the Jesuits. He had grown up in a Jesuit parish and admired the priests he knew there. In his view, if he was to be a priest, he wanted to join the "very best." A few students in classes ahead of him had transferred to the Jesuit novitiate after high school or college. During the Christmas holidays he was interviewed and screened for psychological traits by the Jesuits for half a day and, "I must have passed since they said yes." He was supported in the impending transfer by his mother who "appreciated the boost in status." He waited until late in the school year to announce his intention to peers and faculty because he had heard that the faculty "had not been happy with the guys who jumped ship to the Jesuits before me. I didn't understand the financial implications of the diocese's investment in my education."

As he did concerning his time in the minor seminary, Stephen had no regrets about his short stint with the Jesuits; it lasted but three months. The novitiate was incredibly difficult, "the most challenging thing I ever did for sure, but I also grew there, spiritually and as a young adult with a better sense of how to choose paths in life." The first month for novices was directed toward learning the ropes of the Jesuit novitiate and the Jesuits more generally. The second month was given over to manual labor on the nearby farm that the order operated as a revenue stream. Stephen recalled this as a period in which "I was in the best shape physically that I've ever been in." The third month "got serious." Novices engaged in a thirty-day retreat marked by silence and spiritual reading. "All you thought about was who you were spiritually and how you related to God and whether God was actually calling you to be a Jesuit."

Not uncommonly, the month-long retreat was the deal-breaker for aspirants to the order. Many, often most, were only eighteen or nineteen years of age, trying to wrestle with concepts that were decidedly more adult than they. Stephen began thinking that life within the Jesuits was not for him. Among the difficulties he encountered in his spiritual journey were *flagella et catenae*, Latin for "whips and chains."[59]

A few weeks into novitiate, we all got little cardboard boxes, and in them were these little wire bracelets with barbs. You were supposed to wear them on your ankles or thighs and on your wrists under your cassock. You know, "mortification of the flesh." There was also a little whip, about two feet long, kind of like the cord from a venetian blind, with knots tied in it. You were supposed to whip yourself over your shoulders with it, you know, to atone for your sins. It was all supposed to be symbolic, but it was also serious. We were housed in a dormitory but each of us had a private cubicle with walls part way to the ceiling, so you could hear everything. At 9:00 each night, the lights would flicker, and that meant that we had to take off our cassocks and hang them on the wall in the shape of an M, for Mary. Then the lights would flicker again and that meant it was time for "flagellatio" (whipping). All over the dormitory, you'd hear "wheet,

---

[59] The subject of whips and chains was mentioned as well during my interviews with two other former Jesuit seminarians. One had been horrified by "how medieval it was" and threatened to leave the novitiate. He was appeased by the novice master who told him that it was strictly up to him whether or not to engage in their use. The other seminarian-interviewee saw the whole thing as "no big deal." See also Bowman (2012) and Murray (2012).

wheet, wheet," as all these guys started hitting their backs with their little whips. I couldn't take it. I'd dive into bed and bury my face in my pillow so no one could hear me laughing.

Just as Stephen was concluding that the novitiate was not right for him, the decision to leave was taken from his hands.

I got in trouble. Novices were in the program for two years before they advanced to the juniorate class, third- and fourth-year guys. We never saw those guys except at dinner which was always in silence while a juniorate guy read to us from some spiritual book. Toward the end of dinner, two guys from the juniorate would get up and go to the middle of the room and lie down prostrate. Then they'd start yelling in staccato at the top of their lungs all the sins they'd committed in the past. They were both yelling at once, so you couldn't understand them. It was like they were speaking in tongues at a Pentecostal service. And I couldn't stop laughing! I remember once losing it while looking down at my bowl of ice cream. I was laughing like a hyena. After dinner, another novice said, "[The Novice] Master wants to see you." Master suggested that it would be better for me to go to college and then think again about joining the Jesuits. I couldn't argue with that. That was it. ...My vocation ended when I could not stop laughing.

Second Chance

And then there is my own exit story – the boy/young man who, after years of trying to find the door out of the seminary, mysteriously froze when it was left unguarded. Having missed his chance to depart after high school, he waited two more years before walking away.

To this day, when people ask me why I returned to St. Pius X after high school, I cannot articulate well to myself, let alone to them, my reasons. Graduation from high school in 1965 was the natural break by which I could have ended my seminary career. I had sought to leave each summer prior, only to be checkmated by my mother who now was having a very nice summer, thank you, when, for the first time, her son did not declare his wish to change life course. Why did I not bolt after senior year? I cannot blame that one on Mom.

Part of the non-decision – I did not "decide" to return; I simply flowed back – rested with the vocation "hook." Most of my classmates and I still conceived of vocation more in terms of "seminary" than of "priesthood." Our primary attachment was to an institution in which we felt comfortable even while unhappy and to peers who constituted our major reference group. It was hard to imagine proactively breaking those bonds even as we watched them disintegrating as we grew older. On the one hand, becoming a priest remained too distant and fuzzy an objective to affect us psychologically; we still did not know what priests did beyond saying mass and hearing confessions though we now saw them as decidedly human. On the other hand, it was hard to shake the sense (for most of us, at least a decade old) that we were *supposed* to be there, hiking the arduous sacerdotal trail. Our fear and its accompanying pain and angst resided in that ambiguous and slippery notion of "calling." I personally could not grasp it no matter how I pushed myself. Leaving that which I could neither appreciate nor articulate should have been easy. Instead, for seminarians like me, with the hook set deep in my gut, the notion of departure was daunting, going well beyond worry over letting down my mom.

Looking back, I sense three factors that weighed against my leaving after high school. First, I had had a very enjoyable senior year. I had done well academically. I had had a good year in athletics, and that always was the flame that drew the moth in me. I had enjoyed the theater projects of which I had been a part. Second, the fact that St. Pius was a six-year institution placed me in the position of having to decide about "leaving" as opposed to "not continuing" (though others seemed less bothered by the distinction). Were the next step to have been movement to a new institution (as happened two years later), rather than returning to St. Pius for college studies, I likely would have decided "not to continue." Third, no one explained to seminarians the importance and process of admission to college in the outside world; that was in no way a seminary's objective. It did not occur to me to explore non-seminary options, even though my secular friends were stressing over which college to attend.

More important than the above factors, however, was my failure to anticipate the grand defection that occurred within my class the summer after high school. Eight classmates, each well-liked and respected, decided to make their dash for freedom. I knew beforehand only about two. My best friend, Ethan, had shared with me early in senior year that this would be his last hurrah. He signaled his intent by sleeping in (i.e., missing mass) more mornings than not, which was as close to publicly broadcasting an intention to bolt as could be made in a minor seminary. Another friend and basketball chum, Harmon, was headed to a religious order which, at the time, seemed to me tantamount to "leaving." I knew I'd miss them, but it never occurred to me that six other of my classmates, guys with whom, in so many senses, I had grown up, were headed over the hill. In the way of survival within the institution, none had suggested as much. One classmate-interviewee who also stayed on noted similarly that he had "not been part of that conversation":

That series of guys leaving really shook me. The only world that I knew was the seminary world, and I didn't have a clue. ...

These were guys that I not only felt close to, but it was special.
When they left, it shook me right down to my shoes. It rattled
me so badly that I spent the summer after senior year just sort of
shell-shocked.

We were stunned when we realized toward the end of summer
that our "class" truly existed no more; we had shifted from actual to
nominal cohort. Neither the above interviewee nor I likely would
have continued had we seen this coming or better understood its
impact. Instead, we'd have been asking ourselves what was wrong
with us, which is precisely what we did when we returned in the
fall.

Two more long-time classmates left college studies within a
month after classes resumed, and two more would depart at year's
end. I was close to jumping ship but stayed, primarily because we
had been joined by seven more classmates recruited as "late vocations" (see Chapter Seven). Our new classmates differed from us.
They were essentially good boys, to be sure, but they were older and
had been in and of the world. They were fun at the same time that
they were serious about seminary life. A few were good athletes
and brought some pride back to the class team. Again, we had a
sense of cohesion, almost of cohort. I had new friends to offset, if
not to replace, those I had lost. That said, I knew by mid-year that
I was destined to depart. I simply could not shake my blues and, in
the end, the blues overwhelmed the worries about disappointing.
Exactly as did my classmate-interviewee, I planned "not to continue" after the next natural break, completion of the two-year college curriculum. He recalled:

After senior year, I went back to Pius because I was scared shit-
less. I realized that I knew nothing but seminary life, but that
meant I had no idea how or when I should move into the world

and what I would do. So I traveled all over the U.S. It became a trek into the world I needed to discover. By the time I got back, I knew I was not going to go on after sophomore year [of college]. I had two years to figure out a plan. All I really needed to do was to make sure I got good grades, look around for somebody who was going to take my credits, and I was gone.

At the end of my first year of college, I borrowed several university catalogs from a neighbor, and wrote for application materials – a small act but incredibly liberating. My mother almost certainly saw the responses appear in the mailbox, so I did not have to drop any immediate hints. Early in the fall, once back at Pius, I told her that, after the year was done, I did not plan to go on to the major seminary, and that I was fairly certain that I did not want to become a priest, though, of course, "I could always go back in." The major seminary, I explained, was old, cold, dark, and drab. I had not detected during my visit there any sense of happiness among the guys I knew. (Further, I lamented, "It does not even have a gym, for God's sake!") I explained that, instead, I wanted to go to a regular college, to get a better sense of the world and my options within it. She handled it well and actually talked about the logistics of going to college, though without ever saying she supported my decision. Perhaps she believed that she had given *her* vocation the best shot she could.

During my last year at St. Pius, knowing as I did that I was on the way out, I had problems pleasing people. I was asked by the faculty to assume the office of general prefect. The assignment was considered an honor. The general prefect was tasked with ensuring student discipline and communication between students and faculty, and leadership qualities were assumed. I did not want the job; I wanted to cruise below the radar for the year. But I said yes – seminarians acceded to requests from their leaders (just as priests would be expected to do) – because saying no was effectively to out myself, hardly staying under the radar. Now in the spotlight, I seemed to step into difficulty. One faculty member complained that I was "too aggressive" in sports activities – he was correct, I suspect. Heretofore recognized for keeping my cool in such situations, I recall physically throwing a classmate out of my room when he entered to complain about a work assignment. I also began to push back against some of the less mature priests when they said less-than-mature things, and they in turn complained. Prefect and bad attitude did not go well together.

The topper came early in the semester when I disobeyed a direct order from the Dean of College Students, Father Anthony. The issue was pudding! (Yes, straight out of a Dickens novel, pudding.) At dinner one evening, we were served an awful dessert that no one was eating. Anthony chewed us out, invoking the rough equivalent of reference to children starving in China. Most of the guys held their noses and ate their pudding. I did not. Joking, one of my friends told the dean that I was not doing as directed. Anthony came straight to me and reiterated the command, smiling, sure I'd eat this mess if directly ordered. I looked calmly into his eyes and said, "No Father, I am not going to eat that pudding." The room grew suddenly very quiet. No one, least of all the general prefect, publicly defied his dean. "To my office. Now!" a red-faced Anthony bellowed. Once there, he was fairly kind. "Why are you acting so contrary lately? Why didn't you just eat the stupid pudding? Now I've got to come up with some kind of punishment." He offered three afternoons of painting dorm rooms, and I said fine. He could not figure out what was happening to his prefect, and it was too early to tell him.

I told three good friends later that semester that I was on the way out. The seminary faculty was alerted by the front office that I had asked that my transcripts be forwarded to several colleges.

This triggered an immediate visit from my assigned confessor, a perfectly nice guy with whom I had never before exchanged more than a greeting in the hallway. I told him simply, no thanks. The rector called my pastor, and one night I heard a knock on my door. In walked a priest from my parish, the same gentle soul who had comforted me during my earlier efforts to defect, asking if I had time to talk. I did but told him it would be to no avail. Desperation begets determination; having crossed the line, I no longer worried about pleasing people.

One more task remained: informing my classmates. That became easy when, late in the spring, we were invited into a room to be fitted for the cassocks we were to wear the next year at major seminary. Sacerdotal garb! Able at last to don the priestly uniform, some of the guys were positively giddy. For others, the moment was more sobering. Two of those being fitted already had made up their minds not to move on but had told no one. I was the only one to pass up the fitting room, and that amounted to a very clear declaration. A few classmates stopped by my room later to say that they would miss me. Nobody seemed surprised. Then again, by that point in our seminary career, departures rarely surprised anyone.

At commencement, I received my certificate of completion and listened to speeches about the importance of priestly vocations for the future of the church. I left quietly, scared of the world from which I had been shielded nearly to the point of ignorance. I had spent my adolescence, six years of prime time, engaged to the church, well protected from other suitors. But I also felt hopeful, more than simply relieved, about the prospect of being ordinary, reentering the world, heading off to college. I knew I would never wear a cassock, and this occasioned within me no sadness or doubt. To the contrary, it was my turn to feel giddy.

References

Bowman, Jim. 2012. *Company Man: My Jesuit Life, 1950 – 1968.* Chicago: Little Man Press.

Cornwell, John. 2006. *Seminary Boy: A Memoir.* New York: Doubleday.

Hendrickson, Paul. 1983. *Seminary: A Search.* New York: Summit Books.

Miles, Vincent J. 2012. *Boys of the Cloth: The Accidental Role of Church Reforms in Causing and Curbing Abuse by Priests.* Lanham, MD: Hamilton Books.

Murray, J. Richard. 2012. *Seen and Unseen Worlds: Private Memoirs of a Former Jesuit.* Lanham MD: Hamilton Books.

Thomas, Clarence. 2007. *My Grandfather's Son: A Memoir.* New York: HarperCollins.

PART V

Changing Habits

CHAPTER TWELVE

Makeover

A year had passed since I had left St. Pius X
Seminary. I was having lunch in the university cafeteria during the fall when I spotted a
familiar face. Jack had been in the class behind me at Pius,
a good guy, gregarious, like so many of us. I had not seen
him since my own departure. He was not quite twenty.
As had I, he had decided against moving forward to the
major seminary after his sixth year at Pius, and now he
was struggling to gain his footing in a school a hundred
times the size of the one we had attended. We ate our lunch
and talked of the old days and old crowd. I asked him what
he had been doing in the four months since his exit. He
hesitated a moment, then said he was going to get married. He had met a young woman, four years his senior,
divorced and the mother of two young children. They had
fun together, and he liked the kids. She wanted to marry,
and he thought that would be fine. He was a little worried
about money, but they could get by while he was in school
on what she made at her job. He said all this with a look of
fear in his eyes, but he was not soliciting my opinion. So I

tucked my own year's-worth of worldly experience back in
my pocket, along with my personal inventory of insecurities
and anxieties, and replied, "Wow. Uh… congratulations,"
thinking all the while, "Jack, you are out of your mind."

Most former seminarians understand the notion of transition; you cannot exit a seminary and expect the smooth and effortless assumption of standard social roles. Most of my interviewees also believe that many of the residual effects of the seminary experience are long-lasting; that is true even of those who successfully placed their seminary memories in a virtually impenetrable box. That's what this book is about, and one of the surprises in conducting the research leading to it has been the willingness of former minor seminarians to talk about their past, seemingly relieved at last to bring the box out of the closet.[60] Decades after exiting the institution, a former seminarian can talk for hours about how he got into the seminary, what it was like in there, how hard it was to get out, how difficult the adjustment once out, and the extent to which he feels tattooed by the experience all these years later. We have covered the first three topics in previous chapters. This chapter and the next examine transition and outcome. Transition is a process with a beginning and an end; outcome is open-ended, changing color and shape as experience and age alter one's viewing lens.

Transition

Minor seminarians were not selected randomly from the universe of Catholic boys thirteen years of age; by definition we were different.

---

[60] One interviewee noted when, responding to his concern that he was "different," I assured him that his seminary- and post seminary-experiences were fairly common among former seminarians: "Yeah, but you have the advantage of having talked to some of them."

By the time we got out, we were, or certainly felt, yet more different, several standard deviations from the mean for guys our age. "Not nuts or anything," as one interviewee put it, "but big-time not normal. I mean, what's normal about having been locked away in a seminary?"

Boys and young men who left the seminary during the 1950s through the 1970s did not exactly enter a foreign world. We had occupied that world as young boys and had been sampling it to one degree or another on trips home during school breaks. But transitioning from observer to participant was complicated. Most of us felt out of sync, like an ex-con so long in the pen that he struggles to count his change at a McDonald's. The initial challenge was blending into the crowd as if we belonged in our new surroundings, hoping no one saw us bump into walls. It did not take long to lose our immediate sense of transparency, the feeling that somehow we had "ex-seminarian" stamped on our foreheads. Beyond that, however, we had no guidebook. An interviewee asked and answered, "How do you become normal, kind of? You keep quiet about your past, and you watch what everyone is doing and try to do it too. Fake it till you make it."

Understandably, the shorter the seminary career, the easier the reentry. Part of the challenge in most cases was readjusting to life with one's parents and pursuing education with "normal" adolescents. Former seminarians still in high school began their new life back in the family home.

After I left Pius, I went to [Catholic] High for my last year of high school. I hated it, and just sort of went flat. I was not doing well. My parents let me transfer to [the local public high school], and that's where I finished high school. They accepted some of the credits that [Catholic] High wouldn't take. And it was a breeze because the competition was less serious and because I needed a

break from all the Catholic pressure. I had a good senior year.
(Alumnus, St. Pius X Seminary)

*[Having left during my freshman year] I went back home and
had no real problems. I returned to junior high with the same
kids I had gone to school with before. In the fall, I moved on
to high school just as if I had done it the usual way.* (Former
seminarian from Los Angeles)

Most exiting seminarians who had finished high school or had
stayed a few years longer, lived at home too, at least until they headed
off to college or to military service.[61] The independence and privilege we had experienced as seminarians no longer prevailed; we were
not "on leave" from our life's mission any more, killing time until
our formal vocational pursuit resumed the next fall. Our everyday
world most of the year as seminarians had been a universe away from
parental scrutiny. Even while at home, we had been elsewhere mentally and emotionally. And our parents had been okay with that; it
was what was supposed to happen when God called your son.

We now occupied a new status, at least somewhat dependent
financially upon our folks, living under their rooves, negotiating
turf and time constraints. Independence no longer was taken
for granted. It now was bargained and usually necessitated overt
acknowledgement of the arrangement by word or deed: "You'll
need to get a summer job." "You can't come home so late in front of
your brothers and sisters." "Who gave you the idea that I'm going

---

[61] The military draft was in effect during the seminary boom era. Seminarians who remained after high school were given a "divinity-student"
exemption. Those who left the seminary and went into college received a
"student deferment." Those who did not were drafted, enlisted, or objected
conscientiously.

to pick up after you?" "Your assignment is to make sure the back yard is kept clean and mowed." "Of course, if you don't like the rules here, you can get an apartment and pay your own way."

My own transition back into the home went smoothly enough. While my old neighborhood buddies already were away at college or were moving into jobs and apartments, I was fine living at home – in so many ways, it was as new to me as living away was to them. My folks treated me as a young adult. This was easy for my dad, I suspect, since he likely was happy to see me done with the seminary. My mother did not *appear* to be grieving my decision to leave, though not a word ever was said about it. In fact, it was as if a huge weight had been lifted from the two of us. Minus the anxiety occasioned by the perpetual "staying or leaving" drama, Mom became someone with whom I could chat easily and someone interested in my life in a positive way. Having once surrendered her son to others, she seemed to worry now about losing me again. When a visiting aunt advised her to tell me to move out unless I cut my hair, my mother responded, "But that's exactly what he'll do, move out."

I worked swing shifts as a janitor at the local Air Force base, and dinner would be waiting for me when I returned home at midnight. And Mom would knock on my door every morning to remind me that I had classes to attend at the local state university. I moved into a new form of cruise control for a while, blending in, enjoying the freedom that went with college life and no worries about room and board. Like most of my interviewees, the part of my new life that I most appreciated was the anonymity; none of the other janitors at work cared to know about my prior situation, and mine was but a face in a huge crowd on my college campus.

The first thing about which most former seminarians who transitioned into college reminisce is the quality of their seminary education. No one pretends that the math and science side of it had been suitable; we had a gaping hole there, even, ironically, regarding symbolic logic. But the arts and letters side of our education was more than adequate. We had read a lot and written a ton. Our study habits rested upon exceptional discipline, and our ability to sit through lectures was envied. Tests did not scare us – at least after the initial set we took. Most former seminarians were, as an interviewee noted, "A-student[s] who never studied." College professors loved students who could write, and we could write.

We now had choices. Our years in the seminary had been years of commands and compliance. Someone else had chosen the courses we would take and when we would take them. In our new world, we could experiment and shift direction. We could leave an academic major and pursue another that piqued our interest. We could build our own class schedule. And we had an array of extracurricular activities from which to select. Scary as it was at first, managing our own time was a much-appreciated luxury.

The employment side presented little challenge as well; we were used to following orders and sticking to the task at hand. Even those who went into the service found themselves better able than most to adjust to boot camp and military life.

I went to basic [training] with a guy I think went to [the same seminary] as you. Albert something. You know him? [I did.] Nothing ruffled the guy. He could sleep standing up, I swear. Every break he just went back to his bunk and lay down until it was time to move to the next exercise. It was effortless for him. (Former GI who later became an acquaintance of the author)

It did not take long out of basic training before I had a pretty easy clerical job, mainly typing and filing and keeping things on track in the office. It was simple. Just keep your mouth shut and do your job. (Former seminarian from Hawaii)

Relationships

The greater challenges in reentry lay in developing social relationships and compensating for the inexperience and immaturity that, by definition, characterized nearly every newly-liberated former seminarian. At least for those of us attending college in larger cities, part of our new social world included former seminarians, and even seminarians at home during breaks, with whom we could compare notes and commiserate a bit. On the one hand, we possessed the near-invisibility that we coveted on campus and, for most, in part-time employment. On the other, we needed something more than the marginal acquaintanceships we were forming with fellow collegians and workers. For some, the link to old buddies slowed the merry-go-round enough to provide steadier footing. For others, the old relationships likely retarded social development somewhat.

Most former seminarians regressed a bit and behaved for a while like high school students. Though good boys at heart, they tended quickly to seek out that which they had been denied. They bought "dumb-ass" cars (an interviewee's terminology; in my case, it was a metallic-blue 1959 Triumph TR-3, a great car on those rare days it was not in the repair shop). They went drinking with new college mates or old neighborhood friends, always risking trouble since they were not yet of legal drinking age. A former seminary classmate found himself expelled from his community college after being caught one night drinking beer on campus with a boyhood pal. Another old friend from seminary high-school days took me to parties given by the college fraternity he hoped to join. Fresh from a far more serious fraternity, the seminary, I could not stomach the notion of having to prove myself worthy to associate with a bunch of back-slappers, but I did like their beer. Beer was available from other sources as well; neither of us joined the fraternity.

Almost to a person, former seminarians point to more personal relationships as the most challenging aspect of reintegration. Among the minority who were homosexual, this involved learning to navigate relationships more serious than simple sexual encounters and, prior to the early 1970s, in many ways still taboo. A former seminarian from San Francisco recalled:

> *I wasn't afraid of guys, of course. I knew guys. I went to school with guys. But all of my sex had been secret sex. Now, here I am in college without a clue about how to have a relationship with another guy or even to have sex without one eye on the door. Being gay was still not [socially] okay, but you could have a "friend." But it was hard to know what to do… with the other parts of a relationship. It was like going through adolescence … you couldn't help it emotionally. I was like a thirteen-year-old, demanding, possessive, easily offended… terrible.*

Among the heterosexual majority, transition into "normal" social roles meant learning to interact with young women. We had skipped the process by which most male adolescents form at least an inkling of what might please or displease females with whom they seek basic interaction, never mind a relationship. Seeking to be "normal" meant addressing hormonal drives and blending in socially through having a girlfriend. If you had not made your mistakes as a high school student, you were bound to make them in college or in the workplace. In either venue, the game now seemed more serious.

> *I was so far behind socially when I started college, it was pathetic. I was desperately afraid of girls. It took me a long time to find myself.* (Former seminarian from San Francisco)

> *I was so immature sexually that I was totally at a loss for how to even talk to girls without having impure thoughts. They had*

been so totally off limits that I didn't know how to interact with them. I had to start my junior year of college [after six years in the minor seminary] learning how to have a healthy dynamic with women – at the end of the '60s! It was hideous. And the first time in my life I ever had a conversation with a black woman was in college. It made me realize that I had had no interaction, no experience, with people of color. (Former seminarian from Texas)

Minor seminarians often projected to external audiences a wisdom and maturity beyond their years. I could do that as well as anyone, but I also knew, even then, that my twenty years of life equated, socially, to roughly fourteen; my six years "away" counted for little in my new world. Absent prior experience, former seminarians felt seriously impaired in their understanding of the rules of the relationship game. Those who survived mistakes tended to close the gap somewhat and to perceive patterns that could be avoided in ensuing relationships. However, many who left after three or more years in the seminary dated the first girl they danced with and married the first girl they dated, in some cases at the business end of the proverbial shotgun.

That's what happened to me. I married the first girl I went with in college. When she said she was pregnant, I was not ready for what it meant other than I knew I was supposed to get married. We were just Catholic kids – but not really kids, I guess – who did as we were told, even though we got into the mess we were in because we did not do as we were told. Neither of us went into the marriage knowing a lot. I was really immature, and my marriage did not work out so well as I grew older and changed. We both changed. I look back and see myself as a boy with a family. (Former seminarian from Chicago)

The summer after leaving the seminary, I realized that there was a difference between flying inconspicuously beneath the social radar and spending Saturday nights watching Lawrence Welk with Mom and Dad. I screwed up my courage and asked a few young women on dates – low risk, easy and innocent stuff, like going to movies – as I had done a few times late in my seminary years. Nothing came of it beyond the practice and the acquisition of skills that the average high-school sophomore already possessed, including how to decipher that a young woman might be interested in going out with you in the first place and then how to survive if she rejected the overture.

As I registered for my college classes in late August, I heard that there were dances on campus every Saturday night. That's where I headed the very next Saturday, and that's where I met Lee. I asked her to dance as soon as she walked in the door; that she was nice-looking was secondary to how awkward I felt standing alone while others danced. Lee was two years my junior, a brand new freshman. She was pleasant, a little shy, and obviously smart. We danced several more times (if you can call what I was doing dancing) and agreed to look for each other at the next dance. To cut to the chase, as easily as that, I had acquired a girlfriend. Search over; normality accomplished.

Not quite. As it happened, I learned soon that Lee was rebounding from a recently broken engagement in high school to a U.S. Airman stationed in Sacramento with whom she was to have spent the rest of her life in rural Mississippi. A few weeks after I met her, she disappeared. When I inquired, her folks directed me to a local health facility where she was recovering from a "breakdown" and severe depression.

Lee greatly appreciated my visits – good boys were supposed to visit, right? Even though my secular friends (though not my old seminary buddies) warned me against it, I did what every good boy would do: "I'll carry your bag even though it weighs two thousand pounds." When she got out two weeks later, we started up again. I had no clue what I was getting into and no opportunity to learn through the dating game. I took myself out of circulation before I understood what circulation was. Aside from classes, work, and the occasional night out with the boys, my social calendar (i.e., weekends) revolved around my relationship with Lee. I did not recognize the pitfalls at play. After all, I felt "normal" and inconspicuous socially – or thought I looked so, anyway. The year went by quickly.

Not surprisingly in hindsight, I began to develop interests and a sense of self as other than a former seminarian in my senior year in college, my second year away from St. Pius X Seminary. I expanded my circle of friends, began to recognize signals of interest from young women, and started to think about going to graduate school away from Sacramento. This did not sit well with Lee who wanted to marry. She complained that her mother felt that I was taking her for granted. I was, though that was not clear to me at the time. I was a sixteen-year-old in a twenty-one-year-old's body, projecting to any and all the worldliness of a twenty-five-year-old – fake it till you make it. Marriage was on my mind about as much as running for Congress. What love was – and was not – was a mystery to me. Lee, a perfectly nice and very smart young woman, had done nothing wrong, other than taking up with a young man who did not understand fully that he had an experience gap to close. The seminary had taught me to ignore my own needs and to ride out my problems; indeed, ever the people-pleaser, I almost acceded to her request to tie the knot. Yet, just as it ultimately had at Pius, time would run out on my ability to ignore the specter of a lifetime commitment. The problem – again – was how to leave without disappointing; I still had not learned that to disappoint was okay.

Clarity and courage came with wider vision, and wider vision came with travel. Seeking both to experience the world and to clear my head regarding my love life, I teamed during the summer with an old friend from the seminary to hitchhike from Sacramento to New York and back. We saw the world and had our adventures. I grew clearer about what I wanted. I returned, broke with Lee, rented an apartment, played the field, and pursued a master's degree. That in turn led to a decision to go east to pursue a doctoral degree. I was no longer transitioning from the seminary to a life in my home-town where people invariably asked me where I had attended high school. I was entering a social environment in which no one knew, or cared in the least, who I was or once was. I was reconfiguring what sociologists refer to as my "master status."

Constructing and Managing Identity

A person's master status represents that individual's primary attri-bute in the eyes of others and, perhaps, in his or her own eyes (Hughes, 1963). It bundles biases and expectations regarding one's beliefs, behavior, social responsibilities, and, potentially, place in multiple social pecking orders. It may enhance or constrain free-dom within the spectrum of social action, may signal respect or its absence, and may structure the roles a person chooses or is com-pelled to assume in social spheres. Master status may involve pres-tige or dishonor. It can be variable in its effects in even the tightest of circles; surgeons generally are accorded significant status, for instance, but the woman who works within this elite professional field may not be granted the respect and authority that her male counterpart receives from audiences external and internal.

Master status may open doors or keep them shut, in the extreme signaling hero or goat. The consigner and the consignee of a master status may not see the world through the same lenses, and conflict may ensue, as it sometimes does, for example, when a younger per-son fails to display the social deference normally accorded elders.

An individual's master status may vary across the multiple social units he or she occupies, and it may change over time. In many instances, master status may be managed or even manipulated by virtue of an individual's ability to hold close the fact of the attribute in question (see, for example, Goffman, 1963; Griffin, 1961).

The master status attached to a former priest or nun can be difficult to outrun. Downey (1988) made the point well when she wrote about a former nun with a Ph.D. who had become a university professor, had been married for fourteen years, and was the mother of four children — in other words, someone very far removed from her convent days. The former nun recalled drinking beer with colleagues when a female among them swore, then "turned around to me and apologized." She later wrote of herself and ex-nuns whom she interviewed:

> *Even if the ex-nun is partially successful in deemphasizing her past identity in terms of her own self-image, she is frequently confronted by other people who remind her that she is an ex-nun ... For non-Catholics, the realization that a woman is an ex-nun frequently arouses bizarre ideas, or at least great curiosity about her former life. ... It is difficult for these ex-nuns to disengage from that previous status in the face of such attention and curiosity about who they used to be. ...As she struggles to be accepted as an ordinary woman in society, she constantly has to disprove the label society gives her* (Ebaugh, 1988: 160, 162).

Similarly, the label "spoiled priest" (a man who left the priesthood, especially one who did so to marry) once commonly impacted social and employment chances and, according to a few interviewees, remains in effect today though to a lesser degree. Whether or not accurate, those interviewees' perceptions of negative outcomes nonetheless shape in part how the men view and present themselves — or are permitted to do so — in certain social arenas.

I am careful who I tell. Maybe "stigma" is too strong, but there definitely is something. When you first take a new job, pretty much everyone knows you used to be a priest – it was on your job application. Non-Catholic [co-workers] sometimes comment that my former priesthood explains why I am such a nice person. After a while, some newer hires don't know about it unless someone mentions it. But in one way or another, it's always there. A few months ago, … [the company where I work] put out a little newsletter that had a section on "Where were they five years ago?" and it told what everyone was doing five years before. They left me off. They didn't know what to do with me. (Former priest from San Francisco)

My wife and I volunteered to work at a booth at a big music festival. After the training session, we went to get pizza with everyone. We were having a conversation with a woman at the table and that led to discussing how many children we have. My wife had four children [from her previous marriage]. The woman asked me how many I had. I said I didn't have any, and she asked how come I didn't have any kids. Rose and I looked at each other like how do we answer this question with someone we don't know? The woman could see there was something there. So she said, "What? There's something wrong with the question? What were you? A priest or something?" We just looked at her and smiled and said yes. She got all embarrassed and walked over and pretended to try to climb over a fence. (Former priest from Chicago)

The question presently is whether or not the status of "former seminarian" has similarly meaningful consequences. Such consequences could be real (as, for example, in situations of overt discrimination) or perceived (as in how the former seminarian senses, perhaps inaccurately, that others view him). Though none experienced overt discrimination or even quantifiable harm stemming from his past, most of the former seminarians in this study (see also Hedin, 2003:4) believed that their years in the seminary, if and when revealed, translated to socially pertinent assumptions about them.

My cousin went to dinner with me and my wife. He's a good friend who we go out to eat with all the time. As the food was being served, he said, "Hey, Father Dave, would you say grace?" He was just joking, but I have to admit that it hurt. I left the seminary forty-five years ago, and he was only nine years old at the time. It was a minor *seminary, for Christ's sake, not the real deal. It was as if everything else I had done all these years took a backseat to who I was as a teenager. You can't get away from it. Like it or not, it is a part of how people who know about my past think of me.* (Former seminarian from New Mexico)

When we first got married, my wife told her brother and sister that I had been in a seminary. I imagine she thought that they should know what there was to know about the new person in the family. But she wanted to respect that I kept that stuff pretty private, so she told them not to let on that they knew. And she didn't tell me she told them. So what we end up with is an almost comical bunch of accidental slips – like when a priest character comes on a TV show, and they all glance at me – and me pretending that I had not noticed them glancing. I should have just told them myself at the beginning. (Former seminarian from New Orleans)

Without doubt, not everyone views his seminarian days as a liability in all ways at all times. Few of my interviewees failed to recall times when they have utilized their former identity as an icebreaker. The most common reference was to the manner in which it made them "more interesting" to women they wished to impress.

Women, yeah, but actually anyone that I wanted to get to know or have them notice me. I got a lot of mileage out of regaling people with tales of my time in the novitiate. They couldn't believe it. They really liked the stuff about the chains and the whips. They'd start asking me all kinds of questions about what it was like in there. (Former Jesuit seminarian from Detroit)

Four interviewees related that they had more than once employed their former-seminarian status to their professional benefit. Two noted that many of their successful former classmates had opened doors for them in the business world, and that this generally required an overt disclosure of their past connection. Another, a former diocesan seminarian who hosted a radio show, referenced it on his posted, public biography though he noted that, in everyday life, he most often told people that he had attended a Catholic boarding school. Still another interviewee, a former Jesuit seminarian whose psychology practice involved counseling both individuals and groups in matters of sexuality, believed that proactively revealing his past created "an immediate safe zone" for his clients: "They saw me as empathetic, a listener, someone they could trust."

Some go a bit further in their disclosures of past studies for the priesthood. A former seminarian from San Francisco, for instance, now a university professor, proactively disclosed his past publicly, describing himself in his campus biographical statement as having "studied for the Catholic priesthood (leaving before the vow of celibacy) .... and [having] long since recovered from spending [my] college years wearing a long black dress." In the yet more public spotlight, Jerry Brown, former governor of California (four terms) and three-time presidential candidate, was consistently identified by the media during his years in office as a former Jesuit seminarian. While it is obvious that, under constant media scrutiny, there was little point in not disclosing his past, Brown's three and a half years in the seminary (1956-1960) created for him an added dimension both in terms of his public image and in the manner in which he approached elements of his work (Green, 2013).

> ... *I spent time, many years, in a seminary, a Jesuit seminary, and the focus there was on theology, philosophy, or what they sometimes say is ontology the nature of being.... Well, a lot of things in politics are very relative and somewhat arbitrary, but when we deal with the environment and the fundamental conditions of nature, that's about as close to theology as I think you can get.* (The Climate Reality Project, 2018, quoting Governor Jerry Brown)

Unlike Jerry Brown, most of the former seminarians whom I interviewed tiptoe around their past, careful not to expose too much, evading or stonewalling if somehow the topic is raised. A casual comment by a guest at a dinner party, for example, prompted my wife, sensitive to such matters for obvious reasons, to ask, "Were you in a seminary?" The guest's discomfort was palpable as he at once answered affirmatively and deflected further inquiry through clearly practiced misdirection. An interviewee in this study described a very similar incident:

> *I was at a business convention in Sacramento and was coming back from dinner with a bunch of people from all over the state. We walked by the [Catholic] cathedral, and I mentioned that I remembered singing there for JFK's memorial mass in November 1963. One of the people with me knew that I did not grow up in Sacramento and said, "What are you talking about? Why*

would you be singing here?" I thought, shit! So I started point-ing to interesting buildings and answering questions that no one had asked and mumbling a lot. Somehow I got them off the subject. (Alumnus, St. Pius X Seminary)

Does prior minor-seminary status *really* matter to others, beyond curiosity – "You mean *you* were going to be a *priest?"* or "What was it like in there?" (In the way of perspective, ask yourself how many people say to the man who went to his neighborhood public high school, "You're kidding, right? You were going to be a *pharmacist?* Wow! What was it like in a school like that?") One interviewee in the present study, now the director of a division within state government, put the assumption of a potentially tan-gible seminary impact (or, certainly, concern about it) in stark relief:

Look, when we run a job-placement ad, if I see on an applicant's resume that he was in a seminary, you bet I'd ask him a lot of pointed questions about it. I remember how fucked up some of the guys – a lot of the guys – were in the sem. [He added, laugh-ing,]… Not you and me, of course.

In fact, only one of the interviewees in this study, and none of the published, first-person accounts pertinent to it, cited a specific, personal instance of career impact of the kind suggested above, and that instance easily could be categorized as curiosity-based:

When I first started graduate school, one of my professors had been on the admissions committee and seen my transcripts. He said to me one time: "Didn't you go to some kind of religious school or ministry school?" I just said yes, for a while. Nothing more. He figured out that I did not want to talk about it, and he let it drop. (Former seminarian from New Orleans)

The career-related concern among most interviewees was more general in nature. For example, though no peer or professor ever said as much, when I entered my doctoral program at the University of Massachusetts, I sensed soon that my prior status *could* affect my situation at least to some degree. The primary elements of a graduate student's identity within the social pecking order were number of years in the program and the prestige of the college he or she had attended, unless, as it happened, that graduate student was a former military officer (in the 1970s, even a former ROTC cadet), an ex-convict, or a current or former seminarian, nun, priest, or minister. Beyond the curiosity factor, the individual's religious past was injected quickly into his or her social profile as if somehow it structured the student's identity as a budding academic. "You'd never expect a former Air Force captain to do so well in theory courses." "Mary Alice just got a job at State U. I wonder how she'll do. It'll be interesting. She's an ex-nun." "Yeah, he wrote a good paper on conflict resolution. He used to be a divinity student at the University of Chicago, and it shows." Few of us with such former lives wanted that prior identity to define who we were presently. We kept our mouths shut.

I experienced the same discomfort as a university faculty member, always concerned that I, and my ideas, would be typed or qualified via reference to my past vocational pursuit. When I later became a university administrator in a collectively-bargained institution, I was yet more careful. Faculty union members viewed themselves as laborers engaged in a war against oppressive, corporate-style management. They played hardball within "the struggle": "Nothing personal, but whatever we can do to damage your credibility, we will do." If ever I was tempted to reveal my (at that time, very distant) past, it was not while under threat of photo-shopped images of me in a Roman collar. As another university administrator who had attended a seminary once told me, "Letting my seminary past get out would be political suicide."

In the above sense, I found plenty of company among interviewees worried about the potential career effects of having studied for the priesthood or, as it is commonly put, having been "almost a priest" (Green, 2013; White, nd.). The concern was focused most often upon *how*, rather than whether, disclosure might influence perceptions of the individual within his chosen profession. That is, no one worried about being blocked from pursuit of a line of work. Instead, the concern centered upon *respect* within professions in which regard for one's ideas and work products was the coin of the realm. As one interviewee expressed it, "There was never any animosity detected, nothing that bad, but," he chuckled and held his thumb and forefinger apart, "there's always that little hint of the pejorative."

If, indeed, the effects of former-seminarian status revolve, or are assumed to revolve, around notions of being accepted or judged solely on the basis of what you now do instead of what you once did, we have come full circle, back to the days immediately following departure from the seminary when all former seminarians wanted, *please*, was to be "normal," just a regular guy. In the coming chapter, we examine the longer-term effects of "former-seminarian" status. How "indelible" (to borrow from church parlance) is the mark on one who, as a boy, *studied to be a priest?*

References

Downey, Maureen. 1988. "Former Nun Writes about 'Becoming an Ex.'" *South Florida Sun-Sentinel* (www.sun-sentinel.com/news/fl-xpm-1988-09-03-8802200543-story.html).

Ebaugh, Helen R. F. 1988. *Becoming an Ex: The Process of Role Exit.* Chicago: University of Chicago Press.

Goffman, Erving. 1963. *Stigma: Notes on the Management of Spoiled Identity.* Englewood Cliffs NJ: Prentice-Hall.

Green, Emily. 2013. "Jerry Brown: Latin Scholar and One-Time Almost Priest." *The Atlantic* (https://www.theatlantic.com/education/archive/2013/12/jerry-brown-latin-scholar-and-one-time-almost-priest/282426/).

Griffin, John H. 1961. *Black Like Me.* New York: Houghton-Mifflin.

Hedin, Raymond. 2003. *Married to the Church (Updated Edition).* Bloomington: Indiana University Press. Page 301

Hughes, Everett C. 1963. "Race Relations and the Sociological Imagination." *American Sociological Review* 28: 879 – 890.

The Climate Reality Project. 2018. "California Gov. Jerry Brown: My Faith Compels Me to Act on Climate." (Https://www. climaterealityproject.org/ blog/california-gov-jerry-brown-my-faith-compels-me-act-climate) (June 18).

White, Leslie. Nd. "6 Celebrities Who Almost Became Priests or Nuns." *Beliefnet* (https://www.beliefnet.com/entertainment/celebrities/6-celebrities-who-almost-became-priests-or-nuns.aspx).

CHAPTER THIRTEEN

Grappling with Ghosts

I *went to dinner a while ago with a bunch of people I grew up with. We've been friends since we were in grade school, all these years, and we see each other a lot. The only break was when I went away to the seminary for high school and when we all went away to [different] college[s] .... So, we're sitting around having drinks and people started talking about a guy they knew in high school – I didn't know him; I was in the sem – who wanted to be a priest. And they were saying how good or bad that would have been. And I realized that they were not looking at me while they were talking about it, you know, like I was somehow related to the story. That's when I realized, at least for that moment, they had forgotten it! Honestly, that's the first time in my life that I felt like people who knew me as a kid did not think of the seminary as a major part of me. I was just an ordinary person. It felt incredible.*
(Former seminarian from Milwaukee)

Somewhere between actual reputational effect and wholly imagined (even paranoia-infused) effect rests the truth about the impact of past-seminarian status. The history of a former minor seminarian's vocational career, at least for those students who remained in the seminary for more than two or three years, is a history of a boy or young man desperately wishing to be like others, even though by definition he was not, and he understood that he was not and that he was not supposed to be. The thrill of a trip to town for any reason, the basketball win over an outside team, the proud wearing of the letter-sweater, the sneaking in of the contraband radio, the singing of rock-'n-roll songs while cruising around with pals in a car during breaks, the beers, the simple afternoon's exemption from wearing a tie, the swearing during ball games – any and all were celebration of a momentary step onto normal turf. The return to confinement and regimen following a holiday break at home, on the one hand much awaited because the seminary held one's best friends, was on the other a step away from what was normal.

Upon leaving the seminary, longer-term former seminarians with whom I spoke transitioned into the standard social milieu more easily as they gained the confidence that their unconventional history was not readily apparent. However, in the course of everyday interaction with others, questions would arise that would lead either to disclosure of the seminary background or to suppression of it.

[When I went to college in the fall after leaving the seminary,] I didn't tell a whole lot of people about [my seminary past]. I saw it as a stigma. I didn't want to be different. I wanted to be like them. I didn't want to explain to them that there were a lot of people in the seminary that I had a really good time with, but there also were a lot a geeks there, and I didn't want to be seen as a geek. And my social skills were not well developed, and

I wanted to ask girls out, and I didn't want them to think I was different. I assumed that there was a style, only one way of doing stuff acceptably, and it didn't involve having been in the seminary. (Alumnus, St. Pius X Seminary)

I wouldn't lie if they asked me straight out where I went to high school. But the object was to fit in, not make myself a pariah. (Former seminarian from Nevada)

Success at identity management came with practice, and the transition into everyday society, one to two years in duration for most interviewees, brought the sense within the former seminarian that he now was somewhat normal and that he could manipulate social cues so as to affect normal status in any given moment.

Did the boys and young men in transition perceive the distance between themselves and "ordinary" people inaccurately? Perhaps to a degree (in the sense of over-estimating difference) but otherwise not. Being sequestered for multiple years in fact is not to be ordinary. Possessing a past known to be different is to be different. Being singled out as a point of curiosity is to be considered uncommon and to *feel* uncommon, the more so for a young man whose adolescence in no sense had been routine. Post-seminary days were catch-up time, and what the young man whose social learning process now was telescoped wished for more than anything was to be counted among ordinary people with ordinary backgrounds. He learned how to make that happen – to the extent that he could control how he was perceived.

Longer-Term Identity Management

The process by which former minor seminarians in this study entered the professional or job world mimicked the process by

305

which they had transitioned into standard social roles. By omitting a telling segment of their background, they created a new identity resting solely on present, pertinent data. Did they need to do this? Again, perhaps the need was overestimated, but it likely was not wholly manufactured. Non-disclosure meant that the former seminarian was not typed by variables other than those that governed the socially constructed profiles of "standard" professionals or employees. Reluctance on the part of a former seminarian who had become a teacher to punish an unruly student "appropriately," for example, might more easily (though not necessarily accurately) be explained by others within his professional sphere via reference to biographical information that included former-seminarian status. To control that information was to be professionally (and socially) evaluated solely on the basis of a common measuring stick.

Repetition spawns habit, and habit explains in part the seemingly unnecessarily prolonged utilization of subterfuge and deflection by former seminarians. At some point, one must be sufficiently established no longer to need to manage elements of his past social identity – the fact of keeping something secret is bigger than the secret itself. As an interviewee noted, "I'm fifty-five. I've done well in life. Screw it. I don't worry about it anymore." Yet, most interviewees had moved the needle only a bit, for, while they no longer worried so much about their past, neither did they counter old habits. A former seminarian from New Orleans recalled:

Just a few weeks ago, someone asked where I had gone to high school. Without thinking, I went straight into dodge mode. "I did not stay in New Orleans during those years; I went away to school." And I turned the conversation to something else. I don't need to do that at this point in my life. In fact, I feel stupid. What am I hiding that could really hurt me or anyone else? I just do it without thinking.

Does the former seminarian's automatic effort to control perceptions of his social past signal habit only? It would were he truly to believe he is like others at this point in life. But, judging from the comments of interviewees in this study and many first-person accounts related to it, he's not quite there. He has learned that he can behave like others and can achieve as well as others within routine social competition. Yet, he remains somewhat insecure about his status as normal, about whether or not he is among those old seminary schoolmates who were "fucked up," as the interviewee quoted in the previous chapter put it. Or short of that, is reticence to reveal his past a reluctance to disclose that he once was religious to an extent now deemed "strange" – the more so in an era of a sexual-abuse scandal among practitioners whose adolescent experiences were the same as his?

It is telling that most former seminarians in this study tended to describe (presumably to evaluate) themselves in terms of level of achievement within common social parameters – "good boy makes good." Former seminarians generally strive to succeed. They are focused, intelligent, (too) sensitive, and possess the tools and stamina to exceed the norm in many arenas. And, whether or not they admit it, to be average is, for them, to disappoint not only others but certainly themselves. To be "weird" is worse yet.

> *It's not that I am ashamed. It's not shame. I guess I'm embarrassed. People look at me now as smart and levelheaded, a successful person, even a leader. I'm embarrassed to let them see that part of me that got involved in all that seminary stuff, not just for a week or a year, but for four years! And I guess I'm also embarrassed for my family, my parents. How did they let me get into it? It's sort of creepy. I don't talk about it with very many people.* (Former seminarian from Chicago)

I am far less sensitive today, and I have even brought it up with people in [my profession]. The typical reaction is "You've got to be kidding me." I don't think I ever had a lot of hatred toward it, but I'm not sure I'm totally over it. I'll know that I'm totally over it when I don't feel bad about telling people I was in the seminary. (Former seminarian from Milwaukee)

The above quotes suggest that the ghost that haunts former seminarians is actually two ghosts. The first resides in our concern that others would revise their sense of us were they to learn of our unconventional past. As I noted above, former seminarians arguably often are sensible in withholding elements of their social biographies though, at some point, there seems little reason to continue the subterfuge. That ghost can be vanquished as age brings perspective and freedom to the haunted, much as a recovering alcoholic once hid his past addiction but, with passing years and experience, can now say, "What the hell. I am a recovering alcoholic. If that bothers you, too bad." Whether or not my conclusion, based as it is on my interviews and readings, is valid remains to be seen. While I have met and interviewed former seminarians who have disclosed their past in certain professional and social venues, I have yet to meet one who has put his past readily and candidly on display from point of exit from the seminary, or even at a much later date. In short, I cannot produce the sample of full-disclosers against which to profile the non- or selective-disclosers I interviewed.

The second ghost haunts closer to home, within our sense of self. As young men, we put our seminary past in a box, so high and so far back in the closet, that its effects, if they existed, could be ignored. The emphasis was upon shaping our public rather than our personal identity. We controlled our master status in the public arena and, day to day, we thought of ourselves in those same terms. At some point, however, what was hidden came to the fore for many of us, either flushed out by significant others' questions about what makes us tick or, as happened to me, by personal crises that sent me in search of the roots of my own insecurities and inadequacies. It is to the second ghost that we now turn.

Truth and Consequences

In 1985, twenty members of the St. Pius X Seminary class of 1965 enjoyed a reunion-barbeque at a park in Sacramento. Many brought their wives and children. One who did not commented at the time: "Look at the wives. They are hovering, trying to pick up clues about their husbands and why they are like they are. It's like a mystery that they're trying to solve." The wives likely were on to something:

[My wife] keeps trying to figure out what makes me tick. She always remarks that I am "independent," and it's not a compliment. She's okay that I can take care of myself some, but she feels like I am made of Teflon. Arrows just bounce off me. (Former seminarian from New York)

[My wife] is after me all the time to talk. She's sure our life would be better if I'd just spill my guts! (Alumnus, St. Pius X Seminary)

… [M]y counselor told me that, among other things, my [marital] problem was [four years in] high school seminary [during the 1960s]. He said that is the period when young people experiment and explore with various choices and learn from them, and without that, they cannot determine the outcome of their choices. The outcome of my choice to attend high school seminary seems to have ruined my life for the most part. I feel like I am damaged. (Anonymous [blogger], 2017)

So many former seminarians among my interviewees and in the literature allude to that "something" that we cannot ignore the possibility of a phenomenon with which to contend. Few see themselves as "damaged" (or "nuts" or "fucked up"), as does the individual quoted directly above, but most point to "issues" and "challenges." Most also suggest that they have been unable or unwilling easily to confront, and certainly to speak publicly about, those issues. If they have done so in conversation, it has likely been with old classmates "because most people wouldn't understand." Nearly universally among interviewees, the pattern of transition from seminary to broader social world has involved highly selective disclosure of former-seminarian status throughout work career and most of life more generally. And nearly universally, non-disclosure seems tied not only to managing immediate facts and feelings nested just below the surface but also to storing more deeply in the former seminarian's emotional vault a jumble of experiences, regrets, anger, insecurity, and questions.

In fairness, selective attention to the past, the ability to compartmentalize personal history, and a reticence to explore feelings are not solely the province of former seminarians. Men in general seem (or certainly are accused of being) disinclined to confront feelings and inclined to pursue control of their immediate social environment. But there is something different about men (and women) who experienced adolescence in traumatic, stressful, or unconventional settings and now so often find themselves either walking on eggshells around others or trying desperately to put everything in its proper place: the former member of a reclusive sect (Krakauer, 2003), the adult survivor of an abusive childhood (Walls, 2005), the grown military brat whose early life was rootless (Wertsch, 1991). They know that their adolescence was different. They suspect that some present inclinations and concerns trace to that adolescence. Having stuffed their feelings during adolescence and beyond, they sometimes act out as adults without knowing why. More often, they close their eyes and truck on as (they hope) "normal" adults until someone or something forces them to open the vault.

I know I am terrible about standing up for myself. I mean, I express my opinions and argue about things like sports, but basically I'll be quiet rather than rock the boat about most things. I've been that way all my adult life, I think, in relationships, with my parents, and at work. I swallow my pride and tell myself that it's better to just go along with it, less harm done. Except for my kids... I am too harsh with them. They are not the match that lights the fire. I'm the one who lights it. It's easy because I'm always smoldering inside. (Former seminarian from San Francisco)

There were positives. The sem left me able to deal with lots of things that happened to me in life, challenges. But, if anything, it left me far too unemotional, not able to deal with others' needs or demands. No question, I've had problems with women – the ability to just tune out emotionally. And I can rationalize just about anything I choose to. (Alumnus, St. Pius X Seminary)

... [I]n some ways, the minor seminary ... almost prevented us from being adolescents. ... [S]ome of the most consequential issues of being an adolescent – identity, sexuality, responsibility – were either assumed to have been already answered or were simply not addressed. And all too often, those of us who attempted in our adolescent way to answer them ourselves, ended up on work crew – or worse. ...[W]hatever our chronological age, we were to act like mature young men, adults even. And sometimes I wonder whether the problems some of us have

struggled with as adults would have been less problematic had we been given the freedom to struggle with them as adolescents. (Written communication from priest interviewee from Pittsburgh)

I have no regrets about becoming a priest. I've loved my life. If I could change any part of it, it would be not to be such a people-pleaser. I spent way too much time and energy trying to figure out what people – the priests in the seminary, the people in my parish, and my bishop especially – wanted and trying to give it to them. There was no me. (Priest interviewee from San Francisco)

Lasting Effects

Patterns. I began this project seeking to learn whether or not others who spent time in a minor seminary in the decades following World War II seemed biographically and emotionally like me. The answer, to my way of thinking, is yes. The descriptors of the former minor seminarian – at least one who had more than a limited exposure to life in a seminary – presented below have no direct link to the psychological literature. They are not based upon scales or tested indices. They derive only from the interviews and first-person accounts utilized in this study. More important, taken together, they are neither diagnostic nor therapeutic nor preventative in objective. They seek simply to capture elements of how former minor seminarians, especially those I interviewed, describe themselves.

The profile of the former seminarian (or, more precisely, of my former-seminarian interviewee) has two dimensions, one public and the other personal. Regarding his more public face and especially concerning the work world, the average former seminarian describes himself as achievement-oriented, able to gain a handle quickly on organizational requirements, needs, and goals, to stay focused upon them, and to deliver desired outcomes. He believes that people generally view him as capable of leadership roles. He considers himself a "good guy" who relates well to others, including subordinates, and commands their respect and attention. He describes himself as principled and emphasizes personal integrity. He views himself as an effective communicator.

On the more personal level, the average former seminarian whom I interviewed is cautious about longer-term commitments to people and causes, hesitant to trust his own judgment. That said, once having committed to individual or ideology, he is intensely loyal. He views himself as one who holds secrets close, both his own and those of others, and notes that people refer to him as "very private." He readily admits to "stuffing" his feelings and old wounds. The majority of former seminarians with whom I spoke see themselves as "worriers," acutely concerned about disappointing significant others and thus easily guilt-tripped. Having spent his adolescence in a doctrinal, black-and-white intellectual world, he tends toward concrete opinions. That said, having spent his youth told that thought as well as action matter in adherence to "the rules," he agonizes often over nuances. Nearly to a person, my interviewees noted that communication within the personal sphere, especially stating directly what is bothering them, is not among their strengths.[62]

---

[62] The average interviewee imbibed but saw himself as disciplined in his drinking. Several of the interviewees reported having had "drinking problems" (unspecified) in the past, and a few noted "bad choices" regarding use of cocaine and other substances earlier in their lives. Their numbers and their experiences in this regard did not seem out of line with those of non-seminarians of the same age cohort. There is little to suggest that time spent in a minor seminary produced a tendency toward substance abuse later in life.

According to a counseling psychologist with whom I have consulted (in the interest of full disclosure, she is my wife, Bernadette, and I am her ongoing case study), former seminarians may not quite get past the notion of "special" once attributed to them by parents, church, and school (though not by the seminary faculty and seminary peers). Where they once walked on water, now they swim like regular folks. Having internalized the sense of self as special, later in life and not necessarily consciously, they may expect certain responses from others which, not delivered, can lead to problems in personal or professional relationships. Further, when confronted with the possibility of not being quite so special, they may experience anger or depression.[63] I definitely understand the insight, but am clear that "special" does not signal the expectation of privilege so much as the need for reassurance of the type that boys received while seminarians – that which I pursue in life remains meaningful and good. Disappointment in this regard comes easily.

Here is the clincher regarding the seminary's impact: in both public and personal spheres, and for better or for worse, the average former seminarian whom I interviewed can "do time" as few others can. He can endure considerable stress for considerable periods and still function at a high level. He maintains his poise during crises. As he ages, he understands increasingly that this attribute has not always served him well.

The above characteristics are only partially a product of time spent in a minor seminary, at least for the average of us whose

---

[63] The logic here is undeniable, though no interviewee raised the matter – which carries with it a certain element of catch-22 – and I found no discussion of it in the literature on seminarians. It likely applies more directly to "anointed boys" and "parental offerings" than to "runaways" (see Chapter Five) since the latter generally did not feel "special" prior to entry into the seminary. In either case, not sufficiently aware of the possibility when conducting the interviews, I did not ask interviewees about it.

tenure exceeded three years. There was nothing random about the recruitment process that landed us in the seminary as boys. The church knew exactly the type of child-candidate it desired for priestly studies, and its seminary recruiters homed in upon such boys with laser-like precision. Seminary recruits were special boys, chosen because we were thought to possess just the right characteristics: highly religious, good boys, malleable, obedient, loathe to disappoint, and able to withstand tedium and isolation (for years on end). In short, we carried into our seminary careers tendencies that likely would have produced elements of the above profile later in life had we not experienced our "calling." Through its seminary formula (in both minor and major seminaries), the church converted those tendencies into more enduring character attributes. And, if it could not, especially during the heyday era, it quickly jettisoned its recruiting mistakes.

The church accomplished "vocation formation" in its seminaries through a steady diet of behavioral control and emotional manipulation, an emphasis upon heeding God's call, and a level of social isolation that reinforced our seminarian-sense of self and quashed our impulse to do what ordinary adolescents do – push normative bounds and learn from mistakes. So skillful were seminaries at their task that, cringe though we might at the suggestion, in fact, after the first two years and despite differences in the homes from which we came, those of us who remained in the minor seminary were veritable clones of one another.

The challenge for the church was to hold on to those of us who survived the initial culling process, for, as they did for adolescents generally (and as they would later for priests after Vatican II), brighter lights always beckoned. Here the church failed spectacularly. Most of us (certainly not all) eventually fled the seminary though not before paying a price: the loss of a significant portion of our adolescence, the phase during which most teenagers experiment and develop a sense of self as unique and special in appropriate ways and of responsibility and balanced pursuit of one's own interests as against those of others. Without all the necessary tools, after exiting, we required a crash course by which to recover lost maturational ground. How successful was that crash course has been the focus of this chapter.

I have spent the better portion of my adult life wrestling (sometimes consciously, more often less so) with the fallout from my stint in a minor seminary. The positives (discipline, drive, and endurance) are easily enough enumerated. The negatives are much harder to recognize as derivatives of my seminary years and harder still to address. But the above former-seminarian profile most assuredly captures me and nearly every one of my interview subjects who spent serious time in a minor seminary. We are the distinct product of childhood tendencies taken beyond fair limits during the process of "vocation formation." Differences among us likely developed after we left the seminary, yet, given the highly similar reformation process we have undergone, I cannot even state with any certainty that any such differences are meaningful.

I also have gone through life assuming that those of us who escaped the seminary differ somehow from the smaller number who did not – those poor guys, unable to wriggle off the hook and now living unhappily. My priest-interviewees disabused me quickly of this notion (and the research literature regarding their happiness in life and work supports their position; see Chapter Four). Further, as I interviewed former seminarians and read first-person accounts of those who attended minor seminaries, the distinction between priest and seminary-escapee increasingly became less discernable. Perhaps the reader perceived it sooner than I, but only when I finally assembled the former-seminarian profile discussed above did the obvious strike me: it describes priests from the minor-seminary boom era as well as it describes the rest of us. We possessed the same tendencies during childhood, and we experienced the same adolescence (or the absence of a standard one) while sequestered. Put aside extant issues of celibacy and relationship with God, and we are mirror images.

Former minor seminarians – escapees and priests alike – from America's seminary-boom era are older now and wiser. We've won some battles and lost others. A long line of people and events can lay claim to having shaped significantly today's iteration of who we are. Yet, after all these years, most of us, to a greater degree than we wish, still sit astride the same horse the seminary put us on half a century ago, the horse we could not control, that went where he wished to go. For me, that's okay. Knowing the horse is half the battle for the rider. Mine can still break stride if I'm not careful, galloping as if he were calling the shots. But mostly he's grown older too, and weaker and less headstrong. And I'm a better rider now.

References

Anonymous (Blogger). 2017. "High School Seminarian." *www.ExSeminarian. com/high-school-seminarian/* (May 15).

Krakauer, John. 2003. *Under the Banner of Heaven.* New York: Random House.

Walls, Jeannette. 2005. *The Glass Castle.* New York: Scribner.

Wertsch, Mary E. 1991. *Military Brats: Legacies of Childhood Inside the Fortress.* St. Louis MO: Brightwell.

CHAPTER FOURTEEN

Boys Called Today

*F*or some (I am one), seminaries for boys are a reminder of Catholicism's uncompromising commitment, after World War II, to an eroding culture – blindness with a tinge at times even of cult. Due, for most, minor seminaries are simply a feature of recent church history, probably not a great idea, certainly not worth fighting over. Few Catholics born after 1980 likely have heard of, let alone thought much about, minor seminaries, even though most of the last significant wave of their inhabitants still live among us.

On the ropes and easily forgotten they may be, but minor seminaries are not quite gone. Thus, I find myself reacting to the following passage as I might to a photo of a young person about to scale a cliff in bare feet. I know what the next photos will show.

I have felt called to be a priest for some time now, probably ... three years. Next year, I will be in 8th grade.... My question is with my strong desire to do God's will, if I still feel called to the priesthood when I end my 8th grade year, should I enter a minor *seminary. I am torn because I have this extreme desire to go to a minor seminary but, the pastor of my church says it would be the one thing he wishes he could change about his life and he doesn't recommend it. I extremely feel called to serve Christ through the priesthood and would like to begin, if it be His will, study-ing now. Are there any **traditionally** minded minor seminaries for high-schoolers? ...Please help...!* (Anonymous [blogger], 2013; emphasis original)

Listen to your pastor, kid.

The young writer's plea resurrects images of child-vocations that I and, apparently, the boy's parish priest prefer to leave far behind. I was never as passionate about the seminary or its final product as this boy appears to be though my "vocation" began at about the same age as his. Nor did I have to choose sides as he seems to feel the need to do. The Catholicism of my day was virtu-ally the only brand available, "traditional," the version that charac-terized (and filled) minor seminaries in the 1950s and early 1960s: custom as law, a black-and-white orthodoxy enforced unsparingly, hierarchical authority with a significant gap between the governed and the governors, and a liturgy delivered to, rather than in concert with, the faithful. Times changed and seminaries with them.

Many Catholics today, a sizeable minority, do not celebrate the changed times. For them, the concept of minor seminary symbol-izes a better period, pre-Vatican II. It offers potentially a vehicle by which to generate priests whose ecclesiastical purity and focus (some would say, myopia) could help restore a lost "sense of order" marked by church bells, Latin, incense, and directives from the bishop (Kirchoff, 2017). Moreover, they view a return to traditional minor seminaries as viable – if only someone could afford to under-write them. Attending a former seminarian-friend's funeral a few years ago, I overheard a small cluster of Catholics, adult profession-als, outline their blueprint for action:

> *They can't stop us if we do it ourselves. We don't need permission to build. What we have to do is buy some land, build our own church, and bring in a priest from France. The French know how to do this right. We can establish our own school. If there are enough of us, the bishop will have to recognize us. And if each of us pledges a son to the priesthood, within a generation or so, we'll have our church back.*

For those few young sons now pledged to the traditional priest-hood (see below), the call is exactly that which we former seminar-ians experienced as priests-to-be: beckoned by God and shaped by the seminary – formation as capture, isolation, and production of a lifelong set of responses to directives. It is far easier to accomplish this with children than with adults, as a contemporary minor sem-inary webpage makes clear:

> *... [T]he Church has always recognized that God calls whom He wills when He wills. This often means that those who are called to the priesthood first hear that call in their adolescence or even childhood. In fact, because boys are usually not struggling with the weight of past sins in the way many adult men are, they are even more sensitive to divine grace and thus better able to hear God's call. ... [B]oys who are called to the priesthood need an environment that will help nourish and encourage their vocation. Adolescence is perhaps the most crucial period of devel-opment in a person—not only physically, mentally, and socially, but also morally and spiritually—and as a result, there is no point in one's life when it is more important to be educated in*

accord with one's vocation. (St. José Sanchez Del Rio Minor Seminary, 2019)

Minor Seminaries in New and Old Vestments

Boys – or their parents – seeking a minor seminary in the United States presently must work to find one. They have but four choices.[64] Two have little in common with the traditional seminary I attended (Vitz, 2010). St. Lawrence Seminary High School was established in 1860 and Cathedral Preparatory School and Seminary in 1914. St. Lawrence is a residential school in Wisconsin housing about 200 students, and Cathedral Prep is a day school in Queens, New York, with about 135 students. Neither approximates the pre-Vatican II minor seminary in goal or culture. In fact, each is alive today only because it revised its mission.[65] Both now strive quite successfully to be college-preparatory schools that offer their pupils vocational discernment opportunities, both clerical and lay. Both celebrate the ordinations of past students, but they also make clear that most of their graduates ultimately live their Christian lives as other than clergy.

The remaining two institutions, both residential, available to those seeking a seminary experience for boys are at once much newer and exceedingly traditional: Sacred Heart Apostolic School

---

[64] In 1967, the year I left the seminary, minor seminaries containing high-school students in the United States totaled 160 – 36 diocesan and 86 religious high-school seminaries, and 38 combined high-school and junior-college seminaries (enrolling primarily high-school students, the front end of the six-six seminary model discussed in Chapter Two) (Gautier and Do, 2018). These institutions, and a number of small junior-college seminary programs, held nearly 16,000 boys and young men.

[65] St. Lawrence Seminary High School, at the time St. Lawrence Seminary, also survived a particularly serious and very public scandal involving the sexual abuse of seminarians by faculty and staff members. See Chapter Nine.

(2019), opened in 2005 in Rolling Prairie, Indiana, and St. José Sanchez Del Rio Minor Seminary (2019), established in Mankato, Minnesota in 2008. They mirror each other in apostolic orientation, educating their charges to be missionaries within global religious orders, the Legion of Christ and the Institute of the Incarnate Word, respectively. Each order locates its ethos in John Paul II; each is "Christ-centered," its allegiance to church and to pope steadfast, and its faith anchored in the eucharist, traditional liturgy, and unparalleled devotion to the Blessed Virgin.

Sacred Heart enrolls about 32 students annually, and St. José Sanchez enrolls about 20, though these enrollment figures must be qualified in an important way. The seminaries in question are not the high-school seminaries of my day. They are junior high- and high-school seminaries; Sacred Heart admits eighth-graders and St. José Sanchez admits seventh- and eighth-graders. A quarter of the 54 students in the schools' combined enrollments in 2019 were not yet high-school freshmen.[66] This is as likely a function of the numbers necessary to each institution's financial viability as it is of its ideology. In either case, cradle-robbing by a segment of the church in America has moved deeper into the ranks of the faithful.

Flashbacks

To access the websites of Sacred Heart and St. José Sanchez Del Rio seminaries is to travel back in time. The photos of the seminarians in those institutions are the photos of the minor seminarians of my era – engaging in everything from mass to prayer to study to class to music to sports to field trips to work crew to meals and to leisure. The schedule of daily activities is the schedule within which

[66] The Council of Trent established the rules governing minor seminaries in 1563 (see Chapter Two). The minimum age at which an individual can enroll in a seminary is twelve years.

my classmates and I lived our day. The curricula of the schools are very similar to each other and to the academic offerings we experienced – including mandatory Latin in all years of attendance (not to mention mandatory Greek for three years at Sacred Heart). The rules also remain essentially the same; movement in general and choice of activity in particular are controlled via schedule, mandate, physical boundaries, and direct oversight, as are all forms of communication to and from the outside.

These are highly organized, well-focused total institutions. The likelihood of the vocational seed planted in a child is taken for granted. Cultivation and formation of that vocation are paramount. "Discernment" is less a process than a term employed ex post facto should a boy choose to leave the seminary. Having surrendered its son to the "will of God,"[67] family has been left behind for the most part by that son. Visits to the seminaries by families are permitted but limited in most cases by the cost of travel; most students come from states outside that of the institution. Interaction with outsiders is not uncommon but is highly structured. Students and faculty members travel each year en masse, for example, to witness ordinations within their religious orders.

Allegiance to the religious order is emphasized and reinforced within the seminary, some critics contend, to the point of "cult-"

---

[67] An Idaho parent who sent three sons to a new Legion of Christ seminary (now closed) in California in 2004, for example, explained that "God is attracted to us and for some reason our kids are getting evangelized very young. ... It's God working in their life. It's a stunning thing as a parent" (Rosen, 2004). Similarly, a family living in Mankato, Minnesota in 2010, only a mile from St. José Sanchez Del Rio Minor Seminary, found monthly visits with their son in the seminary unbearable (in terms of the extent to which they missed one another) and ended them. The boy's mother, who worked across the street from the seminary but saw little of him, explained that, though she missed her son, "If that is where God is calling him, that's where he needs to be" (Linehan, 2010).

or "sect-like" control (Cronin, 2009; Rosen, 2004).[68] For the vast majority of hours in the day and months in the year, the seminarian "belongs" to his religious order. He rarely is alone. His point of orientation always is his school and his order. The adults with whom he lives are members of the order. He relies upon peers and upon the order's spiritual advisors for support and for diversion. The good works done by him in the community, often within parishes and programs administered by the order, are performed in groups of boys and men from the order. He lives the order's life, and it is very far from that of an ordinary high-school boy. And then he transitions to the order's novitiate without missing a beat.[69]

As they did in the seminary publications of my day, the photos on these traditional seminaries' websites capture intense concentration and solemnity among students at prayer and study. They also project the unbridled joy of fraternity within the seminary's physical and social bubble. We sense no boredom, mischief, anger, or depression. These boys are experiencing a liberal arts education of high quality[70] within a community of kindred souls under an

---

[68] Both the Legion of Christ and the Institute of the Incarnate Word in recent years also have faced serious scandals involving sexual abuse of or sexual misconduct with seminarians by their founders, Marcial Maciel (sexual abuse of minors) and Carlos Buela (sexual misconduct with adults), respectively (Catholic News Agency, 2016; Donadio, 2010; see also Goodstein, 2012; Berry, 2011).

[69] Sacred Heart reports that half of its graduates proceed forward to the Legion's novitiate or (a small percentage) to a diocesan seminary. Two thirds of the novitiate's current students were Sacred Heart students (Sacred Heart Apostolic School, 2019). These are perseverance rates considerably in excess of those produced by mainstream religious orders in days when traditional high-school seminaries and novitiates were more common.

[70] Sacred Heart is fully accredited. St. José Sanchez Del Rio is not accredited directly but relies upon affiliation with an accredited Catholic homeschool program to structure curricula and to issue credits and diplomas.

umbrella of faith. We can assume, certainly for the sake of argument, that their mentors are all good souls and would never harm or exploit their wards. The boys are happy; their parents are happy; the order is happy. What possibly could be wrong this picture?

What is wrong, I believe, is asking a boy (in the present instance, one as young as twelve) to carry on his shoulders the burden of deciphering and remaining faithful to a call from God to serve as a priest. What is wrong is to carry that burden in an environment that fences out competing ideas and options. What is wrong, as it was during my days in the minor seminary, is the absence of attention to the quality of the emotional development of an adolescent sequestered within a total institution for years. What is wrong is framing the matter of the effects of social isolation only in terms of the boy who "perseveres" – will he be emotionally mature enough as a priest one day to relate to the laity? God forbid, might his physical and emotional isolation increase the possibility of sexual predation after ordination? Finally and most important in the eyes of this former minor seminarian, what is wrong is the persistent treatment of the seminary experience as neutral, if not positive, in its impact upon individuals who choose to depart the institution. It is as if, after thanking God for the chance at discernment, the boy then merges into ordinary life's lanes with nary a scratch, never mind a wreck – no tendency to stuff or bury emotions and to endure difficult situations beyond what is considered "healthy" and no maturational retardation that will make early (and perhaps later) post-seminary social integration difficult.

The good news, at least from my perspective, is that, with the exceptions noted above and despite sporadic efforts to rekindle the traditional minor-seminary model (Korson, 2009), the Catholic Church in America no longer is tapping boys for its future priests. Indeed, the idea of blank-slate boy presently counters notions of what is necessary to the formation of a priest. Dioceses and religious orders now point to self-awareness, maturity, and life experience as critical to seminary success.

Less encouraging is the realization that, since minor seminaries of the traditional, high-school variety remain plentiful through-out the world,[71] the church has not concluded officially that they are unhealthy, if not morally problematic, institutions. As a church official put it regarding seminaries for boys, "There is room for peo-ple to be more liberal or more conservative, without ceasing to be Catholic" (Rosen, 2004). And in the eyes of at least some Catholic leaders, should the dearth of major seminarians and priests con-tinue, minor seminaries should again be considered a viable engine for their production (Korson, 2009; Vitz, 2010). In this light, it appears that we would see minor seminaries for boys in America today if the church could afford them. Financial challenges, rather than the church's clarity regarding the appropriateness of minor seminaries for juveniles, appear to dictate contemporary seminary enrollment as adult enrollment.

Contemporary Seminaries

The Catholic Church has yet to recover from the stampede of so many of its priests and priests-to-be from religious vocations in the final third of the Twentieth Century. The precipitous decline in number of priests, 37 percent fewer today than in 1970 (the combined effect of deaths, retirements, defections, and unpro-ductive recruiting), contrasts sharply with the precipitous,

---

[71] See Kramarek et al. (2017). The exact number is hard to pinpoint due to problematic terminology ("minor" vs. "junior," for example) and the embed-ding of adolescents' programs in college and major-seminary programs. Large numbers appear in Asia, Africa, and Latin America, and many likely serve the same upward-mobility function as did American minor seminaries at one time. Minor seminaries remain common in Spain and Italy as well.

immigration-driven growth (nearly 45 percent) of the Catholic population in the United States during the same period (CARA, 2018). Given its troubles – the demoralizing global sex-abuse scandal (transgressions and cover-up) that worsens daily, the financial fallout stemming from it, and the ongoing culture wars between Vatican II-era "liberal" Catholics and John Paul II-era "conservatives" – the church is unlikely anytime soon to accommodate the needs of the faithful let alone to bask in its former glory (Brown, 2017; Douthat, 2018; Worthen, 2018).

Troubled times notwithstanding, Catholic major seminaries in the United States continue to mint new priests, some 500 of them every year (though half the number produced in 1970 [CARA, 2018]). They emanate from an average yearly population of about 4,650 men (a third the number in 1970) studying in approximately 70 Catholic, primarily residential, seminary programs (free-standing colleges, collaborative colleges, pre-theology programs, and major-seminary theological programs).[72] Most of the candidates for the priesthood (81 percent) within these institutions are diocesan seminarians. Seventy-eight percent of those in major-seminary theology programs are under 35 years of age; 81 percent of those in college-level programs are under 25 years of age. Sixty-three percent of the seminarians at both levels are white; 25 percent are of Hispanic or Asian/Pacific Islander descent. Within the theology-level student population, 13 percent are foreign-born, eight in

---

[72] Changes regarding college-level seminaries are somewhat difficult to track. Junior-college seminary programs once were part of what was commonly called the "six-six" model of minor seminaries (see Chapter Two), though junior-college students in those minor seminaries constituted a minority of their students. Those seminaries were discontinued or absorbed into college-level seminaries, leaving enrollments of college-level seminaries and stand-alone high-school seminaries today to be compared with those of former six-year institutions.

ten of whom are studying for U.S. dioceses or U.S.-based religious orders (Gautier and Do, 2018).

Seminaries today are not the calm, contemplative places we might imagine (Monczunski, 2002; Tobin, 2009). Their inhabitants grapple constantly with doctrinal issues, matters of obedience and conscience, and what has or has not jeopardized their church's future (Hoge and Wenger, 2003: 83-95; Periello, 2017; Reese, 2019). The topic of celibacy remains debated among priests-to-be, though it is doubtful that they soon will see change in the church's position regarding it (Jones, 2018). Similarly, while women now are more active within the church, it is unlikely that we will encounter them in seminaries in the near future (Coday, 2018; Giangrave, 2018). Homosexuals as well surely are feeling less welcome in today's seminaries (Carlin, 2018; Dias and Demczuk, 2019) as conservative priests and seminarians publicly bemoan the loss of "real men" in the clerical ranks (Mason, 2015) and in light of the church's position that men with "deep seated homosexual tendencies" should not be permitted in Catholic seminaries and the priesthood (Berg, 2018b). In short, the matters that roil church waters are not trivial, and seminaries are no place for adolescents (Englert, 2006).

In fact, most Catholic seminaries presently do not accept students under eighteen years of age. College-level seminaries enroll young men who fit the normal age-profile of college-goers; many of these seminarians attend Catholic colleges while residing in seminary "houses." Major seminaries (offering postgraduate studies in theology) require candidates for the priesthood to possess a college degree and, it is hoped, some exposure to the world. Pre-theology programs have experienced growing enrollment as more college or near-college graduates undertake compensatory coursework in preparation for major-seminary studies. Religious orders' novitiates now prefer as well that novices enter with at least some college credits and life experience. The result has been a strong four-year retention rate: 70 percent for college seminaries and 77 percent for major seminaries (Gautier and Do, 2018). The estimated yield (i.e., ordinations) for major seminaries now stands at 14 percent – an annual average of 500 newly ordained priests derived from a yearly average major-seminary population of 3,500 during the past several years. If we look only at fourth-year major seminarians, the yield rate exceeds 90 percent.

Today's seminarians, generally young adults but also older men with "belated vocations," are capable (or more so than adolescents) of making informed choices.[73] While major seminaries once were adult versions of minor seminaries in the sense of containment and formation objectives, they now focus much more upon discernment than previously was the case.[74] Seminary walls also now are more porous, though some critics argue that the culture of seclusion still holds sway (Berg, 2018a). Contemporary seminarians typically spend considerably more time than in the past outside the seminary in internship-like placements that expose them to the challenges and rewards of the ministry.

---

[73] It can be argued reasonably that eighteen years of age does not constitute a level of maturity sufficient for seminary studies. Berg (2018b), for example, suggests that twenty-two years of age might be more appropriate. The point made presently is that eighteen represents a societal age whereby young people are assumed to be sufficiently experienced to vote, serve in the military, and marry.

[74] A former-priest interviewee recalled having no conversations with anyone in the major seminary concerning his reasons for pursuing the priesthood. The closest to such a discussion that he remembered was a major-seminary faculty member's query to a class: "Why do you want to be a priest?" The class bell rang immediately after the question was posed, and it never was raised again. The interviewee often wondered what might have come of his vocation had he been made to answer the vital question.

Major-seminary websites offer testimonials (whose authors likely were not chosen randomly) that convey a sense of pursuit of vocation foreign to those of us who attended minor seminaries and most who attended major seminaries during the boom era. Some excerpts:

Over the past year and a half, I have learned more about my Catholic faith than ever before. When I finally made the decision to apply to the seminary, I felt so free and peaceful. I would recommend to anyone discerning a priestly or religious calling to pursue it. Even if you end up realizing that God is not calling you to a religious life or the priesthood, the time you spend in formation… will be some of the best time of your life. (Diocese of Lafayette, 2019)

…I had been working … for 19 years as a teacher and then administrator. Transitioning from a well-established career and starting over hasn't been easy, but it's been well worth it. God, in His providence has blessed me with the [seminary] community. The faculty, staff, fellow seminarians and students have been a source of ongoing support these last four years. Also, the prayers of family, friends and parishioners have reminded me that I'm not alone on this journey. (St. John's Seminary, 2019)

I began thinking about the seminary during my senior year [in high school]. I was kind of panicking because I was already accepted to college and I was very excited. I spoke with friends and teachers. I did end up going to college and worked as an electrical engineer. But thoughts about the priesthood persisted. After a year, I tendered my resignation. Saying "yes" to the seminary is not a commitment to ordination. It's a commitment to asking God what he wants you to do. I knew I was never going to find the answer unless I went out and searched. (Diocese of Allentown, 2019)

I have said yes to handing over everything that I have, everything that I am, everything that I was, and everything I ever will be to God. ...I hope that it is enough. It's in the hands of God. I hope that he will make it enough. (Christ the King Seminary, 2019)

In short, these are grownups, not offered-up, seduced, or runaway children. They are persons able to comprehend what they are getting themselves into and to know that they can walk away and feel at peace. That is as it should be... and as it always should have been.

References

Anonymous (Blogger). 2013. "Minor Seminaries (High School)?" *Catholic Answers Forums* (www.forums.catholic.com/t/minor-seminary-high-school/317960/ [March]).

Berg, Thomas. 2018a. "Want to Address Priest Sexual Abuse? The Catholic Church Needs to Overhaul Its Seminaries." *Washington Post* (https://washingtonpost.com/religion/2018/10/18/want-address-priest-sex-abuse-catholic-church-needs-overhaul-its-seminaries/).

_____. 2018b. "Getting Formation Right." *First Things* (www.firstthings .com/article/2018/12/ getting-formation-right).

Berry, Jason. 1992. *Lead Us Not Into Temptation: Catholic Priests and the Sexual Abuse of Children.* New York: Doubleday.

Brown, Andrew. 2017. "The War against Pope Francis." *The Guardian* (https://www.theguardian.com/ news/2017/oct/27/ the-war-against -pope-francis.)

CARA (Center for Applied Research in the Apostolate). 2018. "Frequently Requested Church Statistics." *www.cara.georgetown.edu.*

Carlin, David. 2018. "Gay Priests and Indulgence of Homosexuality." *The Catholic Thing* (www.thecatholicthing.org/2018/11/30/gay-priests -and-indulgence-of-homosexuality).

Catholic News Agency. 2016. "Institute of the Incarnate Word Founder Guilty of Sexual Misconduct." *Crux* (www.cruxnow.com/Institute of the Incarnate Word Founder Guilty of Sexual Misconduct) (December 27).

Christ the King Seminary. 2019. *Four Newly Ordained Priests Discuss Their "Yes."* www.cks.edu.

Coday, Dennis. 2018. "Advocates Dismayed by Reaffirming Ban on Women Priests." *National Catholic Reporter* (www.ncronline.org/news/people/ advocates-dismayed-reaffirming-ban-women-priests.) (June 9).

Cronin, Peter. 2009 [1996]. "Legion of Christ as Cult-like Org." *Dialogue Ireland* (www.dialogueireland.wordpress.com, August 31).

Dias, Elizabeth and Gabriella Demczuk, 2019. "'It Is Not a Closet. It Is a Cage.' Gay Catholic Priests Speak Out." *New York Times* (https:// www.nytimes.com /2019/02/17/us/it-is-not-a-closet-it-is-a-cage-gay -catholic-priests-speak-out.html).

Diocese of Allentown. 2019. *Spotlight on Seminarians.* www. allentown-diocese.org.

Diocese of Lafayette. 2019. *Seminarian Testimonials.* www.diolaf.org.

Donadio, Rachel. 2010. "Catholic Order Admits Its Founder Abused Boys Over Decades." *New York Times* (https://www.nytimes. com/2010/03/27/ world/europe/27legion.html).

Douthat, Ross. 2018. *To Change the Church: Pope Francis and the Future of Catholicism.* New York: Simon & Schuster.

Englert, Jonathan. 2006. *The Collar: A Year Inside a Catholic Seminary.* New York: Houghton Mifflin Company.

Gautier, Mary and Thu Do. 2018. *Catholic Ministry Formation Enrollment: Statistical Overview for 2017-18.* Washington DC: Center for Applied Research in the Apostolate (CARA).

Giangrave, Claire. 2018. "Signs Suggest a Turning Point on the Role of Women in the Church." *Crux* (www.cruxnow.com/vatican/2018/03/08/ signs-suggest-turning-point-role-women-church/).

Goodstein, Laurie. 2012. "Leader of Catholic Order Admits Knowing Priest Fathered Child." *New York Times* (https://www.nytimes.com/2012/05/23/ us/leader-of-catholic-order-admits-knowing-priest-fathered-child.html).

Hoge, Dean R. and Jacqueline Wenger. 2003. *Evolving Visions of the Priesthood.* Collegeville MN: Liturgical Press.

Jones, Kevin. 2018. "How Seminaries Help Men Discern the Call to Chaste Celibacy." *Catholic News Agency* (https://www.catholic-newsagency.com/ news/how-seminaries-help-men-discern-the-call-to-chaste-celibacy-66058) (August 26).

Kirchoff, Timothy. 2017. "Is Pope Francis Right about Traditionalists Who Love the Latin Mass?" *America* (https://www.america magazine.org/faith/2017/09/13 / pope-francis-right-about-traditionalists-who-love-latin-mass).

Korson, Gerald. 2009. "Minor Seminaries: Are They Making a Comeback?" *Our Sunday Visitor* (https://www.osv.com/osvweekly (September 23).

Kramarek, Michal J., Thomas P. Gaunt, and Santiago Sordo-Palacios. 2017. *Global Directory of Catholic Seminaries.* Washington DC: Center for Applied Research in the Apostolate (CARA).

Linehan, Dan. 2010. "Teenage Seminarians Explore Their Theology, Vocation." *Mankato Free Press.* (https://www.mankatofreepress.com/news/ local_news/ teenage-seminarians-explore-their-theology-vocation/article) (June 20).

Mason, James. 2015. "The Forgotten Vice in Seminary Formation." *Homiletic and Pastoral Review* (https://www.hprweb.com/2015/07/the-forgotten-vice-in-seminary-formation/).

Monczunski, John. 2002. "The Priesthood in Peril." *Notre Dame Magazine* (https://magazine.nd.edu/stories/the-priesthood-in-peril/).

Periello, Pat. 2017. "The Future of the Priesthood Looks More Hopeful." *National Catholic Reporter* (https://www.ncronline.org/blogs/ncr-today/future-priesthood-looks-more-hopeful) June 21).

Reese, Thomas. 2019. "The Catholic Church's Seminaries Need Reform."
   National Catholic Reporter (https://religionnews.com/2019/02/12/
   the-catholic-churchs-us-seminaries-need-reform/).

Rosen, Laurel. 2004. "Priesthood Prep: A Conservative Catholic Order
   Teaches Boys in Placer County." *Sacramento Bee* February 3: A1, A10.

Sacred Heart Apostolic School. 2019. Rolling Prairie, IN: *www. sacred-
   heartapostolicschool.org.*

St. John's Seminary. 2019. *Testimonials.* www.stjohnsem.edu.

St. José Sanchez Del Rio Minor Seminary. 2019. Mankato, MN: *www.
   iveminorseminary.com.*

Tobin, Thomas J. 2009. "How the Seminary Has Changed." *Rhode Island
   Catholic* (www.thericatholic.com/stories/) (September 24).

Vitz, Daniel. 2010. "Major Arguments for Reviving Minor Seminaries."
   Homiletic and Pastoral Review 111: 8-15.

Worthen, Molly. 2018. "A Conservative Catholic's Case against Pope
   Francis." *Washington Post.* (https://www.washington post.com/out-
   look/a-conservative-catholics-case-against-pope-francis) (May 18).

Epilogue

*S*t. Pius X Seminary – "St. Pius Jailhouse" – opened with a flourish in 1961 in Galt, California. Not long for this world, it closed its doors in 1977. I passed by it on a road trip with a friend in 1978. The sole caretaker of the institution, a Salvatorian brother, showed us around the ghost town frozen in time. "Don't worry," he assured me, though I did not think I was projecting worry, "St. Pius X will rise again." It did, after a fashion. In 1983, the State of California leased (and later would purchase) the property and facility. It serves today as the Richard A. McGee Correctional Training Center, preparing future correctional officers for the State of California's Department of Corrections and Rehabilitation. Among the academy's graduates is a former Salvatorian priest, a good guy. He taught, counseled, protected, and, yes, guarded several generations of seminarians when the same land and buildings held the promise of the priesthood for hundreds of boys in the grip of America's minor-seminary boom.

Personal Seminary Post Mortem

A friend asked me recently whether or not I have exorcised the demon that inspired this book. I have ... pretty much anyway. I now possess answers to questions that I ignored or let confound me for years. I have a context for those answers and a history with which to frame new questions. And, based on the accounts of former seminarians with whom I've spoken extensively and the first-person accounts I have read, I am greatly reassured that I did not imagine the content and quality of my seminary years or their ultimate impact. Nor, importantly, do I feel "damaged" to an extent that disables me. What I have are issues and tendencies attributable to my stint in the seminary; they linger just below the surface; they crash my life's parties more often than I care to admit. As one interviewee offered, "They shanghaied us when we were kids," and there is no way to rewrite that as inconsequential. The study that informed this book sought to describe both the abduction and its outcomes.

Though I feel better now, I have little doubt that I will drift off course at times as elements of my seminary past shape responses to personal issues in ways that I did not anticipate. Nor can I pretend still not to wish that my seminary experience – and, thus, identity as a former seminarian -could be excised from my personal history. No luck there: I recently stumbled upon a 1966 book on the genealogical roots of my father's family, the product of years of exhaustive research by his cousin in days sans computerized data and DNA analysis. There I was, my dad's progeny:

Their son Joseph is a senior St. Pius X Seminary in Galt, California and is studying for the priesthood.

Dagger to the heart. There is no outrunning this. One day in the distant future, some great, great, great niece or nephew, engaged in the same "Who am I, and how did I get this way?" quest that occupies my energies, will immortalize my master status in the "facts" section of my tiny box in the family tree. By then, he or she likely will have to look up the meaning of "seminary."

My hunt for answers has been productive in an important sense. Overall, my anger toward the church, the seminary, and my mother has softened. (I'm giving my dad a pass though, as I've noted in previous chapters, it is hard to understand how he became simply a bystander.) In large part, this owes to a renewed appreciation of the era that made my seminary career likely, the mid-1950s through the mid-1960s. I did as many Catholic boys had done in prior decades in Europe and America: chose a career (vocation) that would provide both economic security and serious social respect – accolades, in fact, with hallelujahs and mighty pats on the back. And the church did what it always had done: sequestered boys who wanted to be priests and who passed muster at entry and through-out the four–to-six-year "trial" and "protective custody" that kept its adolescent seminarians safe from spiritual harm.

Little did the church, seminary faculties, mothers, and the rest of us fathom beforehand that the model of "vocation formation" honed for four centuries had reached the end of the line. How could anyone have suspected such an about-face given that so many boys and young men were beating down seminary doors as the 1950s gathered steam? Who would have guessed that, by the mid-1960s, the new, suburban, middle-class Catholic family would divine alternate paths to economic security and fulfillment, not to mention social status? And who could have foretold the Catholic culture wars spawned by the Second Vatican Council's well-intended attempt to refit the church to the modern world?

If those of us caught up in America's seminary boom were the product of an era, so too were our mothers and fathers who grew up Catholic during the Great Depression and World War II and themselves were reared by parents who believed that priests were special beyond words. Can my mother truly be vilified for wanting her son to be special and herself to earn the prized designation, *mother of a priest*? She did what she had been told (or at least urged) to do, and I imagine that it hurt to surrender her firstborn even as she felt sanctified by the deed.

I can even let myself off the hook a bit after years of assuming responsibility for my vocational fate. What was a child to do in the face of an all-out campaign to get him into a seminary at a very young age, to hold him there as long as possible and, hopefully, years later to transfer him to an "adult" seminary? Minor seminarians had no clue regarding the Mack truck that clobbered them. We were conditioned to frame the entire seminary experience as of our making. It was our vocation; God called us, and we chose to heed or not to heed that call. *Chose.* Really? It has taken years to flush the notion of volition from our personally constructed (though little-shared) emotional biographies. We did not enter seminaries; we were entered into them.

I've abandoned as well my sense of sadness regarding the few seminarians who ultimately became priests, i.e., persevered or failed to escape, depending on your point of observation. While I found the former priests among my interviewees and in most written accounts happier than when they were priests, I also found men who remained in the priesthood quite satisfied with their life choice. I suppose we could chalk it up to dissonance-reduction, yet, as one former seminarian pointed out to me:

> *Maybe we were tricked into the seminary as kids, but who's to say that, as [those who ultimately were ordained] aged out of adolescence, they didn't actually hear and respond to a call from on high? How do you know their vocations eventually were not manufactured, but real? Why shouldn't they be happy?*

He's right; how do I know, and why shouldn't they?

Having reread the above paragraphs, I must confess candidly that I am not nearly as forgiving as these professions of good will suggest. I have mellowed and no longer feel sorry for myself, to be sure. But let's face it; God did not call me. The church did – albeit through my mother. While technically all I had to do was to walk out the door, I recall no seminary priest explaining that option to me, and my mother surely did not. However noble everyone's intentions and however much their worldview was part and parcel of the era in question, the fact remains that the church's approach to vocations cost thousands of boys and young men the better portion of a normal adolescence (granted, with its own attendant miseries and insecurities). That, in turn, came with a life long set of attributes and tendencies. We do not have to deny the reality in question in order to move on. The personal objective at this stage in life for the average former minor seminarian is less to let church, seminary, and would-be mothers of priests off the hook than to come to terms with what happened and to deal with it. I'd like to believe that this is where the present study has taken me.

An interviewee for this study commented that he will know that he is past his seminary experience when he has no trouble acknowledging it to others. The test of my own mettle in my mellower approach to my seminary past and newfound ability to forgive those who trespassed against me lies similarly in my willingness to disclose publicly that I spent six years as an adolescent being (or certainly perceiving myself to be) different, not normal, maybe even "weird." As I noted in Chapters Twelve and Thirteen, it is one thing to come to terms with one's seminary past and another still to let one's ship of secrets hit the rocks. Mine has hit the rocks, so to speak, with the coming-out that this book represents. No turning back now.

Author Index

Subject Index

About the Author

Joseph F. Sheley, once a minor seminarian, is President Emeritus of California State University, Stanislaus. He served additionally for many years as Dean, Executive Vice President, and Provost at California State University, Sacramento. A sociologist and criminologist and author of numerous books and journal articles, he was, prior to entering the administrative field, a faculty member at Tulane University. His research focused generally upon issues of social control, deviance, and public health and more specifically upon patterns of acquisition and use of firearms by juveniles. His wife Bernadette and he make their home in Sacramento, California.

Made in the USA
Monee, IL
30 June 2020